UNDER THE GUNS OF THE RED BARON

THE COMPLETE RECORD OF VON RICHTHOFEN'S VICTORIES AND VICTIMS FULLY ILLUSTRATED

UNDER THE GUNS OF THE RED BARON

The Complete Record of Von Richthofen's Victories and Victims Fully Illustrated

NORMAN FRANKS,
HAL GIBLIN
AND NIGEL McCRERY

GRUB STREET · LONDON

Published by Grub Street
4 Rainham Close
London SW11 6SS

Originally published in hardback in 1995
This new edition first published in paperback 2007

Paintings by Chris Thomas

British Library Cataloguing in Publication Data
Franks, Norman L. R.
Under the guns of the Red Baron : the complete record of
Von Richthofen's victories and victims fully illustrated
1. Richthofen, Manfred, Freiherr von, 1892-1918 2. World
War, 1914-1918 – Aerial operations, German 3. World War,
1914-1918 – Aerial operations, British 4. Fighter pilots –
Great Britain – Biography
I. Title II. Giblin, Hal III. McCrery, Nigel, 1953-
940.4'4943'092
ISBN-13: 9781904943976

Originated in China by Modern Age Repro
Printed and bound in China by
1010 Printing International Ltd

ACKNOWLEDGEMENTS

During the course of the preparation of, and the research for, this book, the authors were frequently and most pleasantly surprised by the amount of unstinting and generous assistance they received from many individuals and organisations. We acknowledge, with gratitude, their valuable input.

In particular, we must express our appreciation to three noted 'aero historians', Stewart K Taylor of Dutton, Ontario, Canada; Bill Evans of Cleveland, Ohio, USA and Sue Fischer of Indianapolis, Indiana, USA.

Stewart's great pride in his country is only matched by his encyclopedic knowledge of the enormous Canadian contribution to the aerial war. He has given freely of that knowledge and has provided us with a number of rare photographs. Bill Evans has studied the von Richthofen 'Saga' for, quite literally, decades and again, his generous advice and practical help have been absolutely invaluable.

Sue Fischer contributed not only her enthusiasm and great expertise but also travelled hundreds of miles and laboured long and hard on our behalf!

And to the many others listed below, our heartfelt thanks..........

D.R. Adam, Lewes, East Sussex.
All Staff, Commonwealth War Graves Commission, Maidenhead, Berks.
All Staff, Liverpool Central and Reference Libraries.
All Staff, Dr. Barnado's Home, Ilford and Clapham.
Adrian Allan, Asst. Archivist, University of Liverpool.
Derek Allen, Saltash, Devon.
Stan Applin, London.
Ian Arnold, Bideford, North Devon.
Carol Arrowsmith, Archivist's Office, Institution of Civil Engineers, London.
John Bailey, Hon. Editor, Western Front Assoc. Essex Branch.
David Baldwin, Stafford, Staffs.
Victoria Bannister, Southport, Lancs.
David J. Barnes, Ramsbottom, Bury.
Mr. and Mrs. F. Bennett, Dorking, Surrey.
Mike Blackburn, St. Helens, Lancs.
Cliff Blood, Prestwich, Manchester.
Mr. and Mrs. B. J. Boultbee, Huntingdon, Cambs.
W.K. Brookes, Senior Asst. Registrar, University of Nottingham.
John Bruton, *Nottingham Evening Post.*
Roland Burke Savage, Archivist, Clongowes Wood College, Naas, Co. Kildare, Eire.
Hugh Butterworth, Braunton, North Devon.
Diana Chardin, Manuscript Cataloguer, Trinity College Library, Cambridge.
David Cheetham, Nottingham.
Frank Cheesman, Margate, Kent.
Neil Clarke, Southport, Lancs.
Alan Clay, Carlton, Nottingham.
G.M. Clutterbuck, Dursley, Gloucs.
Dr. Jamie Cottis, Archivist, Magdalen College, Oxford.
Peter Cunniffe, Bonymaer, Swansea.
Geoff Davies, Alumni Office, University of Manchester.
Alex Dawson, *Leicester Mercury.*
Jeff Day, Chard, Somerset.
Jacques DeCeuninck, Tournai, Belgium.
Maria Delfgou, Archivist, Chigwell School, Essex.
Department of Documents, Imperial War Museum, London.
Dr.Roger Dye, Department of Engineering, University of Manchester.
Jim Edgar, Newton Stewart.
Mrs. J.E. Edgell, Librarian, Hon. Society of the Middle Temple, London.
Robert Elwall, Photographs Curator, British Architectural Library, London.
John Evans, Pembroke Dock, Dyfed.
Major David Evans, T.D., Hon. Secretary, Liverpool Scottish Museum.
John Field, Librarian and Archivist, Westminster School, London.
Mr. Finbow, Saxmunden, Suffolk.
Stuart Fraser, *Plymouth Evening News.*
Phillipa Giles, Saundersfoot, Pembroke.
Lou Gottfreund, Southport, Lancs.
Lee Granville, *Honiton News.*
Mrs. J. Granshaw, Secretary to Bursar, Felsted School, Dunmow, Essex.
Barry Gray, W.W.1 Historian, Hertford, Herts.
Russell Guest, Writer and Historian, Melbourne, Australia.
Brenda Hand, Hon. Secretary, Western Front Association, Devon Branch.
Elmer J. Hankes, Minneapolis, Minnesota, USA.
Bill Hannam, Hebden, North Yorkshire.
Mrs. A. Hartley, Team Librarian, Stockport Central Library.
David Harrison, *Bristol Evening Post.*
B.D. Hankins, Deeping St. James, Lincolnshire.
Jan Hayzlett, Fort Collins, Colorado, USA.

Dr. T.A. Heathcote, Curator, Royal Military College, Sandhurst, Surrey.
Derek Henderson, Journalist, *North Devon Journal*, Barnstaple, Devon.
Hon. Archivist, Campbell College, Belfast
Mrs. Hulse, Department of Local Studies, Sheffield Central Library.
Information Department, British Film Institute, London.
Keeper and Staff, Public Records Office, Kew, London.
Kevin Kelly, Sunderland, Tyne and Wear.
Jim Klobuchar, Feature Writer, *Star Tribune*, Minneapolis, Minnesota, USA.
Dr. W.A. Land, Secretary, Orders and Medals Research Society, Australian Branch, Sydney, N.S.W., Australia.
Douglas Latter, Bristol, Gloucs.
James Lawton, Librarian, Shrewsbury School, Shrewsbury, Salop.
Andrew Leigh, General Manager, The Old Vic Theatre, London.
Stuart Leslie, Scarborough, North Yokshire.
James Leslie, Ballymoney, Co. Antrim.
Ian Livesley, Southport, Lancs.
Clive Lucas, O.B.E., Sydney, N.S.W., Australia.
Alaister MacPherson, Hon. Archivist, Haileybury College, Herts.
Malcolm McGregor, Esher, Surrey.
N.W.R. Mellon, Headmaster, King Edward VI School, Stratford on Avon.
Paul Morris, Blackpool, Lancs.
Ms. I.G. Murray, Archivist, Hon. Society of the Inner Temple, London.
The Newspaper Library, British Library, London.
Mike O'Connor, Aero Historian, East Sussex.
Neal O'Connor, Princeton, N.J., USA
John J. Parry, Liverpool.
Andrew Phillips, O.J. Liaison Officer, Old Johnian Society, Leatherhead, Surrey.
Vic Piak, *Nottingham Evening Post.*
Simon Pile, Blackpool and Liverpool.
Catharine Prance, Bideford, Devon.
Gillian Prince, Doncaster, South Yorkshire.
Registrar, The University of Wales, Aberystwyth, Dyfed.
Keith Rennles, Sutton, Surrey.
Alex Revell, W.W.1 Historian, Hatfield, Herts.
Mrs. J.E. Ritchie, Ayr, Ayrshire.
Bruce Robertson, Writer and Historian, Chippenham, Wiltshire.
Bob Rogers Jnr., Viet Nam Veteran (U.S.M.C.) and W.W.1 Historian, Stone Mountain, Georgia, USA.
Harry Rudd, Hightown, Merseyside.
Graham Sacker, Cheltenham, Gloucestershire.
Dr. Derek Scales, Director of Studies, St. Lawrence College, Ramsgate, Kent.
Michael Schoeman, Vlaeberg, South Africa.
W.O.Simpson, Membership Secretary, The Cheltonian Society, Cheltenham, Gloucestershire.
Gordon Smith, Bonnyrigg, Midlothian.
Barry Stead, Public Inquiries Assistant, National Archives of Canada, Ottawa, Ontario, Canada.
Mr. and Mrs.Stevenson, Brecon, South Wales.
Pat Stewart, Spalding, Lincolnshire.
James A. Stuart, Hollywood, Co. Down.
Roland Symons, Hon. Archivist, Monkton Combe Junior School, Combe Down, Bath.
Geoff Taylor, Birmingham.
Roy Thornley, Warrington, Cheshire.
Mrs. A. Toner, Assistant Archivist, Trinity Hall, Cambridge.
Brian J. Turner, Leigh on Sea, Essex.
Nick Watson, The *Worcester Evening News.*
M.A. Weaver, Hon. Archivist, Woodbridge School, Suffolk.
David West, O.B.E., T.D., Hon. Archivist, Marlborough College, Marlborough, Wiltshire.
Ann Wheeler, Librarian, Charterhouse College, Surrey.
Brian Wilks, Secretary, Old Worksopian Society, Worksop, Nottinghamshire.
James Wilson, Cardiff, South Wales.
Derek Winterbottom, Archivist, Clifton College, Bristol.
Peter Yeend, Hon. Archivist, The King's School, Parramatta, N.S.W., Australia.

CONTENTS

INTRODUCTION

Baron Manfred von Richthofen: even now, nearly 80 years after the exploits that made him a household name and ensured him a permanent and leading role in the history of WW1 aviation, the universal enthralment with this one man continues.

Much has already been written about his life, his squadron, his group, his aeroplanes, his violent death. The first attempts to list and identify his 'victims' – the pilots and observers unfortunate enough to find themselves under his guns – were made nearly 70 years ago. Some of the flyers concerned were correctly identified, a number were not. Guesses and assumptions (always necessary in a reconstruction treatment of this nature) have, with time, gained credence beyond the merit of the evidence upon which they were based.

The authors of this book, always conscious of the many difficulties, set out to review completely the available evidence - documentary, visual, anecdotal - to arrive at the hoped for, 'definitive' list. By a series of processes of elimination involving the study of contemporary maps, time checks, place names, RFC, RNAS, RAF and Jasta records, combat reports, etc, we have assembledwhat we believe to be the most comprehensive list of the Baron's victories ever compiled. Next, we set out to achieve something which had never before been attempted, to put the flesh on the bones to the identities of the many young men who comprise the cold statistics. Our quest for the photographic images and personal details of the pilots and observers who fought von Richthofen has covered most corners of the planet and we have been helped, in no small measure, by the huge and abiding interest in the exploits of this Ace of Aces that still exists worldwide.

Having conquered the last of the elements, mankind almost immediately employed his new-found ability to fly in the waging of war. The reporting of this new phenomenon, a 'War in the Air', also presented a fresh challenge to the contemporary chroniclers of the period. In their search to project a suitable image, journalists chose, paradoxically, to equate the exploits of the brave men who flew and fought in this new element with the knights of Arthurian legend. As with the knights of old, the passage of time has not dimmed the aura of mystique and romance which came to surround these daring young men. Although the war was fought on many fronts, it is the events on the so-called Western Front which, above all, fire the retrospective imagination. And, of those engaged in the skies above those pockmarked and sanguineous fields of France and Flanders, none has captured that imagination more than Cavalry Captain Manfred von Richthofen of the German Air Service – 'The Red Baron'.

Manfred von Richthofen's arrival on the Western Front as a fighter pilot in the late summer of 1916 came at an auspicious time for the new fighter arm of the German Imperial Air Service. From the opening day of the Battle of the Somme on 1 July 1916 – a day on which the British Army suffered 60,000 casualties (most occurring in the two hours following the initial assault at 0730), a whole series of further attacks had been attempted, each of them intended to achieve the long hoped for 'breakthrough'. All failed.

The scale and enormity of the losses to the British Army on that first day alone can be best illustrated by a comparison: when all the casualties of the Crimean War (1854-56), the Boer or South African War (1899-1902) and the Korean War (1950-53) are added together, the total does not match those suffered on that first July day! Further weeks and months of bitter fighting occurred in the area of the Somme-Delville Wood, Fricourt,

Guillemont, Flers Courcelette, emotive names to WW1 historians even now.

From mid-1915 until the Somme offensive, the German Air Service, with its nimble Fokker Eindekker monoplane fighters, had carved their own chapter of history in the skies of France. Few in number, many two-seater Flieger-Abteilung (aviation section) had two or three Fokkers attached for use as protection flights for the two-seaters and hunting sorties against British and French aircraft. Pilots who showed an aptitude and aggression in flying these monoplanes soon began to make names for themselves with the general public in Germany, and RFC and French Air Service personnel quickly came to know them too. Wintgens, Parschau, Frankl, Berthold, Immelmann and Boelcke were perhaps the more famous; their exploits were followed by an adoring public, conferring upon them a status comparable to present-day pop stars or sporting heroes. When Max Immelmann fell in action in June 1916, Oswald Boelcke was immediately withdrawn from war flying, lest he too should fall. However, by the time the Somme fighting was at its height, Boelcke's ideas on how to develop the fighting arm of the German Air Service had been accepted by the High Command. From the late summer the fighting aeroplanes would be grouped together into Jagdstaffeln – hunting sections – to provide air protection and to seek out and engage the Allied aeroplanes that daily flew over the German positions on the Western Front. Recalled to active duty, Boelcke was given command of Jagdstaffel Nr.2 (shortened to just Jasta 2) in September 1916, with an almost entirely free hand to select pilots for his new Jasta. Amongst those he asked for was a young former Uhlan cavalry officer turned airman, Manfred von Richthofen.

In the air over the Western Front – the line to the north held by the British, the Belgians helping to hold the northern edge by the Channel coast, and by the French to the south – the Allies had enjoyed comparative superiority, able to patrol above the lines, if not with impunity, then with limited opposition. Despite the depredations during the Fokker period of supremacy, the RFC in particular had not been deterred from carrying out its declared policy of pursuing its offensive across the lines into enemy territory. Now, as the battle on the ground began to stultify, the air war hotted up. German resistance to, and interference with, British photo-reconnaissance patrols and artillery liaison sorties intensified.

Now flying was to become an even more hazardous occupation for the chosen elite who were the pilots, observers and gunners of the Royal Flying Corps and Royal Naval Air Service. They had to contend not only with mechanical and structural failures, which could and frequently did imperil their young lives, poor weather and a prevailing west to east wind, but now, also, came the hunters. Spawned in the Fokker period and now concentrated into an elite,these hunters were a product of an enemy with an inventive, implacable, fiercely courageous and militaristic ethic and whose sole raison d'étre was the enemy's destruction. Encouraged by honours, awards and the resultant fame in the Homeland, all were keen to emulate their late or contemporary heroes such as Immelmann or Boelcke.

Over those late summer and early winter days of 1916, the fledgling Jasta pilots honed their skills and tactics, and despite their great mentor Boelcke falling in combat (by collision in an air battle on 28 October) most were more than ready to engage their British and French counterparts in the first major campaign of 1917, the Battle of Arras, in early April.

Manfred Albrecht Freiherr von Richthofen was born on 2 May 1892, the second of four children of Baron Albrecht and Kunigunde von Richthofen. Their first child had been a daughter, Ilse (Elisabeth Luise Marie, born 1890), later followed by Lothar Siegfried (1894) who was also destined to become a successful fighter pilot; Karl Bolko, the third son, arrived in 1903. Manfred was born into a world and family of privilege. Richthofen was a Prussian name, tracing its origins to Bernau, in Brandenburg. By the mid-seventeenth century the family had grown and become settled in Silesia, around Striegau, Jauer and Schweidnitz. His father had served in the Leibkürassieren-Regiment Nr.1 in Breslau, reaching the rank of Rittmeister (Cavalry Captain), but had been forced to retire on medical grounds. Manfred's mother also had a notable family background, her line stemming from the Falkenhausen military family, descending from the Frankish line of the House of Hohenzollern. Kunigunde was the daughter of the wealthy von Schickfuss und Neudorff family. A not readily known fact is that other members of the Schickfuss und Neudorff family also had connections with flying: an older uncle was badly injured in a crash in France in June 1915 while training to become an observer; and cousin Oskar flew with Jasta 3 in 1917 but was killed in action on 5 June.

Manfred entered the military cadet training school at Wahlstatt, just outside Liegnitz in August 1903, at the age of eleven. A good student, he endured six years of strict Prussian training, progressing through to the senior academy at Gross-Lichterfelde near Berlin. Graduating as an officer candidate in 1911, he was assigned to his choice of cavalry unit, the Kaiser Alexander III Uhlan Regiment Nr.1, and commissioned the following year after completing the war school course in Berlin. He joined his regiment in Militsch, which today is in Poland (Milicz), north-east of Breslau. When war came he made his first cavalry patrols on the new Russian front, but his unit was soon on its way to France where he saw his first actions and received his first decoration – the Iron Cross 2nd Class. It was the first of many honours.

At this stage, Manfred had little interest in flying, but as the war progressed and the trenches became a permanent feature from the North Sea coast to the Swiss border, the traditional roles of the cavalry – reconnaissance of the enemy's positions, the occasional gallant charge with sabre and lance, and the harassment of a retiring army – no longer obtained. Now it was the aeroplane that made the reconnaissance sorties, flying over the trenches with their barbed-wire entanglements, where cavalry could no longer operate or even survive against the new and deadly weapon of twentieth-century war, the machine gun.

Like so many others, bored with the enforced inactivity over the winter of 1914-15, his cavalry training no longer of value, he requested a transfer to the Air Service (the Fliegertruppe), which was eventually granted in May 1915. First trained as an observer in Cologne, within weeks he was assigned to Feldflieger-Abteilung 69 (FFA69) which was in the process of being formed on the Russian front, but given the name Brieftauben-Abteilung Ostende or BAO (carrier-pigeon section Ostende) to hide its true identity! FFA69 operated initially with Albatros BII machines, before later taking on the superior Albatros CI two - seaters. Then, in August, came a posting back to France and to BAO. Operating over the Western Front, von Richthofen had his first aerial encounters with the Allied airmen he was soon to face in deadly conflict for 17 months. He and his pilots now began to meet opposing airmen more regularly and his gunfire sent a French Farman down, and although it force-landed and tipped nose first into a shell hole on the French side, von Richthofen and his pilot were unable to get confirmation of an aerial victory.

Not long afterwards, Richthofen had a chance encounter with Oswald Boelcke, already an airman of note with four victories to his name. Unable to resist asking the fighter pilot how on earth he did it, Boelcke replied with the famous words, 'It is quite simple. I fly right up, take good aim, then he falls down.' Manfred was soon asking his pilot to show him how to handle and fly an aeroplane, and by 10 October had achieved his first solo flight. He next requested formal pilot training and was sent to Doberitz, just east of Berlin, where his instruction began.

During his training he and the rest of Germany were beginning to hear more and more of the achievements of Boelcke, Immelmann and the other aces. On 12 January, Boelcke and Immelmann received the coveted Orden Pour le Mérite – the famed Blue Max – Germany's premier award for bravery in war.

A pilot at last, von Richthofen was assigned to Kasta 8 of Kagohl Nr.2, commanded by Boelcke's brother Wilhelm. Piloting an Albatros two-seater, the embryo pilot had to complete a period of two-seater work before being considered competent to fly the single-seater Eindekker. Despite this he actually engaged a French Nieuport Scout on 26 April 1916. He claimed it went down to crash, but once again there were no independent witnesses to confirm it, although this and another unconfirmed victory that day were recorded in the German daily communiqué.

By now Manfred was urging his commander to permit him to fly the single-seat Eindekker but although this was finally permitted, another pilot, flying the sole machine of the unit was hit in an air fight, damaging it before Manfred could show any aptitude with it.

When Immelmann was killed and Boelcke taken away from the Front, Manfred's idea of asking Boelcke if he could transfer to his unit was frustrated. Instead, with the opening of a Russian offensive, Kagohl 2 was sent to the Eastern Front where Manfred continued to fly the two-seater Albatros CIIIs. By the summer of 1916, and the mighty Somme offensive in France, Boelcke was at last recalled to the Front. Permitted to select for the most part his own pilots for his new Jasta 2, Boelcke remembered the keen von Richthofen from his earlier meeting and asked him to join him. Von Richthofen needed no second urging.

Jasta 2 had been formed on 10 August 1916, von Richthofen arriving at the unit's base at Bertincourt, on the Somme front, on 1 September 1916. At first they had no aircraft, although Boelcke had a single Fokker DIII biplane fighter in which he scored his Jasta's first successes. As will be described later, the fledgling fighter pilots were successful on their first day of actual combat, 17 September, von Richthofen being amongst those who scored. With his first confirmed victory, von Richthofen received the coveted Ehrenbecher (victory cup) presented to every pilot after achieving his first victory against the enemy. This led von Richthofen to commission a Berlin silversmith to make small victory cups on which was engraved the date and type of his subsequent victories. Sixty were made before silver became less than readily available and prohibitively too expensive.

Manfred von Richthofen was to remain with Jasta 2 until he was given command of Jasta 11 on 14 January 1917, at the same time as he was awarded the Orden Pour le Mérite. He led his new command with distinction, especially through April 1917, his unit being the highest scoring Jasta during the Arras battles. He had achieved 16 victories with Jasta 2, and by the end of April had increased this total to 52, leaving the Front on leave as the highest scoring fighter pilot of the German Air Service, living or dead.

Von Richthofen returned to the Front in June 1917, adding four more kills to his tally, by which time it had been announced that he would command the first ever fighter Jagdgeschwader – JG Nr.1 – comprising four fighter staffeln, Jastas 4, 6, 10 and 11. He brought down his 57th victory on 2 July but was wounded on the sixth and again had to leave the Front. He did not return until August 1917, and when he did he was never quite the same again. Although he led JG1 with courage and fortitude, his former rate of scoring dropped, so that by the end of November his total had only increased to 63. Returning from leave in March 1918, in time for the great German Offensive (The Kaiser's Battle), Manfred von Richthofen led JG1 in the desperate air battles over the Somme battlefields, and recovering some of his earlier verve, scored 17 victories in a month before he fell in combat on 21 April. With a total victory score of 80 he had become and would remain, the highest scoring fighter pilot of any of the belligerent nations who fought in the skies during the world's first air war.

What follows are the details of those 80 air combat 'victories'. We have endeavoured to give as much detail as possible of the actions themselves and of the factors that finally decided our choice, one way or the other, where doubt existed. We have corrected some errors of identity which have gained coinage over the years and, where no absolute certainty still exists, offered our own reasoned identification, backed by the appropriate research. As the reader will glean, we have, in a very few instances, concluded that the 'victories' were not absolute – the 'victims' escaped not only with their lives but with their machines, also.

However, the authors wish to emphasise that in no way whatsoever do we wish to cast doubts on the authenticity and genuineness of the Baron's claims. On the contrary, he appears to have been meticulous in this regard, even when his reputation was such that he could, indeed, have taken 'liberties'. It is simply that in these few cases – and only after long hours spent poring over maps, studying locations, comparing times and taking absolutely nothing at face value – we believe the Great Man was mistaken. Understandably and certainly not uniquely, in the heat and fear of battle he made claims and assumptions which were not always correct.

And so we present eighty 'victories' in the light of the facts as we see them and, with them, the stories of the men who found themselves 'Under the Guns of the Red Baron'.

NORMAN FRANKS MORDEN, SURREY.

HAL GIBLIN HIGHTOWN, LIVERPOOL.

NIGEL McCRERY WEST BRIDGEFORD, NOTTINGHAM.

PLEASE NOTE: THE AUTHORS WOULD WELCOME ANY ADDITIONAL INFORMATION FROM READERS ON THE VICTORIES AND VICTIMS DETAILED IN THE BOOK, AND ESPECIALLY PHOTOGRAPHS FOR POSSIBLE USE IN THE FUTURE.

17 SEPTEMBER 1916

VICTORY NO.1

FE2B NO. 7018
11 SQUADRON
ENGINE NO. 701 WD 7061
GUNS: 16382; 12795

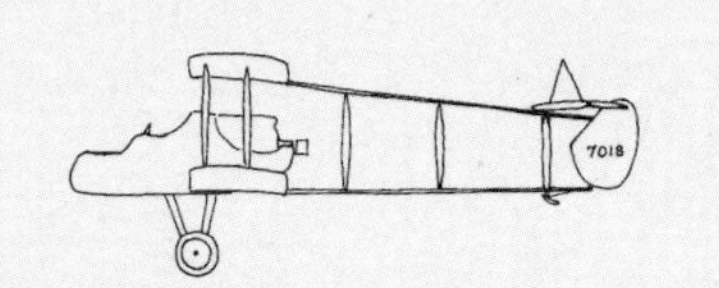

VON RICHTHOFEN'S Combat Report:
Vickers No.7018 • Motor No.701
Machine guns Nos.17314, 10372
near Villers Plouich, 1100 hrs.

When patrol flying I detected shrapnel clouds in direction of Cambrai. I hurried forth and met a squad which I attacked shortly after 1100. I singled out the last machine and fired several times at closest range (ten metres). Suddenly the enemy propeller stood stock still. The machine went down gliding and I followed until I had killed the observer who had not stopped shooting until the last moment.

Now my opponent went downwards in sharp curves. At approximately 1,200 metres a second German machine came along and attacked my victim right down to the ground and then landed next to the English plane.

BARON VON RICHTHOFEN

WEATHER: BRIGHT MORNING WITH CLOUDS IN THE AFTERNOON.

3rd Brigade RFC mounted a bomb raid against Marcoing Station, with four bomb-carrying BE2d aircraft of 12 Squadron (flown without observers on this occasion due to the bomb load) escorted by six FEs of 11 Squadron. 12 Squadron were based at Avesnes-le-Comte, 16 km west of Arras, 11 Squadron at the nearby airfield at Izel-le-Hameau (known also as Le Hameau). Marcoing was just to the south-west of Cambrai, a direct distance of about 48 kilometres from the two squadrons' bases.

As we now know, this day was the first time Boelcke's fledgling fighter pilots in Jasta 2 got in amongst the RFC machines. Until now, mainly due to aircraft being in short supply, only Boelcke had scored victories for his new unit, seven since the beginning of September. An eighth had been downed by Otto Höhne on the 16th (an 11 Squadron FE2b), and on the morning of the 17th Erwin Böhme had scored his first and the Jasta's ninth (a Sopwith 1½ Strutter of 70 Squadron).

It was the first time Jasta 2 had flown as a unit, and they found the BE and FE aircraft over Marcoing, and fell on them. Boelcke attacked the leading FE, crewed by Captain D B Gray and Lt L B Helder, which came down at Equancourt where the two men set fire to their aeroplane (7019) before being captured. Hans Reimann brought down 2/Lt T P L Molloy and Sgt G J Morton (4844) south of Trescault, while von Richthofen shot down his victim at Villers Plouich. Thus the fight had drifted some way south of the target area.

It seems that Morris landed the FE onto a German airfield at Flesquiéres, north of Villers Plouich, back nearer Marcoing. After making a poor landing nearby, Richthofen joined a group of men running to the FE and watched as the dying pilot and dead observer were removed.

In all the raiding force lost four FEs and two BEs. Jasta 4 had also engaged the British aircraft – the latter reported around 20 hostile aircraft in this engagement – and claimed one FE at Equancourt, while ground fire accounted for the two bombing aircraft.

In this fight, Sergeant A Clarkson, observer to Sergeant Thompson of 11 Squadron, claimed one enemy aircraft (reported as a Roland) as shot down 'out of control'. Clarkson would fall to von Richthofen before the month was out.

It is of interest that the gun numbers as shown on the RFC loss report form do not tally with those noted on Richthofen's combat report, although the (part) engine number does. Either there was a mix-up over souvenirs, or a clerical error on the loss report forms. Von Richthofen was flying Albatros DII Nr.491/16.

MORRIS,
LIONEL BERTRAM FRANK
SECOND LIEUTENANT
11 SQUADRON; 3/ROYAL WEST SURREYS

BORN IN 1897, Morris lived with his parents at 'Merle Bank', Rotherfield Road, Carshalton, Surrey, close to where his father owned and ran a tobacconist shop. On 13 May 1915, at barely eighteen years of age, he was selected, along with hundreds of other middle class boys, for induction into the Inns of Court Officer Training Corps (No.2/3601). His training progressed well and he was commissioned into the West Surreys, 'The Queen's Royal Regiment', on 20 August 1915. He immediately and successfully applied for transfer to the Royal Flying Corps. After gaining his Royal Aero Club Aviators Certificate (No.2334) on 25 January 1916, he was appointed Flying Officer in April 1916 and proceeded to his Squadron in France shortly afterwards. Still barely alive when he was extricated from the wreck of his FE2b under the excited and fevered gaze of von Richthofen, who had landed as close to his victims as he could, Morris died before the ambulance could deliver him to the nearby German Military Hospital. He was nineteen years of age. He is buried in the Porte-de-Paris Cemetery, just outside the old city walls of Cambrai, France (Fr.598).

REES,
TOM
CAPTAIN 11 SQUADRON; 14/ ROYAL WELSH FUSILIERS

BEFORE THE WAR, Tom Rees lived with his parents, Thomas and Alice Rees, at their home at Cefnbrynich, Defynog, Brecon. A brilliant scholar, he entered Aberystwyth University College in 1912. As an enthusiastic member of the University Officer Training Corps, Tom had to be restrained from 'joining up' as soon as the war started. Good counsel prevailed but nothing could stop him from entering the Army immediately after he graduated as a Bachelor of Arts. Commissioned into the Royal Welsh Fusiliers on 21 January 1915, he was gazetted to the 14th (Service) Battalion of his regiment which largely comprised volunteers (Pals) from the northern coastal area of Wales, mainly the counties of Caernarvon and Anglesey. Rees's academic abilities and soldierly qualities ensured his early promotion to Lieutenant. Shortly after proceeding to France with his battalion in November 1915, he successfully applied for a transfer to the Royal Flying Corps. Following a brief period of training in England, he recrossed the Channel to join 11 Squadron at the Front. Unlike his pilot, Rees was killed in the air during the fight with von Richthofen, ironically on the very day his promotion to Captain was announced. The members of Jasta 4 showed their respect for a gallant foe by burying him with full military honours. The Rees family suffered the death of another son in November 1916. John Rees and his father were cutting down a tree which fell on John. It was during John's funeral that news arrived of Tom's death. Tom is buried in Plouich Communal Cemetery, France (Fr.667). He was 21.

23 SEPTEMBER 1916

VICTORY NO.2

MARTINSYDE G.100 No.7481
27 SQUADRON RFC
ENGINE No.417 WD 2389
GUNS: 4060; 17074

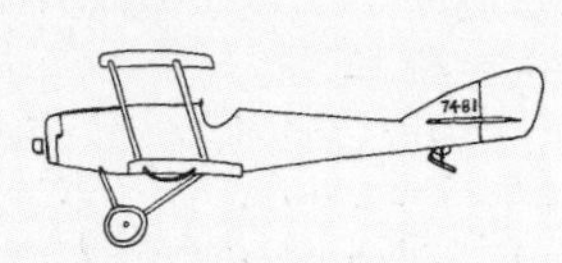

VON RICHTHOFEN'S Combat Report:
1100 hrs. One-seater Martinsyde, GW No.174
1100 air fight above Bapaume. Adversary dashed, after 300 shots, mortally wounded, near Beugny (Street Bapaume – Cambrai) to the ground.
Two machine guns recovered, will be delivered. Dead occupant buried by 7th Infantry Division.

BARON VON RICHTHOFEN

WEATHER: BRIGHT AND CLEAR ALL DAY; GROUND MIST IN EARLY MORNING.

The previous day had seen the end of the Battle of Flers-Courcelette, on the Somme, which had begun on the 15th. The 22nd had seen Sergeant Bellerby in trouble too, flying G100 No.7263 during a bomb raid to Havrincourt Wood, from 27's base at Fienvillers, north-east of Amiens. At 1645, when over Velu, he had become slightly separated from the Squadron formation and was immediately pounced on by three enemy aircraft which came up under his tail. Bellerby turned and fired a few rounds from his rear-facing gun and the enemy aircraft banked steeply and went down. However, his Martinsyde was hit and returned badly damaged.

On the 23rd he was part of a six-man formation that took off at 0840 to carry out an Offensive Patrol (OP) between Bapaume and Cambrai. The area is notable for the long straight road which runs slightly north-west from Bapaume to Cambrai for a distance of 28 kilometres – Beugny being 6 kilometres from Bapaume.

At 0930, flying at 11,500 feet, Captain O T Boyd leading the patrol (in A1564) saw a biplane with blue upper wings and dived on it, firing 50 rounds. The EA dived very steeply with Boyd following but he could not catch it. After making for another EA, Boyd then saw Second Lieutenant L F Forbes collide with an EA, the German going down out of control. Afterwards, another Martinsyde was seen going down, under control, in the direction of Douai, smoke coming from its fuselage.

Meantime, Lieutenant P C Sherran (A1567) also witnessed the collision just west of Cambrai, and also saw Forbes making for the lines. In the event, Forbes managed to get back to 24 Squadron's base at Bertangles, north of Amiens, but having difficulty with his damaged machine he hit a tree, injuring himself and wrecking his aeroplane.

As 27 Squadron fought their way back from Cambrai, several more enemy aircraft attacked but they were driven off. Sherran also saw the Martinsyde going down under control, but trailing smoke, near Le

Transloy. Another was seen heading down near Marcoing.

The Squadron had run into five scouts from Jasta 2 which shot down three of the Martinsydes, Second Lieutenants E J Roberts, O C Godfrey and Sergeant Bellerby, claimed by Leutnants Erwin Böhme, Hans Reimann and von Richthofen. Forbes had deliberately rammed Hans Reimann's aircraft, the German falling to his death. (Forbes later became Air Marshal Sir Leslie Forbes having won the MC in WW1.) The remaining two RFC pilots returned to Fienvillers. Boyd too later rose to Air rank.

Although the translation of von Richthofen's report clearly shows 1100 hrs (twice), Jasta 2 records the time of his and Reimann's kills at 0950 (German time). Böhme's victory was unconfirmed by the Germans and was probably Roberts, who would have come down just inside British lines (near Le Transloy), while Godfrey, well known pre-war as a sporting motor-cyclist and Tourist Trophy rider, was killed by Reimann over Bus, just south of Bertincourt. Reimann crashed near Noreuil at 0955.

After landing back at Lagnicourt, which is only 4 kilometres north-east of Beugny, von Richthofen drove to the crash site and took a souvenir showing the letters 'GW' and the number '174'. The number may have been part of the surviving serial 7481 but more probably this with the GW represented the part-number of a component, the Martinsyde having been built under a sub-contract with the Grahame-White Aviation Coy.

Von Richthofen was flying Albatros DII Nr.491/16.

BELLERBY, HERBERT

SERGEANT (No.17018) 27 SQUADRON

HERBERT BELLERBY volunteered for service with the Royal Flying Corps in 1915. The son of Henry and Mary Bellerby, he was living with his parents at their home at 49 Warren Road, Chingford, Essex when war was declared. He had been educated at Bancrofts School, Woodford Green, and worshipped regularly at St Peter and St Paul, Chingford, where today his name appears on the memorial for those who fell in the Great War.

A man of maturity and experience, Bellerby was quickly picked out for pilot training. His body was recovered by men of the 7th German Infantry Division but his burial place was lost in the subsequent fighting which raged backwards and forwards across the area. Bellerby is commemorated on the Arras Memorial to the Missing, France. He was twenty-eight years old.

30 SEPTEMBER 1916

VICTORY NO.3

FE2B NO.6973
11 SQUADRON RFC
ENGINE NO.634 WD 6994
GUNS: 2144; 11003

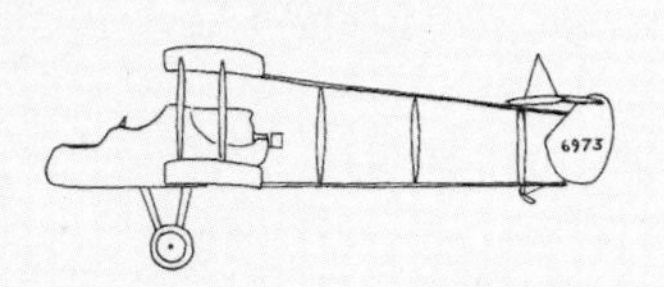

VON RICHTHOFEN'S Combat Report:
1150 hrs, near Lagnicourt.

About 1150 I attacked, accompanied by four planes of our Staffel above our aerodrome at Lagnicourt and at 3,000 metres altitude, a Vickers squadron. I singled out a machine and after some 200 shots, the enemy plane started gliding down towards Cambrai. Finally it began to make circles. The shooting had stopped and I saw that the machine was flying uncontrolled.

As we were already rather far away from our front lines, I left the crippled plane and selected a new adversary. Later on I could observe the aforementioned machine, pursued by a German Albatros machine, crash burning to the ground near Fremicourt. The machine burnt to ashes.

BARON VON RICHTHOFEN

WEATHER: BRIGHT AND FINE ALL DAY, WITH OCCASIONAL CLOUDS IN THE AFTERNOON.

Despite another pilot appearing to follow his victim down, credit for the destruction of this FE went to Richthofen. 11 Squadron had been providing escort to bombing machines from 12 and 13 Squadrons against Jasta 2's airfield, while other RFC fighters – Nieuport Scouts and Moranes of 60 Squadron – were also in the vicinity.

However, these did not prevent von Richthofen from bringing down 6973, although Lieutenant S F Vincent of 60 Squadron witnessed an FE going down in flames at 1045 hrs, south-east of Bapaume (British time one hour behind German time). However, Vincent's location seems a little out as Fremicourt is about 4 kilometres due east of Bapaume. It was the only success claimed by Jasta 2 on this day.

The FE gunner, Sergeant Clarkson, despite considerable experience as an air gunner (having already been credited with three victories, one being in the action with Jasta 2 on 17 September), was unable on this occasion to fend off the attacker.

Von Richthofen was flying Albatros DII Nr.491/16 and once more he was able to secure a souvenir from what remained of the smashed and burnt aircraft. It was a presentation aircraft purchased with money raised by the people of Malaya, with 'Malaya No.22' painted on the nacelle.

Right: Von Richthofen's friend and mentor, Oswald Boelcke – leader of Jasta 2.

LANSDALE,

ERNEST CONWAY

LIEUTENANT 11 SQUADRON ARMY SERVICE CORPS

ALTHOUGH ORIGINALLY a native of Goole, Lansdale was living with his family at 3 Hawthorn Villas, Grove Road, Ilkley, Yorkshire when war broke out. Lansdale had completed his education at Ilkley Grammar School and, after leaving, had secured a position as a representative with Leigh and Pierce Ltd, Wholesale Provision Merchants, for whom he travelled extensively. He was in Denmark on business in August 1914, but returned home and was ready to join the Army immediately upon the declaration of war. Not surprising, in view of his civilian calling and experience, he was given a commission in the Army Service Corps on 16 October 1914, and posted to the 57th Divisional Train where his father, Major Matthew Ernest Lansdale, was second-in-command. Young Lansdale was promoted Lieutenant on 12 June 1915, going to France for the first time in January 1916. In July of that year, thoroughly bored with the similarity of his Army duties to those of his civilian profession, he applied for a transfer to the Royal Flying Corps. After flight training in England, he was sent to 11 Squadron in France on 17 September 1916. Less than two weeks later he died in German hands after falling under the guns of von Richthofen. Lansdale is buried in Bancourt Communal Cemetery, France (Fr.306). He was twenty-one years of age.

CLARKSON,

ALBERT

SERGEANT (No.3049) 11 SQUADRON

ALBERT CLARKSON WAS born and brought up at Lonsdale Road, Burnley, Lancashire. After leaving school, he served and completed an apprenticeship as an electrician with a local company. As soon as he was able, he volunteered for service with the Royal Flying Corps and was accepted on 23 January 1915. In the August of 1915, Clarkson's parents moved to Blackpool, taking up residence at 56 Shaw Road. In the meantime, Albert had successfully undergone training as an observer and was flying operationally in France. Reports following his death credited him with numerous encounters with enemy machines and "having accounted for three German aeroplanes". By a tragic coincidence, Clarkson's father had died on 16 October 1916, and news that her son was missing, presumed killed, was received by Mrs Clarkson at the very moment her husband's funeral entourage was about to leave Shaw Road in Blackpool for his burial in Rosegrove Cemetery, in their original home town of Burnley. Sergeant Albert Clarkson is buried in Bancourt Communal Cemetery in France (Fr.306). He was twenty-two years of age.

7 OCTOBER 1916

VICTORY NO.4

BE12 No.6618
21 Squadron RFC
Engine No.25226 WD 5730
Guns: 16442; L6920

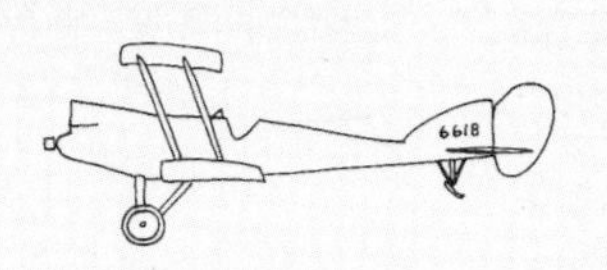

VON RICHTHOFEN'S Combat Report:
Machine type: New and not seen up till now.
Plane No.6618: A two-deck plane (biplane) with 12 cyl. Daimler Motor No.25 226.

0910 hrs, near Equancourt.

About 0900 I attacked at 3,000 metres altitude and accompanied by two other machines, an English plane near Rancourt. After 400 shots enemy plane dashed downwards, the pilot having been mortally wounded. Occupant: Lieutenant Fenwick, killed by shot in the head.

Baron von Richthofen

Weather: low clouds and strong winds – stormy all day.

The BE12 was a fighting scout version of the BE2c; the only difference was that the front cockpit was closed over and a gun was mounted on the port side of the fuselage (some also had a gun on the top wing, set to fire over the propeller), and a 140 or 150 hp engine was fitted rather than a 90 hp. With the obvious moves by the Germans to mount fighter patrols to engage Allied two-seater reconnaissance and artillery spotting aircraft, there was a desperate need to increase fighter types, the BE12 being a stop gap. It was not effective.

Five 21 Squadron BE12s took off from their base at Bertangles at 0730, to fly an Offensive Patrol led by Captain R Neville. Neville and Lieutenant J A Stewart's aircraft each carried 112 lb bombs, the other three acting as escort. The patrol flew to the Ytres area, south of Bertincourt. Jasta 2 were again sent up from Lagnicourt, Neville spotting them at around 0800 between Bus and Ytres, and began attacking the two bombing aircraft. Stewart (6564) dropped his bomb on a dump at Ytres and dived. His aircraft was shot up and he was wounded, but got back despite also encountering severe ground fire, making a forced landing at 18 Squadron's base at Lavieville, west of Albert. Lieutenant Fenwick died instantly from von Richthofen's fire and fell at Equancourt, south of Ytres. Richthofen mentions first attacking this machine near Rancourt, which is some way to the south-west of both Equancourt and Ytres, so he must have chased Fenwick some distance before the BE went down, 8 km to the north-east. His was the only claim by Jasta 2; Boelcke claimed a French Nieuport on another sortie.

Again von Richthofen was able to view the wreck and cut from it the aircraft's serial number, the first of many such trophies, which he fixed to the wall of his hut at the airfield. Provided the downed aircraft had not been totally smashed or burnt, Richthofen often took other souvenirs: a gun, a smashed propeller, a flare pistol or some other easily removable object. Many of these eventually found their way to the family home at Schweidnitz which became the 'Richthofen Museum'.

Von Richthofen was flying Albatros DII Nr.491/16.

FENWICK,
WILLIAM CECIL
SECOND LIEUTENANT 21 SQUADRON

BORN IN 1897, William Fenwick was the son of Mr and Mrs C F Fenwick of 3 Tring Avenue, Ealing, London W 5. He was educated at Hamilton House School, Ealing and Christ Church, Oxford. Gazetted Second Lieutenant to the Royal Flying Corps, he was trained at the Central Flying School, Upavon and took the usual gunnery course at Hythe. He was awarded his 'Wings' and, almost immediately afterwards, posted to 21 Squadron at the Front. Although he was the Fenwicks' only son, eleven of his cousins served in the Great War, of whom five were killed and nearly all were wounded. Fenwick's body was never found and he is commemorated on the Arras Memorial to the Missing, France.

Below: The wreckage of Fenwick's BE12 6618.

10 OCTOBER 1916

UNCONFIRMED VICTORY

FE2B No.4292
25 SQUADRON RFC

VON RICHTHOFEN'S Combat Report:
1800 hrs, Roeux, near Arras.

About 1800 I attacked squad of Vickers at 3,500 metres altitude six kilometres to the east of Arras above Roeux. After having singled out a Vickers at whom I fired 300 shots, the enemy plane began to smoke and then started gliding steeper and steeper. I followed always shooting. The enemy propeller was only going very slowly, and clouds of black smoke were coming from the motor. The observer did not shoot any more at my machine. In this moment I was attacked from the rear.

As was ascertained later on, the plane crashed to the ground and the occupant was killed.

BARON VON RICHTHOFEN

The Germans not only had a strict code about claiming and crediting air victories, they did not have a system of sharing victories. From his report it seems pretty certain that von Richthofen had caused this FE two-seater substantial damage and, had he not been forced to break off combat, would have gained a further victory. However, as he did break off, this allowed the doomed FE to be attacked by another German aircraft.

The FE was then engaged by a two-seater crew from Flieger-Abteilung 22 (FA22), crewed by Vizefeldwebel Fritz Kosmahl and Oberleutnant Neubürger, operating on the German 1 Armee front. This was Kosmahl's third awarded victory, which he claimed above Roeux. He would gain two more victories while flying two-seaters, then become a single-seat fighter pilot with Jasta 26. He would bring his score to nine before falling mortally wounded following a fight with 60 Squadron, on 22 September 1917. He died four days later.

Von Richthofen's near victims had been Second Lieutenant Moreton Hayne and Lieutenant Arthur H M Copeland of 25 Squadron. Hayne, a former Lancashire Fusilier, was killed, Copeland, Canadian ASC, was taken prisoner. They had been part of a bomb raid to Oppy, one of two attacks made by the Squadron on this date, and 4292 was their only loss. In the translation of Richthofen's report, the locality of this fight was twice noted as Boeux, but the correct spelling is Roeux, which is on the Scarpe River, six kilometres east of Arras.

Right: Fritz Kosmahl of FA22 won a disputed claim with Richthofen for the downing of this 25 Squadron FE2b.

16 OCTOBER 1916

VICTORY NO.5

BE12 No.6580
19 Squadron RFC
Engine No.25188 WD 5693
Guns: 14543; L6632

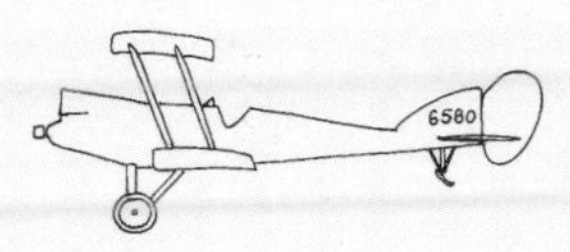

VON RICHTHOFEN'S Combat Report:
0500 hrs, near Ytres.
BE one-seater No.6580.
Daimler Motor, No.25188.
Occupant: Lieutenant Capper (sic).

Together with four planes I singled out above Bertincourt an enemy squadron at 2,800 metres altitude. After 350 shots I brought down an enemy plane.

Plane crashed to the ground, smashed. Motor can probably be secured.

Baron von Richthofen

Weather: fine with occasional clouds.

Once more the poor BE12s were being used for a task far beyond their real capabilities, this time by 19 Squadron, mounting a bomb raid on Hermies railway station. Hermies is just south of that long straight Bapaume to Cambrai road, approximately mid-way. From their base at Fienvillers, 19 Squadron would have to fly 60 km (as the crow flies) to carry out IXth Wing's orders.

The Squadron put up eight aircraft, led by Captain C R Tidswell (6620), the others being Second Lieutenants J Thompson (6580), Smyth (6643), R Watts (6622), A B Drewery (6594), Hope (6637), J D Canning (6588) and C G Baker (6619).

They took off at 1425, but the force was reduced to seven when one BE dropped out with engine trouble and landed at Vert Galant airfield at 1500. West of Havrincourt Wood the BEs got into a fight with three enemy fighters and Canning saw Thompson apparently going to help two other BE12s. He flew past Canning who was then engaged himself and he did not see Thompson again. Second Lieutenant Baker identified what he later recorded as a red doped aircraft (Nieuport type) and two Rolands. The red aircraft and one Roland remained behind Baker but he kept them at bay with his rear gun. Baker then had to change drums on his rear Lewis, and in doing so lost control and began to spin down, but this effectively lost the two German aircraft and he then flew home.

In the event, Cecil Robert Tidswell (1st Dragoons) aged 36, was shot down and killed, along with Thompson. Tidswell had seen action in South Africa in 1902, having joined the cavalry the previous year. He held the Queen's South Africa Medal with five clasps. Although there is no doubt that Richthofen brought down Thompson, and later salvaged the serial number to prove it, who shot down Tidswell is not so clear. Jasta 2 credited Richthofen with his kill at 1700 hours, and Boelcke with a DH2 at 1745, but this was a machine of 24 Squadron.

The mystery which surrounded von

Richthofen's victory for some time was the assertion that the pilot had been Lieutenant Edward Capper. Lieutenant E W Capper was certainly a member of 19 Squadron at this period but had not flown on this operation. Capper in fact survived flying with the Squadron until he was shot down and killed by Kurt Wolff of Jasta 11 (Richthofen's Jasta by then) on 14 April 1917. It was obviously a case of Thompson flying with something of Capper's with him – a borrowed coat, gloves, helmet, map, or some such – but which von Richthofen found when he cut the serial number from the wrecked BE. As Thompson had not been long with the Squadron, and it appears this was about his first war flight, it would be natural for him to have been loaned something until he got his own things together, and a map seems the most likely, or perhaps he'd left his gloves in his room.

Once again we have a problem with the combat report translator, who obviously thought Ytres was a spelling error for the more famous Ypres, and changed it to the latter. Ypres, of course, was more than 85 kilometres to the north of von Richthofen's fight.

It is interesting, though, that Second Lieutenant C C Baker should see a red aircraft. RFC airmen often referred to the Albatros Scouts as Nieuport types, the Albatros DIII (which came to the Front in January 1917) having similar interplane struts and wing construction to the Nieuport's unusual sesquiplane configuration, the lower wing being less than half the chord width of the upper. However, the difference abruptly ends forward of the wings, the Nieuport having a rotary engine, the Albatros an in-line one. Von Richthofen was again flying his DII Nr.491/16 on this occasion but it has not been recorded that he used red colouring to his aircraft until after his 14th victory. There is nothing to suggest Richthofen was flying the red aircraft Baker saw, but nevertheless, in view of his later fame in flying a red machine, this early suggestion that either he or another pilot of Jasta 2 was flying such a coloured machine is fascinating. At this time a reddish-brown was used as camouflage.

THOMPSON,

JOHN

SECOND LIEUTENANT 19 SQUADRON DCM, MID

ALTHOUGH ORIGINALLY from West Bromwich in the Midlands, Thompson was living with his widowed mother at 28b North End Road, Hampstead, London in 1914. Volunteering immediately upon the outbreak of war, Thompson was admitted to the Honourable Artillery Company (Infantry) on 24 August 1914. After training he was sent to join the 1st Battalion of his regiment on the Western Front on Boxing Day, 1914. A period in the trenches followed until, on 16 June 1915, he was wounded in the Battle of Hooge on the Ypres Salient. Two days later he was evacuated home to a Military Hospital in England. For his gallantry during the battle and earlier, he was first Mentioned in Despatches (*London Gazette,* 15/10/1915) and later awarded the Distinguished Conduct Medal (*London Gazette* 14/1/1916 Citation 11/3/1916):

'1412 Lance Corporal J. Thompson, HAC, TF. For conspicuous gallantry. Although wounded, he advanced with his platoon to the first line of a threatened flank and refused to leave his men till he had led them back at the end of the day'.

Shortly after he recovered from his wounds, Thompson gained his Royal Aero Club Aviators Certificate (No.3082) on 23 May 1916 and was commissioned into the Royal Flying Corps before returning to France with 19 Squadron. John Thompson is buried in Lebucquière Communal Cemetery Extension, France (Fr.245). He was twenty-three years of age.

25 OCTOBER 1916

VICTORY NO.6

BE12 No.6629
21 Squadron RFC
Engine No.303 WD 3583
Guns: 17334; L6327

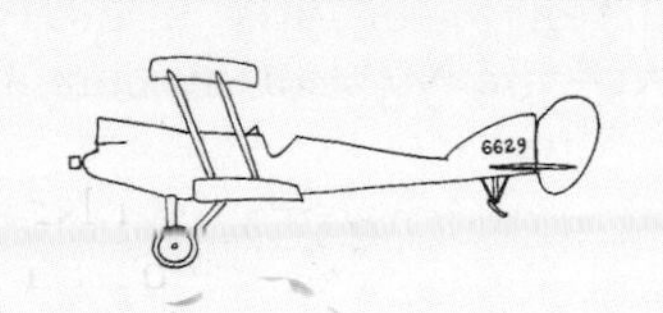

VON RICHTHOFEN'S Combat Report:
0935 hrs, near Bapaume. BE two-seater.

About 0900 I attacked enemy plane above trenches near Lesboefs. Unbroken cover of cloud at 2,000 metres altitude. Plane came from the German side and after some 200 shots he went down in large right hand curves and was forced back by the strong wind to the south end of Bapaume. Finally the machine crashed.

It was plane No.6629. Motor dashed into the earth, therefore number not legible. Occupant, a Lieutenant, seriously wounded by a shot in the bowels. Plane itself cannot be brought back, as under heavy fire.

As I first saw the enemy plane there was no other German machine in the vicinity, and also during the fight no machine approached the scene of action. As the enemy plane started to go down, I saw a German Rumpler machine and several Halberstadter planes. One of these machines came down to the ground. It was Vizefeldwebel Müller of Jagdstaffel 5. He claims to have discharged first at 300 metres and then at 1,000 metres distance, some 500 shots at enemy plane.

Afterwards his gun jammed and the sight of his gun flew away. Quite apart from these curious circumstances, a child knows that one cannot hit a plane from such a ridiculous distance. Then a second plane, a Rumpler, came down, also claiming his share of the loot. But all other planes were perfectly sure that he had not taken part in the fight.

Baron von Richthofen

Weather: fine with occasional clouds.

As previously mentioned, the German system of air victories did not allow for sharing, therefore any claims by more than one pilot had to be agreed by 'higher authority' and the victory assigned to a single victor. Thus does von Richthofen declare in his report what he thinks of others trying to secure his victory for their own.

In this instance, von Richthofen was given the victory some days later following arbitration. Vizewfeldwebel Hans Karl Müller of Jasta 5, nevertheless, was no novice in air combat, having downed his seventh opponent just three days earlier. He would gain two more before the year was out, but a serious abdominal wound on Boxing Day 1916 ended his operational flying.

Five BE12s of 21 Squadron had taken off from their base at 0745, led by Captain E F Norris, to fly an Offensive Patrol. Eight hostile aircraft had been spotted between Velu, Villers au Flos and Fins. Before 21 Squadron had a chance to engage, they were seen to be driven down by four Nieuport Scouts, but then came up again and met 21 Squadron's BE fighters as they were heading back to the lines. It was in this fight that Fisher was hit and brought down in the front lines. The 11th AA Battery reported a BE12 north-east of Maricourt being closely pursued by a German biplane, at 15,000 feet. Lesboefs is six kilometres due south of Bapaume and Maricourt is to the south-west.

Von Richthofen was flying Albatros DII Nr.491/16. Second Lieutenant Fisher had joined the Squadron on 9 October and had lasted just 16 days. *(cont.)*

FISHER, ARTHUR JAMES

SECOND LIEUTENANT 21 SQUADRON

AMONGST THE FIRST to volunteer, Fisher joined the 23rd (County of London) Battalion, The London Regiment (TF) as a private soldier (No.3158) in September 1914. He was eventually picked out as potential officer material and posted to the Inns of Court Officer Training Corps on 23 October 1915 (No.6/6980). Gazetted as a temporary Second Lieutenant on the General List, he was attached to the Royal Flying Corps and selected for pilot training. He was awarded his 'Wings' and posted overseas in September 1916. Shortly after his arrival in France, he was sent to 21 Squadron and presented himself for duty on 9 October 1916. Just sixteen days later, he was dead. His Commanding Officer, Major R Campbell Heathcote (ex Cameron Highlanders) had the unpleasant duty of writing a letter of condolence to Fisher's parents who were, respectively, the Superintendent and Matron of the Clapham branch of Dr Barnado's Homes in Clapham High Street, London. Fisher is buried in Bancourt Communal Cemetery, France (Fr306). He was twenty-one. After her husband's death in the mid-twenties, Mrs. Fisher moved to 76 Victoria Road, Clapham Common, London SW4. She named her new home, 'Bancourt', after the cemetery in which her son lay buried.

Above: BE12, single-seat version of the BE2c.

3 NOVEMBER 1916

VICTORY NO.7

FE2b No.7010
18 Squadron RFC
Engine No. 399 WD 2371
Guns: 1405; 4438

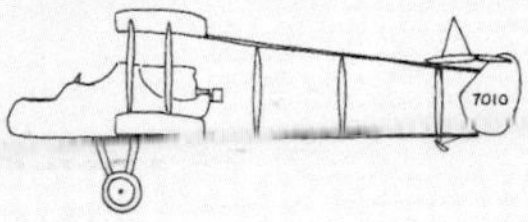

VON RICHTHOFEN'S Combat Report:
1410 hrs, north-east of Grevillers Wood.
Vickers two-seater No.7010.

Accompanied by two machines of the Staffel, I attacked a low flying plane at 1,800 metres altitude. After 400 shots, adversary dashed to the ground. The plane was smashed to pieces, inmates killed.

As the place where plane fell is under heavy fire, no details can be ascertained as yet.

Baron von Richthofen

Weather: very strong winds all day, low clouds in the morning; clearing in the afternoon.

This was the first aircraft shot down by von Richthofen following the death of his friend and mentor, Oswald Boelcke.

Despite von Richthofen's remarks concerning the location of the crashed FE and that no details could be confirmed, he at least found the serial number, making it fairly clear he was the victor over this 18 Squadron machine. This is important due to the time that had elapsed between the British aircraft taking off and Richthofen's recorded combat time.

The British Squadron had taken off from its base at Lavieville, west of Albert, at 1135 to fly a 'Hostile Aircraft Patrol' along the 5th Army front. As von Richthofen timed his combat at 1410 (ie: 1310 British time), the FEs had been nearing the end of their patrol time when he picked off 7010.

From way behind the British trenches, an AA battery reported seeing an FE2b, with two enemy aircraft attacking, and under hostile shell fire, going down out of control east of Engelbelmer, beyond Beaumont Hamel. Beaumont is ten kilometres west of Grevillers Wood, which itself is four kilometres west of Bapaume.

Captain S F Heard with 2/Lt G Doughty (in FE2b 4879), leading 18's patrol, were also in action with these aircraft, identified as Halberstadt Scouts, over Gommecourt. They counted ten enemy machines at varying heights, going for the BEs. George Doughty hit one with a burst and it turned east but they were then engaged by another from behind, but this too flew off when Sydney Heard turned his FE towards it.

Doughty would meet Richthofen again, on 20 November. Von Richthofen was flying Albatros DII Nr.491/16. *(cont.)*

BALDWIN,

CUTHBERT GODFREY

SERGEANT (No.24130) 18 SQUADRON

CUTHBERT GODFREY BALDWIN, a qualified and practising solicitor, lived at 2 Priory Villas, Frien, Barnet, Middlesex in the early months of the war. He was born in Byer's Green, County Durham, on 14 February 1888, the son of the Reverend Alan Godfrey Baldwin, vicar of Burnopfield, Co Durham and his wife, Margaret. He received his education at Newcastle Grammar School and Elm Park School, Shotley Bridge. Moving south, he became an articled clerk with Crossman, Block, Mathews and Crossman of Gray's Inn, London before being admitted as a solicitor in July, 1912. Undertaking a course of flying at Hendon at his own expense, he joined the Royal Flying Corps in January 1916 shortly before he was awarded a Royal Aero Club Aviators Certificate (No.2423) on 9 February 1916. He was promoted to Sergeant and joined 18 Squadron in France on 14 September 1916 less than two months before his death. His body was never found and he is commemorated on the Arras Memorial to the Missing, France. He was twenty-eight years of age.

BENTHAM,

GEORGE ANDREW

SECOND LIEUTENANT 18 SQUADRON; 7/EAST SURREY REGIMENT

GEORGE ANDREW BENTHAM was born in 1894, the eldest of the three sons of Mr and Mrs Bentham, 92 Ritherdon Road, Upper Tooting, Balham, London, S W. Educated first at Monkton Combe Junior School (1907), he next went on to the senior school in 1908 where he was, quote, 'quite a games player. In cricket, a slogger quite devoid of all style, useful as a run-getter and a very plucky fielder'. He left Monkton Combe in 1910 and entered the business world. Immediately upon the outbreak of the war, he enlisted as a private soldier (No.7331) in the 10th (The City of London) Battalion, Royal Fusiliers, with whom he was sent to France on 31 July 1915. After service in the trenches, he returned home for training and eventual commissioning into the Royal West Kent Regiment on 18 March 1916. Transfer to the 7th Battalion, East Surrey Regiment followed, before, shortly afterwards, he was again transferred, this time at his own request, into the Royal Flying Corps. After completing his training, he was posted, on 10 October 1916, as an observer on probation to 18 Squadron, then stationed on the Western Front. His machine was last seen crashing 2,000 yards behind the enemy lines. His body was never found and he is commemorated on the Arras Memorial to the Missing, France. He was twenty-one years of age.

9 NOVEMBER 1916

VICTORY NO.8

BE2c No.2506
12 Squadron RFC
Engine No.941 WD 22082
Guns: 11375; 15947

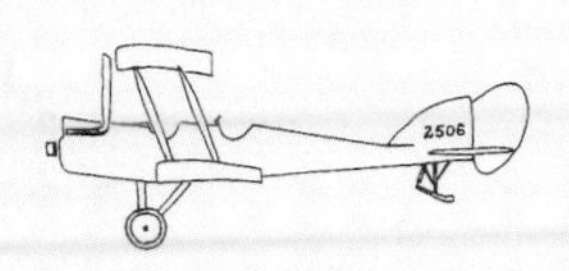

VON RICHTHOFEN'S Combat Report:
1030 hrs, BE two-seater, No.2506. Motor: Daimler, No.22082. Occupants: Seriously wounded, pilot very seriously; observer, shoulder.

Above Beugny. About 1030 I attacked, with several other planes, enemy bombing squadron above Mory at 2,500 metres altitude. After preceding curve fight, my victim crashed to the ground near Beugny.

Baron von Richthofen

Weather: bright and clear nearly all day.

Left: BE2c.

Despite the original translator of the combat report stating the locations as 'Bengny' and 'Nory', the area of action is well established; Beugny as we have seen before is on the straight Bapaume-Cambrai road, where victory number two fell, and Mory is six kilometres north of Bapaume.

The target for the RFC on this morning was the sugar factory at Vraucourt, six kilometres north-east of Bapaume, with 11 Squadron's FEs, 29 Squadron's DH2s and 60 Squadron's scouts as escort. In all, 3rd Brigade sent out 16 bombing aircraft escorted by 14 fighters. This force was intercepted by an estimated 30 German aircraft (aircraft from Jastas 1 and 2) and the escorting machines fought them but in doing so, went below the bombers as more German aircraft arrived. The raiding force claimed three hostile aircraft brought down, but they lost two BEs and another pilot returned wounded, despite an attempt by 11 Squadron to help them. One 11 Squadron FE came down just inside British lines, its pilot wounded and the observer dead. One 60 Squadron pilot, Lt A D Bell-Irving MC, was also wounded but came down safely inside British lines, while two DH2s of 29 Squadron were brought down, one pilot being lost, the other wounded.

As the BEs were once more flying with just a pilot, the observers being left behind in lieu of a larger bomb load, it has occasionally been thought that von Richthofen brought down this BE with the usual two-man crew, referred to as Lieutenants Cameron and Knight, this, of course, being compounded by Richthofen's own reference to both pilot and observer in his report. However, Cameron was flying 2506 and Gerald Featherstone Knight (Devon Regt and RFC) 2502. Knight was taken into captivity, brought down by the new leader of Jasta 2, Oberleutnant Stefan Kirmaier. He landed on a village green behind Mory in the middle of a large number of Germans so was captured immediately. However, he later effected an escape and was back in England in autumn 1917. It had been his first show as a pilot (he'd had six months as an observer) and continued on the raid despite a rough engine.

Two other BEs were seen to go down, one over Mory – this was Kirmaier's – and another over Sapignies, which was probably that flown by Second Lieutenant T Hayes also of 12 Squadron (in 4589), who was wounded in the thigh but got back. Hayes was attacked from behind just east of Adinfer Wood and hit by a bullet which had passed through a steel strut in the fuselage and then through the back of his seat. The BE's 'curve fight' obviously put the machine further to the south-east as it came down near Beugny. Hans Imelmann got one of the DH2s, Jasta 1's Leutnant Hans von Keudell the other.

Von Richthofen was flying Albatros DII Nr.491/16.

CAMERON,
JOHN (OR IAN) GILMOUR
SECOND LIEUTENANT 12 SQUADRON; QUEEN'S OWN CAMERON HIGHLANDERS

CHRISTENED 'JOHN', but with a personal preference for the Scottish version 'Ian', 'Ian' Gilmour Cameron was born on 23 September 1897, the elder son of Surgeon Major James Cameron and his wife Mary, of 'The Fountain', Loanhead, near Edinburgh. A keen athlete of powerful build, he was educated at Leeswade, Edinburgh Academy (Rugby XV and shot put) and the Royal Military College, Sandhurst (Rugby XV) whence he was commissioned into the Cameron Highlanders on 22 December 1915. He successfully applied for transfer to the Royal Flying Corps in January 1916, and gained his Royal Aero Club Aviators Certificate (No.2624) on 25 March 1916. Served with the Expeditionary Force in France from June 1916. He died from his wounds in the Dressing Station at Beugny and is buried in Achiet-le-Grand Communal Cemetery, France (Fr.518). He was nineteen years old.

20 NOVEMBER 1916

VICTORY NO.9

BE2c No.2767
15 Squadron RFC
Engine No.23011 WD 879
Guns: 7330; 7258

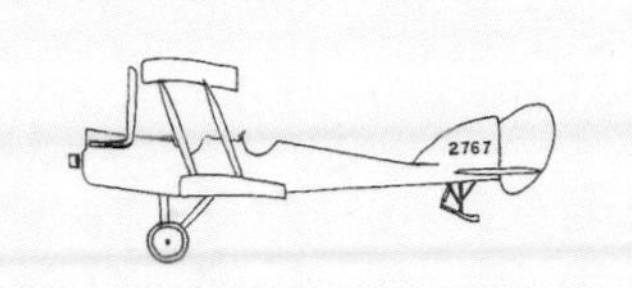

VON RICHTHOFEN'S Combat Report:
Jagdstaffel Boelcke. 0940 hrs, south of Grandcourt. Vickers two-seater.

Together with several machines of our Staffel we attacked, on the enemy side above Grandcourt at 1,800 metres altitude, several low flying artillery planes. After having harassed a BE two-seater for a time, the plane disappeared in the clouds and then crashed to the ground, between the trenches south of Grandcourt. The machine was taken immediately under artillery fire and destroyed.

Baron von Richthofen

Weather: low clouds, strong winds and showers.

What is immediately interesting in this report, is that while Richthofen says he shot down a BE two-seater, he initially reports it as being a Vickers two-seater. In view of a number of controversies that still persist concerning von Richthofen's victims, it is important to point out here two things. Firstly, that one must not assume totally that von Richthofen, or for that matter any other WW1 pilot, can be relied on absolutely to know or identify his adversary. Human error in the heat of combat when each side is trying to kill the other must be recognised and understood. (See also victory No.15). Secondly, the fact is that German pilots in general, throughout WW1, often reported aircraft or aircraft types by a type name rather than its actual name, or by positive identification. Because in 1915 the RFC used a pusher type (ie: the engine was behind the pilot, pushing the aircraft forward) two-seater fighter, the Vickers FB5 'Gunbus', this led to the Germans calling the later FE2 series of aircraft, a Vickers or Vickers type, two-seater. Even the DH2 and FE8 single-seater pusher types could be, and were, often called Vickers types; they also spelt it Vikkers on occasion.

As far as Jasta 2 is concerned, two British BE2s were claimed shot down on this day, one by Oberleutnant Stefan Kirmaier at 0900, the other by von Richthofen at 0910. Kirmaier claimed his fell north of Miraumont on the German side, von Richthofen's south of Grandcourt in the front line trenches.

It doesn't help that Grandcourt and Miraumont are within about three kilometres of each other, or that the claims are within 10 minutes of each other. A 15 Squadron BE2c (No.2767) had taken off from its base at Clairfaye Farm, Lealvillers (11 km north-west of Albert) at 0650 to fly an artillery observation sortie. At between 0830 and 0845 it was seen being driven down by a hostile aircraft, but seemingly under control, gliding down over Miraumont followed then by one enemy machine. At 0950 this

Left: Crashed 15 Squadron BE in German hands.

machine was seen on its back on the ground (position given as R.4a.37), and its crew's last wireless message had been received at 0829. On the face of it, this seems to have been Kirmaier's victim, in that the times are nearer, and Kirmaier said his BE went down over Miraumont. The crew of this BE, Second Lieutenant J C Lees (Royal Scots Fusiliers and RFC), and Lieutenant T H Clarke (AOD and RFC) were both taken prisoner, which naturally indicates they came down inside German lines or close enough to the Front not to have been able to scramble across into the Allied trench system.

There are no other reports of men or machines being lost on this day in RFC records (other than Richthofen's next victory), so it must be assumed that for once the Germans gave credit for two victories whereas only one was actually brought down. The clue here, one suspects, is in Richthofen's remark that '...the plane disappeared in the clouds and then crashed...' This would seem to indicate that in losing sight of it, the BE either escaped totally and unseen by Richthofen, or that Kirmaier then attacked it or another BE, and also made a claim. The closeness of time and place might support this latter theory. The only problem, then, is that von Richthofen states the BE was shelled and destroyed, whereas a later RFC report says the/an aircraft was seen on its back at 0952, almost an hour later. There are no other BE losses recorded except an 8 Squadron BE, but this was well(?) inside British lines. This BE, No.2762, was crewed by Second Lieutenants C Holland RFC (SR) and C H Keefe (Norfolk Regt/RFC). They were on an artillery patrol and at 0900 (note the time) they landed to assist a machine (type not noted) which had landed in an open field with nobody near to render assistance. When taking off again, a gust of wind caught the machine and turned it onto its back. The crew were not hurt and the only damage was a broken propeller, rudder, and top edges of wings. The position of this crash – and supposedly the 'other' aircraft – was noted as E.26.a. 8 Squadron were based at Soncamp, near Sombrin, on the southern Arras front. Was this the machine seen on its back, and was it confused with 2767? There is no suggestion that the 'other' aircraft was either sufficiently damaged to warrant an aircraft casualty report, or its pilot/crew were even injured.

In any event, it seems pretty certain that 2767 was the only loss and that both Richthofen and Kirmaier received credit for it. Floyd Gibbons was in contact with Clarke in 1927, and Clarke's remarks seem to confirm that he, for one, was aware at the time that they had not been brought down by Richthofen. Clarke wrote: 'The Germans themselves gave me a name which I now forget, but which was certainly not Richthofen's, as the name of the Flight Commander of this German flight ...' This seems to indicate Kirmaier, which is probably the name Clarke had forgotten. Clarke went on to state that they had been conducting a shoot on German batteries from 6,000 feet, and that a bullet had stopped their engine; also that although Lees had been shot through the leg, this had made no difference to their being forced to land.

When he returned from Germany, Clarke said that they were sent up at dawn in a very strong west wind, which rendered escape impossible once they were hit. He recalled being assailed by five German fighters and after a time their engine was hit and Lees wounded in the right leg. The engine failed at 800 feet and with the wind against them they could not reach the lines. The machine was crash-landed on the outskirts of Miraumont, this same town being mentioned by Lees when he too came home at the end of 1918.

Once on the ground they could not burn the machine as it took some time to get the wounded Lees from his cockpit and then soldiers arrived. Clarke believed the BE had been shelled afterwards, for officers he had known in 1916, whom he met after the war, told him they had seen their machine lying upside-down, indicating it had been blown over by shell fire, although this story seems to be confused with the 8 Squadron machine seen on its back.

There was certainly plenty of air action

Painting opposite: Victory No.1

Painting overleaf: Victory No.6

D.491/16

this morning. One 4 Squadron BE2c (4593) was doing a shoot with the 13th Siege Battery between Pys and Le Sars and shortly before 0900, the crew, 2/Lt D K Sworder and Lt C B Bird MC, observed the two hostile scouts attack a BE over Grandcourt. These two scouts, having driven down the BE, then came towards 4593, and attacked from the rear. The leading scout was allowed to approach within close range before being engaged by the rear gun, which then jammed. Sworder rapidly spiralled down until Bird had fixed the gun. The same German machine attacked again and Bird felt sure he'd hit it; it certainly turned east and went down until lost in some ground mist. The second machine was also engaged but soon broke off and followed the first Halberstadt. Undoubtedly this was Kirmaier and Richthofen, but was the BE the one both of them later claimed? The British crew seem certain they had seen them bring down a BE before they were engaged.

Another 15 Squadron BE2c (2766) was also in on the act: 2/Lt J S Brown and 2/Lt Bradford saw two Halberstadts attack '...one of ours over Irles. It appeared to be hit but under control and was gliding over Miraumont followed by the enemy ...' Brown and Bradford gallantly engaged the enemy machines and drove them off after firing three drums of Lewis at them. They then watched as the BE made a landing in position R4.a. All these actions were in the same general area.

Von Richthofen was flying Albatros DII Nr.491/16, but the RFC crews might still identify the type as a Halberstadt.

Below: With Jasta 2, a smiling von Richthofen, with (left to right): Stefan Kirmaier, Staffelführer, Hans Imelmann, and Hans Wortmann.

CLARKE,
THOMAS HENRY
LIEUTENANT 15 SQUADRON; ARMY ORDNANCE CORPS

TOM CLARKE, a qualified mechanical engineer, who originally hailed from Little Lewisford, near Salisbury, Wiltshire, was working in Buenos Aires, Argentina when the war came. He became one of the tens of thousands of British patriots who returned home from South and Central America to fight for the old country. Commissioned into the Army Ordnance Corps, Clarke first crossed to France in April 1916. Transfer to the Royal Flying Corps quickly followed and, after the usual training, he soon found himself back in France with 15 Squadron. Taken prisoner after being forced down behind the enemy lines, Clarke spent more than two years in a German camp before being released for repatriation on 17 December 1918. After the Armistice and his return to civilian life, Tom Clarke moved to the capital, where he formed and ran his own company: Clarke and Bruce Limited, Engineers, Number 7 Wharf, Amberley Road, Paddington, London W9. Clarke always contended that he was not shot down by von Richthofen and stated that his opponent – who, in appearance, had looked nothing like the Red Baron – visited him in his cell shortly after his capture. From the description Clarke gave, his visitor was, undoubtedly, Kirmaier, the Commanding Officer of Jasta 2. But, as neither spoke the other's language, the reason for the visit was never entirely clear! After the Second World War, Clarke's business, Clarke and Bruce Ltd, traded from 71 Bartholomew Close, London EC1, having evolved from pure engineering into dealing in motor accessories.

LEES,
JAMES CUNNINGHAM
SECOND LIEUTENANT 15 SQUADRON; ROYAL SCOTS FUSILIERS

JAMIE LEES, the second son of Andrew and Mrs Lees, lived, prior to the outbreak of the Great War, with his parents at 'Carrick Lodge', Carrick Road, Ayr. As well as being a partner in the firm of Macpherson and Lees of Cairnhill, Garvan, Lees managed two farms in Wigtownshire. He volunteered as soon as the war came and, after serving as a trooper in the Ayrshire Yeomanry for more than twelve months, was commissioned into the Royal Scots Fusiliers on 21 October 1915. He next successfully applied for transfer to the Royal Flying Corps and, after the appropriate training, was appointed Flying Officer with effect from 16 August 1916. Shot through the leg in the fight with von Richthofen or Kirmaier, Lees was taken prisoner by German troops in the area of the crash site and remained incarcerated until New Year's Day 1919, when, on that special day for all Scots, he was at last repatriated. Lees returned to farming after the war, married and fathered two children both of whom, tragically, pre-deceased him. His daughter died in her teens and his son was killed in a flying accident whilst training with the RAF in 1943. Jamie Lees served his country again in the Second World War, volunteering first for the Local Defence Volunteers before going on into the newly formed Home Guard. For this service, he added the Defence Medal to the British War Medal and the Allied Victory Medal he had been awarded for the Great War.

Left: The badge of the British Latin American Volunteers.

20 NOVEMBER 1916

VICTORY NO. 10

FE2B NO.4848
18 SQUADRON RFC
ENGINE NO.295 WD 1359
GUNS: 3085; 1365

VON RICHTHOFEN'S Combat Report:
1615 hrs, above Grandcourt.
Vickers two-seater, fallen near Grandcourt, No.4000 Motor No.36574. Plane cannot be secured as under fire. Occupants: One killed: Lieutenant George Doughty. Lieutenant Gilbert Stall (sic), seriously wounded, prisoner.

Together with four planes, I attacked a Vickers two-seater type above the clouds at 2,500 metres altitude. After 300 shots adversary broke through the clouds, pursued by me. Near Grandcourt I shot him down.

BARON VON RICHTHOFEN

WEATHER: LOW CLOUDS, STRONG WINDS AND SHOWERS.

Today saw the first occasion von Richthofen scored two kills in one day. Despite him recording the serial number of his victim as being 4000, rather than 4848 (4000 was the serial given to a 160 hp Sloane-Daniel machine) and the second crewman being recorded as Gilbert Stall, rather than Gilbert S Hall, there is no doubt this was the Baron's victim. Oddly, though, the engine number on the loss report bears no relation to that on the German's report. Also, as Richthofen named Doughty first, it has often been wrongly assumed that he was the pilot.

Little is known from the British side about 18 Squadron's action, other than that Hall and Doughty were flying a front line Defensive Patrol. They had taken off from Lavieville at 1315, operating over the 5th Army front, their assigned patrol line being Warlencourt-Beaucourt-Gommecourt. Warlencourt is just west of Bapaume, the patrol line thus heading due west for eight kilometres to Beaucourt, then a further eight kilometres north-west to Gommecourt. Grandcourt, the same area he had downed his morning victory, being two kilometres east of Beaucourt, the area is unquestioned. As von Richthofen timed the combat at 1615 German time, 4848 would have fallen at 1515 British time, ie: two hours into their patrol.

As we saw earlier (victory No.7) Doughty had been in the combat on 3 November and had helped drive off Jasta 2. Five days later, he and Captain Heard, again flying 4879, had an indecisive fight with a hostile scout over Gommecourt at 1300, which had been attacking a BE, and drove it off.

Von Richthofen was flying Albatros DII Nr.491/16. *(cont.)*

HALL,
GILBERT SUDBURY
SECOND LIEUTENANT 18 SQUADRON

G S Hall was born at 'Greenaleigh', Matlock, Derbyshire, on 28 December 1890, and lived there with his parents for most of his short life. He was educated at Mill Hill School in London (1905-08) before going on to Burton Bank College where he qualified as an engineer. Commissioned into the Royal Flying Corps on 13 December 1915, he gained the Royal Aero Club Aviators Certificate (No.2286) on 16 January 1916. Proceeding to France shortly afterwards, he was slightly wounded and obliged to return to England for treatment and rest. Fully recovered, he returned to the Front to join 18 Squadron on 7 November 1916. Following his confrontation with von Richthofen, he was taken to a hospital in Cambrai by his German captors where he lay desperately ill for ten days before finally succumbing to the effects of his wounds on 30 November 1916. He is buried in the Porte-de-Paris Cemetery, just outside the old city walls of Cambrai in France (Fr 598). He was twenty-five years of age.

DOUGHTY,
GEORGE
SECOND LIEUTENANT 18 SQUADRON
13/ROYAL SCOTS

George Doughty, the son of George and Betty Doughty of 2 Albert Place, Leith Walk, Edinburgh, was born in 1895. He was commissioned into the 13th (Service) Battalion, The Royal Scots (the First of Foot), before subsequently and successfully applying for transfer to the Royal Flying Corps. He arrived for service with 18 Squadron on 7 August 1916, a little more than four months before his death. Qualifying formally as an observer on 9 October 1916, he was granted a short leave from 18th to 24th of the same month. Doughty is buried in Achiet-le-Grand Communal Cemetery Extension, France. He was twenty-one years old.

23 NOVEMBER 1916

VICTORY NO. 11

DH2 No.5964
24 Squadron RFC
Engine No.6138 B 540
Gun: 14563

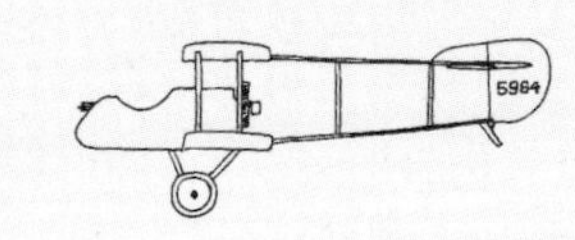

VON RICHTHOFEN'S Combat Report:
1500 hrs, south of Bapaume.
Vickers one-seater, plane lying near Bapaume.
Occupant: Major Hawker, dead.

I attacked, together with two other planes, a Vickers one-seater at 3,000 metres altitude. After a long curve fight of three to five minutes, I had forced down my adversary to 500 metres. He now tried to escape, flying to the Front. I pursued and brought him down after 900 shots.

Witnesses: Leutnant Wortmann, Leutnant Collin, etc.

Baron von Richthofen

Weather: fine all day.

If Manfred von Richthofen was starting to make a name for himself, this victory certainly elevated his name and standing with the German High Command.

Lanoe Hawker was already a well known figure, not only to the British but to the Germans too, so to have conquered him would have given any German flyer more than a moment of acclamation. Hawker had been credited with seven air combat victories of the period, but his last had been the previous September. Although he had brought 24 Squadron out to France in February 1916, he found little time to fly in combat, and indeed, it was not deemed necessary by RFC HQ for any squadron commander to fly and endanger himself because, by this time, someone of Major rank was far more valuable in a command position. Hawker had, nevertheless, flown whenever possible, and although he found his match on this occasion, it was not so much a case of being out-fought, as finding himself at a disadvantage over hostile territory with the need to get back across the lines or be taken prisoner.

The DH2s of 24 Squadron had done much to overcome the Fokker Eindekker period of early 1916, and there were a number of experienced and dedicated fighter pilots with this unit. On this occasion, the Squadron had sent off three DH2s (originally four but one aborted with a rough engine) from their base at Bertangles at 1300 to fly a Defensive Patrol over the 4th Army front. The three were Hawker, Captain J O Andrews (5998) and Lieutenant R H M S Saundby (5925), all very experienced men. Indeed, Andrews and Saundby would survive WW1 and rise to high rank in the RAF, both to Air Vice-Marshal, with Saundby being knighted.

At about 1350, the patrol spotted two hostile aircraft, identified as Roland two-seaters, at 6,000 feet north-east of Bapaume, and Andrews, who was leading, drove them east but then saw two strong hostile patrols approaching high up. Andrews was about to

Left: DH2.

Right: The famed 'Ehrenbecher' (Victory Cup) given to airmen after their first victory.

retire when he saw Hawker dive past him and continue the pursuit of the former aircraft. The DHs were immediately pounced on by the higher aircraft, one of which was seen to come down behind Hawker, but Andrews managed to drive this aircraft away, but in doing so, exposed himself to another hostile attack, the engine and fuel tank of his fighter being hit, forcing him to disengage and head straight for the lines. A last look back revealed Hawker engaged by a German fighter at 3,000 feet.

Robert Saundby had assisted Andrews by forcing another enemy machine from his tail, then engaged a second, firing three-quarters of a double drum of Lewis ammunition at it from 20 yards range. The enemy machine fell out of control for 1,000 feet and then continued down vertically. He then realised he was alone and as the enemy aircraft had moved eastwards, he too headed back to the lines.

History records a classic duel between Richthofen and Hawker which lasted for some minutes, neither pilot gaining an advantage over the other. Hawker knew, however, that he would finally have to make a dash for the front line if, seeing he was now alone, he wasn't to fall prey to other aircraft apart from his immediate antagonist, or run the risk of running out of both fuel and ammunition. Hawker would also be aware of the prevailing wind, which generally blew from west to east, so any prolonged action would result in his aircraft being blown further and further inside German territory. We can see, however, that Hawker had only been out an hour, so his fuel would have been sufficient for some further period, but he would not have liked being over enemy territory alone. Andrews had gone back damaged, and Saundby, after his actions, had lost sight of his CO and had also decided to go home too.

Hawker finally made a bid for the lines, the fight having now descended to around 150 feet, which allowed Richthofen a good burst at the British scout. A bullet hit Hawker in the head and that was that. The dead pilot crunched into the ground 250 yards east of Luisenhof Farm, at the time no more than a shell-shattered ruin, 1.25 km south of Bapaume, on the Flers road.

Some German Grenadiers, occupying the cellars of the ruined farm building, buried him and later Richthofen acquired the serial number of the DH and Hawker's Lewis gun which he mounted in his room.

Von Richthofen was flying Albatros DII Nr.491/16.

HAWKER,
LANOE GEORGE
MAJOR 24 SQUADRON, VC DSO; ROYAL ENGINEERS

LANOE GEORGE HAWKER, a national hero at the time of his death, was born on 31 December 1890, the second son of Lieutenant H C Hawker, RN, and his wife Julia, of Home Croft, Longparish, Hampshire. It was originally intended that he follow his father into the Royal Navy and he was sent to the Royal Naval College, Dartmouth. Unable to sustain the exacting academic requirements in that establishment, he decided upon a change in career and was successful with his application to enter the Royal Military Academy, Woolwich. From Woolwich, he took a commission in the Royal Engineers in July 1911. He learnt to fly at Hendon and was awarded the Royal Aero Club Aviators Certificate (No. 435) on 4 March 1913. Attachment to the Royal Flying Corps followed and he went to the Front with 6 Squadron in October 1914. He served as a Flight Commander on the Western Front and became a Companion of the Distinguished Service Order for gallantry in the spring of 1915, *London Gazette*, 8/5/1915:

'For conspicuous gallantry on 19 April 1915, when he succeeded in dropping bombs on the German airship shed at Gontrode from a height of only 200 feet under circumstances of the greatest risk. Lieutenant Hawker displayed remarkable ingenuity in utilising an unoccupied German captive balloon to shield him from fire while manoeuvring to drop the bombs'.

He was invited to Buckingham Palace to receive the DSO from the hands of the King. Next came the award of the ultimate in accolades, the Victoria Cross, *London Gazette*, 24/8/1915:

'For most conspicuous bravery and very great ability on 25 July 1915. When flying alone he attacked three enemy aeroplanes in succession. The first managed eventually to escape, the second was driven to the ground damaged, and the third, which he attacked at the height of about 10,000 feet, was driven to earth in our lines, the pilot and observer being killed. The personal bravery shown by this officer was of the very highest order, as the enemy's aircraft were armed with machine guns, and all carried a passenger as well as a pilot'.

Again, Hawker received an invitation to the palace for the presentation of the Victoria Cross by King George V. The citation for the award of the VC should be read by the modern reader with an appreciation of how the world at large perceived aviation in July 1915. Certainly, greater aerial feats have since gone unremarked and unrewarded but hindsight can distort history. Contemporary perception is what mattered. Hawker, the first British ace, was a national hero and his defeat in an aerial duel was a damaging blow to public morale and a psychological, as well as a physical, victory for the German side. Hawker was buried alongside his crashed machine at Luisenhof Farm, two miles south of Bapaume, but the site was subsequently lost and he is commemorated on the Arras Memorial to the Missing, France. He was in his twenty-sixth year.

11 DECEMBER 1916

VICTORY NO. 12

DH2 No.5986
32 SQUADRON RFC
ENGINE No.30372
GUNS: 13980; 11924

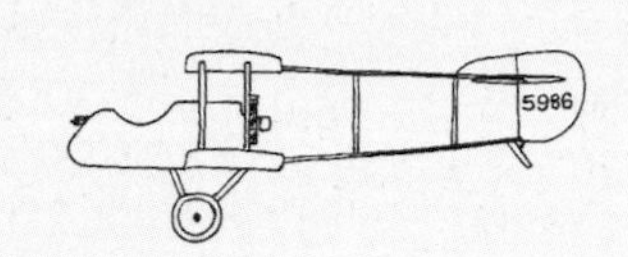

VON RICHTHOFEN'S Combat Report:
1155 hrs, above Mercatel, near Arras.
Vickers one-seater, No.5986. Rotary Motor 30372.
Occupant: made prisoner, wounded, Lieutenant Hund (sic).

About 1145 I attacked with Leutnant Wortmann, at 2,800 metres altitude, and south of Arras, enemy one-seater Vickers squadron of eight machines. I singled out one machine and after a short curve fight I ruined the adversary's motor and forced him to land behind our lines near Mercatel. Occupant not seriously wounded.

BARON VON RICHTHOFEN

WEATHER: FINE MORNING WITH SOME MIST; RAIN LATER.

Despite the misspelt name, there is no dispute about this second victory over a De Havilland 2 pusher scout. 32 Squadron, at Lealvillers, north-west of Albert, had taken off at 0920 hours to escort six FE2b aircraft of 23 Squadron from Vert Galant which had been assigned to bomb dumps and the railway sidings around Morchies, east and north-east of Mory, right in Jasta 2's backyard.

That Hunt's DH2 was a well used machine with around 230 hours on its service record had little to do with it being hit and brought down by von Richthofen, despite a suggestion in the RFC Communiqués that Hunt had been forced to land with engine trouble. He undoubtedly had, but the 'trouble' came from bullets, not mechanical problems. Also, according to Hunt when he returned home in November 1918, he had been wounded in the liver. He also said he came down at Henin – presumably Henin-s-Cojeul, just east of Mercatel.

Hunt had been flying with 32 Squadron since July, so was fairly experienced by this date. He had been in a number of combats, and had claimed one enemy aircraft shot down on 15 October, shared another out of control on 16 November and a scout in flames on 23 November. He had taken over command of B Flight just a week prior to his last sortie, although this had not yet been confirmed in rank.

According to Corporal C W Dalton, one of 32's ground crew airmen, Hunt had just adopted the use of two Lewis guns on his machine instead of the usual one (and possibly carrying more ammunition drums). He had been flying this 'mock-up' for the first time on this day, and one wonders if the performance of his DH2 was impaired by the extra weight imposed by the second gun. With the DH2 already inferior in performance to the Albatros, Richthofen must easily have out-turned Hunt – '... curve fight ...' on this occasion.

This fight must also have drifted north somewhat, for Mercatel is 16 km north-west of the Morchies area; it was also Jasta 2's only kill. Von Richthofen was flying Albatros DII Nr.491/16.

HUNT, BENEDICT PHILIP GERALD

LIEUTENANT 32 SQUADRON; 2/1 SHROPSHIRE YEOMANRY

PHILIP HUNT was born on 6 December 1894, the son of Rowland and Mrs Hunt of Boreatton Hall, Baschurch, Shrewsbury. The Hunts were a well known county family, their 'seat' at Boreatton having been established for many generations. Philip's father was the Member of Parliament for the South Shropshire Division (1903-18). Educated at Shrewsbury (1909-12), Philip was granted a commission in the Shropshire Yeomanry on 22 October 1914, before transferring to the Royal Flying Corps in the following year. He was awarded his Royal Aero Club Aviators Certificate (No.2225) on 14 December 1915. Such was Hunt's social status that the news that he was not, as previously feared, 'killed in action' but instead a 'prisoner of war', was reported in the 'Court Circular' column of *The Times* of 1 February 1917. Wounded and taken prisoner on 11 December 1916, he was held in a German prison camp until April 1918 when, because of illness, he was exchanged across the border into neutral Holland. Although still interned and restricted by the Dutch, he no doubt enjoyed a much more pleasant regime of confinement until he was finally repatriated on 18 November 1918. Married in 1920, he and his wife Gwendoline were to have two daughters. He served as a Major with the Royal Army Service Corps in the Second World War and lived with his family in Southampton until his death on 7 October 1958, at the age of sixty-four.

Below: The officers of 32 Squadron, RFC (1916) including, on the extreme right, Lt P B G Hunt.

20 DECEMBER 1916

VICTORY NO. 13

DH2 No.7927
29 Squadron RFC
Engine No.30413 WD 4134
gun: 19234

VON RICHTHOFEN'S Combat Report:
1130 hrs, above Menchy.
Vickers One-seater, No.7929. Motor: Gnôme, 30413
Occupant: Arthur Gerald Knight, Lieutenant RFC killed. Valuables enclosed; one machine gun taken.

About 1130 I attacked, together with four planes and at 3,000 metres altitude, enemy one-seater squadron above Menchy. After some curve fighting I managed to press adversary down to 1,500 metres, where I attacked him at closest range (plane length). I saw immediately that I had hit enemy; first he went down in curves, then he dashed to the ground. I pursued him until 100 metres above the ground. This plane had been only attacked by me.

Baron von Richthofen

Weather: fine all day.

On this occasion von Richthofen, by his last comment, ensures that no other pilot was able to 'horn in' on his victory. This is probably due to several pilots making claims against these DH2s, which had taken off from their base at Le Hameau, 14 km west of Arras, at 0945. Their assigned duty was an Offensive Patrol to Rollencourt and Gommecourt and they had therefore been so engaged for over half an hour before the five Jasta 2 pilots attacked them (at 1030 hrs British time).

Although Richthofen's was the only confirmed victory, four more of the British scouts were badly shot about: A2588 flown by 2/Lt O F C Ball, A2614 2/Lt W H Britton, A2552 2/Lt H B Hurst and 5956 2/Lt A N Benge. Three had got back to Le Hameau but Hurst had been forced to make an emergency landing south of Beaumetz.

Despite the translator of Richthofen's report showing 'Menchy', this should have read Monchy (Monchy-au-Bois) just seven kilometres north of Gommecourt, Beaumetz where Hurst force-landed being a further six kilometres north of Monchy. Observers from behind the British lines had seen Knight's DH2 brought down in a spinning nose dive east of Adinfer Wood in Square X28, Adinfer Wood being two kilometres east of Monchy-au-Bois.

This third DH2 fighter brought down by Richthofen in succession, despite the inferiority of the type compared to the Albatros, had an equally experienced air fighter at the controls. Gerry Knight had gained his eighth victory four days before his own demise, having been previously with 24 Squadron under Hawker VC. He had already been awarded the DSO and MC for his prowess. Thus we can see that while von Richthofen was easily able to dispatch slower and more vulnerable two-seaters, as was his job, he could equally engage and overcome experienced fighter pilots within the ranks of the Royal Flying Corps.

He flew Albatros DII Nr.491/16.

KNIGHT,
ARTHUR GERALD
CAPTAIN 29 SQUADRON DSO MC MID

'GERRY' KNIGHT, an ace with eight victories at the time of his death, was born in Bedford, England on 30 July 1895. He spent his early years in Canada, completing his formal education at Toronto University. Returning to England, he took up residence with relatives at 4 Cambridge Road, Southampton. Determined to fly, he obtained his Royal Aero Club Aviators Certificate (No.2063) on 11 November 1915. After the usual training with the RFC, he was sent to join 4 Squadron in France in February 1916. The following June saw him transfer to 24 Squadron which was under the command of Major Lanoe Hawker, VC DSO. Knight and Alfred McKay, a colleague in 24 Squadron, were indirectly responsible for the death of the great German pilot Oswald Boelcke on 28 October 1916. On patrol over the Somme trenchlines, Knight and McKay's DH2s were attacked by Germany's leading ace (40 victories). A momentary lapse in concentration on the part of either Boelcke or his good friend, Erwin Böhme, resulted in a sickening contact between their two machines as they dived in on their prey. Although Böhme's machine escaped comparatively unscathed, Boelcke's upper wing broke away, with the inevitable consequences. A brilliant and resourceful pilot himself, Knight flew throughout the first Battle of the Somme, winning both the DSO and the MC. Military Cross, *London Gazette*, 14/11/1916, Page 11058:

'For conspicuous skill and gallantry. He has shown great pluck in fights with enemy machines, and has accounted for several. On one occasion, when a hostile machine was interfering with a reconnaissance, he attacked at very close range, and brought down the machine in flames'.

Distinguished Service Order: *London Gazette, 11/12/1916, Page 12101*:

'For conspicuous gallantry in action. He led four machines against 18 hostile machines. Choosing a good moment for attack he drove down five of them and dispersed the remainder. He has shown the utmost dash and judgement as a leader of offensive patrols'.

As the First Battle of the Somme came to an end in November 1916, Knight was transferred to 29 Squadron as a Flight Commander. Sadly, Knight was due to go on ten day's leave had he returned from his last patrol. The final official recognition of his skill and resource came one month after his death when he was Mentioned in Despatches in January 1917. He is buried in Douchy-les-Ayette British Cemetery, France (Fr.927). He was still only twenty-one years of age.

20 DECEMBER 1916

VICTORY NO. 14

FE2B NO.A5446
(MALAYA NO.11)
18 SQUADRON RFC
ENGINE NO.791 WD 7151
GUNS: 16021; 17924

VON RICHTHOFEN'S Combat Report:
1345 hrs, above Moreuil.
Vickers two-seater: A5446. Motor: Beardmore, No.791
Occupants: Pilot Lieut. D'Arcy, observer, unknown, had no identification disc. Occupants dead, plane smashed, one machine gun taken, valuables please find enclosed.

About 1345 I attacked, together with four planes of our Staffel, at 3,000 metres altitude, enemy squadron above Moreuil. The English squadron had thus far not been attacked by Germans and was flying somewhat apart. I had, therefore, the opportunity to attack the last machine.

I was foremost of our own people and other German planes were not to be seen. Already after the first attack, the enemy motor began to smoke; the observer had been wounded. The plane went down in large curves. I followed and fired at closest range. I had also killed, as was ascertained later on, the pilot. Finally the plane crashed on the ground.

The plane is lying between Queant and Lagnicourt.

BARON VON RICHTHOFEN

WEATHER: FINE ALL DAY.

The British Squadron had left their base at St Leger-les-Authie, situated 12 kilometres south-east of Doullens (having moved from Lavieville ten days earlier), at 1115. They were to fly an Offensive Patrol along the British 5th Army Front but an hour and a half later, they ran into Jasta 2.

In spite of von Richthofen making certain in his report that he was alone when he attacked A5446, his four companions were not far away for they too fell on the FEs. In all 18 Squadron lost three of their number, the other two falling to Hans Imelmann and Hans Wortmann, at 1345 and 1405 hrs (German time) respectively, north-east of Beugny and over Sapignies. With these locations being further west in relation to von Richthofen's victim, his combat report confirms that the others made their attack after his as the FEs fought their way back to the lines.

The other missing crews were Lieutenants C H Windrum (Royal West Kent Regt & RFC)/J A Hollis (East Yorks & RFC), A5452, both prisoners, and Reginald Smith (East Surrey Regt & RFC)/Harold Fiske RFC(GL), 4884, both killed. There is a time discrepancy, in that in the RFC casualty report, it says A5446 was last seen near Le Transloy at 'about' 1315, heading south. If the time is accurate, this would put them still in the air, half an hour after Richthofen had said he shot them down, at 1245 (German time for the claim being 1345).

There is no way of knowing, however, if the RFC report actually refers to this FE or one of the other 18 Squadron machines. However, as Richthofen states his victory crashed with a dead observer and a dying pilot, we can discount the possibility that his victim might have been A5452, as both crew were taken prisoner, or 4884, which fell in flames with both men dead. As the crash site is virtually within walking distance of Jasta 2's base at Pronville, it is inconceivable that Richthofen didn't visit it.

Von Richthofen did in fact secure the rudder of A5446 as well as a machine gun; the FE was a presentation aeroplane built with money provided by the people of

Malaya, the 11th machine built by such donations, and it carried 'Malaya No.11' on the nacelle. There is a note in the few remaining Squadron records that D'Arcy was Duty Officer on this day, and one wonders if he should have been flying while assigned this duty? If he had stayed on the ground he would have survived his 18th day with the Squadron. Richthofen was flying Albatros DII Nr.491/16.

D'ARCY,
LIONEL GEORGE
LIEUTENANT 18 SQUADRON
3/CONNAUGHT RANGERS

An Irishman, Lionel D'Arcy was born in 1888 and lived in New Forest, Ballinamore Bridge, County Galway, a county of which his father was Deputy Lord Lieutenant. He was educated, like the rest of the D'Arcy family, at Clongowes Wood College (1902-06), Naas, County Kildare. He was commissioned into the Connaught Rangers on 29 October 1915, and joined the 6th Battalion of his regiment in France on 3 June 1916. Service in the trenches followed and on the night of 26/27 June 1916 he led one of two special consolidation parties, each consisting of one officer, two NCOs and 52 men, in support of a raid after the blowing up of two craters in the Hulloch Sector, near Loos. The operation was a success and nearly one hundred of the enemy were killed. D'Arcy was keen on joining the RFC, and with this in mind, learnt to fly at his own expense. He obtained his Royal Aero Club Aviators Certificate (No.3448) on 27 August 1916, and, exactly two months later, was accepted into the Royal Flying Corps. After the usual training, he was posted to 18 Squadron in France on 2 December 1916. Ironically, D'Arcy was Squadron Duty Officer on 20 December and, had he so chosen, need not have flown on that fateful day. His body was never recovered and he is commemorated on the Arras Memorial to the Missing, France. He was twenty-eight years of age.

WHITESIDE,
REGINALD CUTHBERT
SUB-LIEUTENANT 18 SQUADRON ROYAL NAVAL VOLUNTEER RESERVE: NELSON BTN. ROYAL NAVAL DIVISION

Surely one of the few sailors (*not* Royal Naval Air Service) to serve with the Royal Flying Corps, Whiteside was an Ulsterman from Kilmallock. He was the younger son of the Reverend W C and Mrs Whiteside who, at the time of the Great War, were living at 'Rose Bank', South Benfleet, Essex. After his son's death, the Reverend Whiteside took his family to a new 'living' in Onehunga, New Zealand. Reginald Whiteside had been educated at Campbell College, Belfast (1909-1914) where he became Senior Prefect and Head Boy of the school. He was in the Rugby XV and was Football Captain, winning his Inter-Provincial Football 'Cap' in 1914. After leaving school, he obtained a position in the Hong Kong and Shanghai Bank. He next sought, and was granted, a commission in the Royal Naval Volunteer Reserve in October 1915, being posted to the Nelson Battalion of the Royal Naval Division. Comprising largely Royal Navy reservists, the Royal Naval Division was the brainchild of Winston Churchill who, faced with a surfeit of sailor reservists, formed them into infantry battalions for service in the trenches on the Western Front and in the Gallipoli campaign. Whiteside, however, opted for the Royal Flying Corps and, after training, he was attached, on 28 October 1916, to 18 Squadron, then at St Leger-les-Authie, as an 'observer on probation'. His grave was never found and he is commemorated on the Arras Memorial to the Missing, France. He was twenty-one years old.

27 DECEMBER 1916

VICTORY NO.15

DH2 No.5985
29 Squadron RFC
Engine: ?
Gun: ?

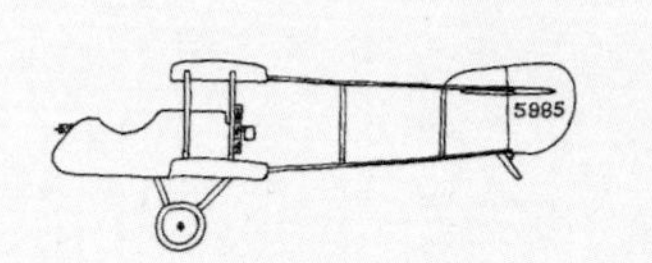

VON RICHTHOFEN'S Combat Report:
1625 hrs, above Ficheux, south of Arras.
FE two-seater was smashed, number etc, not recognisable.

At 1615, five planes of our Staffel attacked enemy squadron south of Arras. The enemy approached our lines, but was thrown back. After some fighting I managed to attack a very courageously flown Vickers two-seater. After 300 shots, enemy plane began dropping, uncontrolled. I pursued the plane up to 1,000 metres above the ground. Enemy plane crashed to ground on enemy side, one kilometre behind trenches near Ficheux.

Baron von Richthofen

Weather: mist in the morning, clearing later.

Almost total mystery seems to have surrounded this victory, and even today there is still a question mark. The whole problem stems from Richthofen's claim that his adversary was an FE two-seater – ie; an FE2b. The problem for historians is that there are just no obvious FE2b losses for this day, certainly not crashed (smashed!) behind the front lines to the south of Arras. An 18 Squadron FE (A5433) was brought down by an Albatros west of Sailly, but this was at 0930. In fact the only 'loss' of an FE this day occurred much further north, 22 Squadron having had a scrap with Halberstadt Scouts around Zonnebeke shortly before noon, so the time is out too. This machine, A36, also caught fire as it came down at Berthen and was completely burnt out after landing, so it doesn't tally with Richthofen's victim at all on three counts.

It is apparent that none of the early historians came up with any firm identity. Indeed, Floyd Gibbons makes little reference to it, nor did 'Vigilant' (Claud Sykes) in his book on Richthofen. Even Richthofen himself goes into little detail, merely writing to his mother that No.15 fell on this date, although as it 'came down' on the British side, he had little to say about it in any event.

Later historians came up with an 11 Squadron crew, Captain J B Quested MC and his observer, Lieutenant H J H Dicksee (FE2b No.7666) who were forced down inside British lines, but this was also in the morning – 1120 – and the machine was not smashed! They in fact were in a fight with Jasta 1, shot down the ace Gustav Leffers, and were then hit by Vizefeldwebel Wilhelm Cymera, near Chérisy (at 1220 German time). Chérisy is on the right part of the Front, situated ten kilometres south-east of Arras, although to come down inside Allied lines they had to have landed way to the west of this locality; in fact they came down at Wancourt, six kilometres south-east of Arras, which is 12 kilometres to the east of Ficheux.

There are simply no other candidates, especially in the mid to late afternoon, so one begins to look around for another suitable possibility. Things appear a little clearer when one discovers that the DH2s of 29 Squadron had a fight in the afternoon. Although the difference between an FE2b and a DH2 is obvious, the latter being a single-seater, at least to the Germans both were 'pushers', both were known as Vickers types, and both were referred to as 'gitterrumpf' ('lattice-tailed'), ie: rear booms and spars rather than a fuselage. It was not unknown, therefore, for both to be confused.

If one takes Richthofen's report and compares it to the one submitted by Flight Sergeant J T B McCudden MM, CdeG, a number of things fit. McCudden stated: 'Going east of Arras I saw five HA. Lt Jennings attacked an HA and another HA was approaching from behind. I fired about 15 shots and drove him off. He turned and came towards me, firing. I opened fire at 100 yards and after about eight shots my gun stopped, due to cross feed. As the hostile machine was engaging me at close range, I turned on my back and dived vertically, in a slow spin and in this way regained our lines. At 800 feet over Basseux the HA left me. I quickly rectified the stoppage and followed the HA across the trenches at 2,000 feet. Owing to his superior speed and climb he out distanced me and rejoined his patrol at about 5,000 feet. The hostile patrol then withdrew.'

Six DH2s had taken off at 1350 to fly an Offensive Patrol between Arras and Monchy (-au-Bois) but two had dropped out with engine problems, followed by a third shortly afterwards. The remaining three continued over the lines near Arras, then patrolled north and south, about a mile east of the lines: Captain Harold James Payn RE and RFC (7849), Lieutenant Alexander Jennings RFA and RFC (5957) and McCudden. There were some Nieuports of 60 Squadron nearby, but they were further east and much higher. At 1500 hrs five Albatros Scouts were seen climbing up and by that time they were in a position to engage; the DHs were near Adinfer, flying at 10,000 feet. Payn began the fight, but then had pressure problems and had to break off. One of his last sights was of McCudden spinning down at low altitude, and when he landed back at base, reported that the Flight Sergeant had been shot down. Jennings was shot up in the fight, but returned unhurt, but he too saw McCudden spinning down. It was a surprise to everyone when McCudden later returned totally undamaged, word having already been passed round that he'd been lost. Jennings' machine was damaged, but he did not go down, and he was flying this DH a few days later.

McCudden had been with 29 Squadron since the summer, so was pretty experienced. The fact Richthofen noted that the British machine was '.. very courageously flown ..' acknowledges that the British pilot was no novice, and we know how great he was to become. Added to this is the time, somewhere between 1500 and 1515 according to McCudden, around 1615 to 1625 (German time) noted by Richthofen, and the location. Ficheux is about six kilometres south-west of Arras, Basseux is about four kilometres further west. Bearing in mind that Richthofen had watched and followed his spinning 'victim' fall from 10,000 feet to 800 feet, he and most other pilots would assume the machine was within a few seconds of smashing into the ground. Richthofen says he left it at 1,000 metres, and it could be argued that the final sentence of his report is auto-suggestion, ie, it must have crashed, so why not say so!

Richthofen would then have rejoined the others, as McCudden observed, but there is no suggestion that Richthofen either saw or was even aware of McCudden's renewed presence, and in any event McCudden was unable to re-engage. In McCudden's book *'Flying Fury'*, he records the events of this action with little deviation from his combat report. All he does add is that when he did recross the lines, he saw some FE2s being engaged by hostile machines before returning home. That might be significant in relation to the later claim/confirmation of Richthofen's kill.

Richthofen's witnesses on this occasion were two AA batteries. Did they in fact see the DH2 spinning down, and merely identify it as a 'lattice-tail', and/or did they also see the FEs in action with some German fighters at about this time, and assume they were all of the same type? Being asked to acknowledge a victory, they may well have confirmed seeing a 'pusher' going down over the British side, in the region of Ficheux, and Richthofen would have his claim verified. It is significant too, that at this particular time, Richthofen, having been recently disappointed at not receiving the Pour le Mérite after his eighth kill, the number required for this prestigious award having been doubled to 16, was anxious to gain the magic 16 before someone 'moved the goalposts' again. This, together with seeing an opponent spin seemingly uncontrolled for 9,200 feet, would certainly convince him that No.15 was in the bag. Human nature might well have taken over when he wrote the last sentence in his report. He wanted it confirmed.

If it was indeed McCudden that Richthofen 'shot down' this day, and the evidence is pretty good, it is surprising that his DH2 did not collect a single hit from the 300 Richthofen fired at him; his only reason for going into a spin was that his gun had jammed and he was being pressed too closely for his liking. As McCudden stated in his book, Payn had attacked the hostile machines and then two went after Jennings, McCudden then attacking the nearest one. This could obviously be the 'After some fighting ...' that Richthofen mentions. One reason Richthofen did not follow his victim down below 1,000 metres, as McCudden describes, was that the German machine came under AA fire from the British side. He would not necessarily want to mention this in his combat report, nor presumably would he hang around over the enemy side of the lines while being fired at from the ground. In his haste to clear the British lines he may be forgiven for his rather optimistic conclusion.

The German aircraft seen taking off and climbing from Croiselles were probably Jasta 12, as their actual aerodrome was at Reincourt, just to the east. Jasta 2 were at Pronville, just to the south-east of Reincourt. However, Jasta 12 were equipped with Fokker D1s, so while McCudden may have seen German aircraft climbing from this area, they were probably Jasta 2, but if they were Jasta 12, they certainly did not engage them.

Any suggestion that Richthofen's victim may have been a French Farman is also discounted, as the only Farman lost this day was a type F42 of Escadrille F.5 (Sgt Fusier/Lt Thamin) way down on the Verdun front.

Von Richthofen was flying Albatros DII Nr.491/16.

McCUDDEN,
JAMES THOMAS BYFORD
SERGEANT (No.892) 29 SQUADRON (VC, DSO & BAR, MC & BAR, MM, Croix de Guerre(Fr))

BORN IN GILLINGHAM, Kent on 28 March 1895, James was the younger son of serving soldier Quartermaster-Sergeant William H McCudden, Royal Engineers, and his wife Amelia. He received his education locally at the RE School, Brompton Barracks, before, in 1910, enlisting in the Royal Engineers as a boy bugler. Three years later, at the age of eighteen, he joined his much admired older brother, William, one of the original members, in the newly formed Royal Flying Corps. Promoted to 1AM by the time war broke out, McCudden crossed to France on 24 August 1914 in a Blériot flown by Lieutenant de la Ferte. In the early months of the war and armed only with a rifle, he flew as a gunner with Lieutenant Conran. Promoted to Corporal in November 1914, and to Sergeant in April 1915, he was at last posted as an 'Observer' in July 1915. Personally presented with the Croix de Guerre by Général Joffre himself on 21 January 1916 (the award was not, apparently, 'gazetted'!), his advancement to Flight Sergeant occurred two days later. The following month he was sent to Farnborough for pilot training and gained his Royal Aero Club Aviators Certificate (No.2745) on 16 April 1916. A 'natural' pilot, he was himself instructing at the Central Flying School within days of qualifying! In July 1916 he returned to France, ferrying a BE2d to St Omer before being posted to 20 Squadron. McCudden's brilliance is most simply illustrated by working through the *London Gazettes* that chronicled his progress as a scout pilot par excellence. His 'consistent gallantry, courage and dash' were quickly acknowledged by the award of the Military Medal (*London Gazette* 9/12/16, page 12049) and he was commissioned shortly afterwards on 1 January 1917. The first of his two Military Crosses came next (*London Gazette* 12/3/1917, page 2479):

'For conspicuous gallantry in action. He followed a hostile machine down to a height of 300 feet, and drove it into the ground. He has shown marked skill on many previous occasions, and has destroyed two hostile machines and driven another one down out of control'.

By then an Acting Captain (1 May 1917), his second Military Cross was announced in the *London Gazette* of 27 October 1917, page 11108 (Citation, *London Gazette* 18/3/1918, page 3418):

'For conspicuous gallantry and devotion to duty. He took part in many offensive patrols, over thirty of which he led. He destroyed five enemy machines and drove down three others out of control. He showed the greatest gallantry, dash and skill'.

The cataloguing of his deadly brilliance continued with his creation as a Companion of the Distinguished Service Order announced in the *London Gazette* of 4 February 1918, page 1600 (Citation, *London Gazette* 5/7/1918, page 7887):

'For conspicuous gallantry and devotion to duty. He attacked and brought down an enemy two-seater machine inside our lines, both the occupants being taken prisoner. On another occasion he encountered an enemy two-seater at 2,000 feet. He continued to fight down to a height of 100 feet in very bad weather conditions and destroyed the enemy machine. He came down within a few feet of the ground on the enemy's side of the lines and finally crossed the line at very low altitude. He has recently destroyed seven enemy machines, two of which fell within our lines and he has set a splendid example of pluck and determination to his Squadron'.

The second DSO came in the second month of the new year, *London Gazette*, 18 February 1918, page 2156 (Citation London Gazette 18/7/1918, page 8438):

'For conspicuous gallantry and devotion to duty. He attacked enemy formations both when leading his patrol and single handed. By his fearlessness and clever manoeuvring he had brought down thirty-one enemy machines, ten of which have fallen in our lines. His pluck and determination have had a marked effect on the efficiency of the Squadron'.

The award of the ultimate accolade to the former boy bugler was inevitable and its announcement in the *London Gazette* of 2 April 1918 (page 3997) came the day following the foundation of the Royal Air Force:

'His Majesty the King has been graciously pleased to approve of the award of the Victoria Cross , etc. 'For

most conspicuous bravery, exceptional perseverance, and a very high devotion to duty. Captain McCudden has at the present time accounted for 54 enemy aeroplanes. Of these 42 have been definitely destroyed, 19 of them on our side of the lines. Only 12 out of the 54 have been driven down out of control. On two occasions he had totally destroyed four two-seater enemy aeroplanes on the same day, and on the last occasion all four machines were destroyed in the space of one hour and thirty minutes. While in his present Squadron he has participated in 78 offensive patrols, and in nearly every case has been the leader. On at least 30 occasions, whilst with the same Squadron, he has crossed the lines alone, either in pursuit or in quest of enemy aeroplanes. The following incidents are examples of the work he has done recently: on 23 December 1917, when leading his patrol, eight enemy aeroplanes were attacked between 1430/1550 and of these two were shot down by Captain McCudden in our lines; on the morning of the same day he left the ground at 1050 and encountered four enemy aeroplanes and of these he shot two down; on 30 January 1918 he, single-handed, attacked five enemy scouts, as a result of which two were destroyed. On this occasion he only returned home when the enemy scouts had been driven far east; his Lewis gun ammunition was all finished and the belt of his Vickers gun had broken. As a patrol leader he has at all times shown the utmost gallantry and skill, not only in the manner in which he has attacked and destroyed the enemy, but in the way he has during several aerial fights protected the newer members of his flight, thus keeping down their casualties to a minimum. This officer is considered, by the record he has made, by his fearlessness, and by the great service which he has rendered to his country, deserving of the very highest honour'.

On 6 April 1918, McCudden was received by the King at Buckingham Palace and presented not only with the Victoria Cross but also with the Bar to his MC and with the DSO and Bar. Promoted Major the following July, James Thomas Byford McCudden, VC, DSO & Bar, MC & Bar, MM, CdeG(Fr) was killed, like so many others of his colleagues, in a simple flying accident when, after an engine stoppage, he side-slipped into the ground. It was 9 July 1918, and he was on his way to take up an appointment as the Commanding Officer of a crack scout squadron on the Western Front. He is buried at Wavans British Cemetery, France (Fr. 1525). He was still only twenty-three years of age.

Below: The insignia of the Croix de Guerre being pinned to the chest of the then Sergeant J T B McCudden by the Supreme Commander, Général Joffre.

4 JANUARY 1917

VICTORY NO.16

SOPWITH PUP NO.N5193
8 SQUADRON RNAS
ENGINE NO.584(?)
GUN: L5178

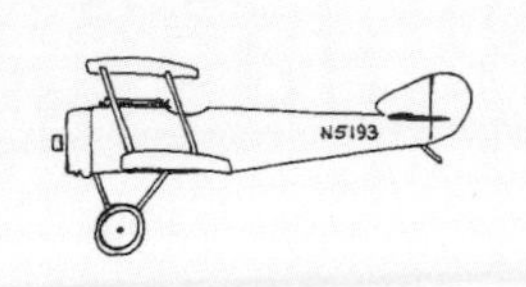

VON RICHTHOFEN'S Combat Report:
1615 hrs, near Metz en Coûture.
Sopwith one-seater (lying south of this place), No. LTR5193.
Motor: 80 hp Le Rhône No.5187.
A new type plane, never seen before, but as wings broken, barely discernible.
Occupant: Lieutenant Todd, killed, paper and valuables enclosed.

About 1615, just starting out, we saw above us at 4,000 metres altitude four planes, unmolested by our artillery. As the archies were not shooting, we took them for our own.

Only when they were approaching we noticed they were English. One of the English planes attacked us and we saw immediately that the enemy plane was superior to ours. Only because we were three against one did we detect the enemy's weak points.

I managed to get behind him and shot him down. The plane broke apart whilst falling.

BARON VON RICHTHOFEN

WEATHER: LOW CLOUDS AND RAIN IN THE MORNING; BRIGHT IN THE AFTERNOON.

This was von Richthofen's last kill while with Jasta 2 'Boelcke'. The Sopwith Pup had arrived in France – but only a single prototype – in May 1916 and a few were operating with 1 Naval Wing, but the first squadron to be equipped with the new type was 8 Naval Squadron in October, which had arrived to support the RFC.

No.8 Squadron was based at Vert Galant on the 26th of that month, 32 Squadron leaving to make room for it. Vert Galant was situated on the right-hand side of the main Doullens-Amiens road, about 20 km from Amiens itself. 23 Squadron's FEs were on the other side of the road. 8 Naval began operations in the second week of November.

The Pup was to be an improvement on the DH2 and FE8 single-seaters and along with the Nieuports would take the brunt of the early 1917 combat actions. On this day, Jasta 2's first encounter achieved success for von Richthofen, although a second Pup was also lost, A626, flown by Flight Sub-Lieutenant J C Croft, who became a prisoner, victor or circumstances unknown.

According to their Flight Commander, Roy Mackenzie, there had been no flying till the afternoon due to bad weather but this had cleared a bit allowing a patrol of four to fly. Croft and Todd failed to return and Mackenzie * recorded: 'I'm afraid one of them was shot down by three Huns, as a wing was seen floating downwards by Little.' [FSL R A Little, a future ace.]

The Naval pilots had taken off at 1430 to patrol Achiet-le-Grand, Grevillers and Guedecourt, the two missing airmen last seen in combat with seven hostile aircraft east of Bapaume between 1500 and 1515 hrs.

Todd came down where indicated, which is just south of Havrincourt Wood, and Richthofen secured the fuselage-marked serial number for his collection. Von Richthofen was flying Albatros DII Nr.491/16.

(cont.)

* Flight Commander C R Mackenzie DSO was killed in action on 24 January 1917, brought down by Leutnant Hans von Keudell of Jasta 1.

TODD,
ALLAN SWITZER
FLIGHT LIEUTENANT 8 SQUADRON(RNAS)

VON RICHTHOFEN'S FIRST 'victory' of the New Year was also the first Canadian to fall and, as Todd was born in Georgetown, Ontario on 18 April 1886, he was also one of the oldest of the Baron's victims. The adopted son of a Toronto doctor, J D Todd, MD of 476 Brunswick Avenue, Toronto, Allan Todd was educated in the local public school system. After the completion of his education, he secured a position in the Sporting Goods Department of the Toronto branch of the giant Canadian retail chain, Reid's. A keen member of the Queen's Own Rifles Militia, he became an expert shot, winning the title of Champion Revolver Shot of Canada in 1908, 1909 and 1910. He volunteered for the Royal Naval Air Service and began his pilot training at the Curtis School in Toronto in June 1915, gaining his Royal Aero Club Aviators Certificate (No.1725) three months later on 4 September 1915. Todd, with hundreds of other Canadian volunteers, arrived in England on the giant Cunarder, the SS *Mauretania*, in October 1915. He served with No.1 Wing, RNAS, first in Dover and then in Dunkirk, undertaking an intensive programme of flying patrols involving fleet protection, bombing, photo reconnaissance, etc, so intense, in fact, that he was unable to take up his first posting to 'Naval 8' Squadron because of stress. After a short break and against advice (thirty was too old for the scout pilot game, his friends counselled) he at last joined Naval 8 on 1 December 1916. Younger men than he fell to the Baron and it is pointless to speculate how much his ageing reactions contributed to his allowing von Richthofen to get behind him. His body was never recovered and he is commemorated on the Arras Memorial to the Missing, France. He was thirty years old.

23 JANUARY 1917

VICTORY NO.17

FE8 No.6388
40 Squadron RFC
Engine No.30445 WD 4166
Gun: 14510

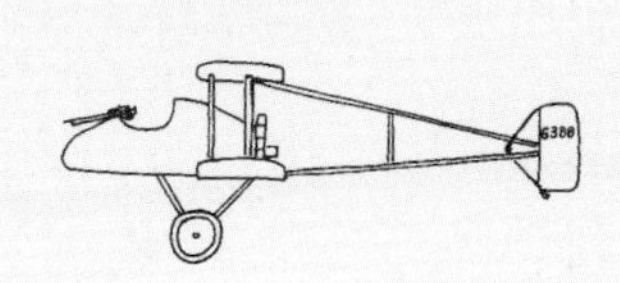

VON RICHTHOFEN'S Combat Report:
1610 hrs, above trenches south-west of Lens.
No details, plane fell on the enemy's side.

About 1610 I attacked, together with seven of my planes, enemy squadron, west of Lens. The plane I had singled out caught fire after 150 shots, fired from a distance of 50 metres. The plane fell, burning. Occupant fell out of plane at 500 metres height.

Immediately after the plane had crashed on the ground, I could see a heavy black smoke cloud rising. The plane burnt for quite a while with frequent flares of flame.

Baron von Richthofen

Weather: fine all day.

By this date, the FE8 – a machine very much in the mould of the DH2, with a pusher-type engine and forward gondola in which the pilot sat with a full and unobstructed forward field of fire from a single Lewis gun – was fast becoming obsolete. Indeed, the FE8 was soon to be replaced with the Nieuport Scout, just as the DH2 would soon be phased out of operational squadrons in France.

Nevertheless, in experienced hands, the FE8 could defend itself to a point, and John Hay was no novice. On the morning of his last day he had shot down his third German aircraft, an Albatros C-type two-seater. Flying 6388 on a line patrol west of La Bassée, he had downed this opponent at 1015.

After lunch, 40 Squadron mounted another line patrol, flown to support a photographic two-seater machine to the Lens area. Taking off at 1312, Lieutenant E L Benbow (7627) engaged an Albatros two-seater at 1345, south of La Bassée, and drove it away eastwards.

Just short of two hours into their patrol, which would have been nearing its completion, 'Lobo' Benbow saw eight hostile aircraft west of Lens, 2,000 feet below and, with another FE, attacked. He had no sooner started firing than his gun jammed and, turning to remedy this, he was attacked by a red machine from head-on. Benbow immediately dived and evaded his attacker, got his gun going again, and headed back, only to find the enemy aircraft heading off east.

Meantime, Hay had been shot down – timed at 1505 – after being seen in combat with five enemy fighters. His FE8 was seen to fall in flames and later his body was recovered by Canadian troops, two miles east of Aix Noulette. Other witnesses reported seeing the pilot jump from the burning aeroplane, rather than fall as in Richthofen's report. It was not an unusual occurence for pilots and/or observers to jump from their burning craft during WW1. They did not have parachutes (only the Germans having access to a parachute apparatus during the last months of the war) but preferred a quick end to being slowly and painfully burnt to death in aircraft which, once set alight, burned most readily, being a very combustible mix of wood, doped fabric, oil and petrol.

Aix Noulette is on the Bethune-Arras road just to the west of Lieven, itself in the present suburbs of Lens. Jasta 11, of course, were operating from an airfield at Brayelles (La Brayelle), just outside the western edge of Douai, so his future actions and combats would be a little further north than hitherto. With the spring offensives fast approaching, Richthofen and Jasta 11 would be ideally situated to take advantage of the increased air combat over the Arras front, and especially over Vimy Ridge.

Von Richthofen was flying an Albatros DIII Nr.789/17. It was his first success in the new, more streamlined DIII – Benbow thought the enemy machines were Rolands – but although they became the standard German fighter for much of 1917, they initially suffered wing failures.

HAY,

JOHN

SECOND LIEUTENANT 40 SQUADRON

An Australian, 'Jack' Hay was born on 22 January, 1889, at Double Bay, an 'up market' suburb of Sydney, New South Wales, the son of William and Isabella Hay and scion of an influential family founded by his great, great uncle name-sake, Sir John Hay, who had landed in Australia from England in 1838. He was educated at Shore, the Sydney Church of England Grammar School. At the time of the outbreak of the Great War, Jack was living in Warren, a lush grazing area in the Central West of New South Wales. Arriving in England early in 1916, he gained his Royal Aero Club Aviators Certificate (No.3039) on 2 June 1916, and volunteered for service with the Royal Flying Corps. Posted to 40 Squadron in France, he proved a brave and resourceful scout pilot, accounting for three of the enemy before he met his own nemesis. His body was recovered by Canadian troops and he is buried at Aire Cemetery, France(Fr 31). He was twenty-eight years and one day old. Jack's mother donated a bell, inscribed with her son's name, to the Carillon built in 1923 by Sydney University to commemorate the sacrifice of its students in the Great War.

Below: FE8 single-seat pusher scout.

24 JANUARY 1917

VICTORY NO.18

FE2B NO.6997
25 SQUADRON RFC
ENGINE NO.748
GUNS: ?

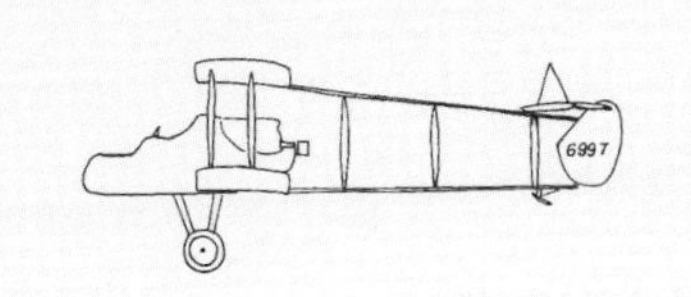

VON RICHTHOFEN'S Combat Report:
1215 hrs, west of Vimy.
Fixed motor; Plane No.6937 (sic); Motor No.748.
Occupants: Pilot – Captain Craig (sic). [Obs] Lieutenant McLennan (sic).

Accompanied by Feldwebel [Hans] Howe, I attacked, at about 1215, the commanding plane of an enemy formation. After a long fight I forced my adversary to land near Vimy. The occupants burnt their plane after landing. I myself had to land, as one wing had cracked at 300 metres. I was flying an Albatros DIII.

According to the English crew, my red painted plane is not unknown to them, as when being asked who had brought them down, they answered: 'Le petit rouge'.

Two machine guns have been seized by my Staffel. The plane was not worth removing as it was completely burned.

BARON VON RICHTHOFEN

WEATHER: FINE ALL DAY.

Of interest here is that despite the fire, only the forward gondola had been consumed, for Richthofen was able to recover the serial number from the tailplane. Although the report notes this as 6937, the trophy clearly shows 6997, the aircraft in which this crew were brought down. Even the German Nachrichtenblatt recorded 6937.

Germans often had difficulty with English names, thus the report notes Craig rather than Greig, and McLennan rather than MacLennan. It is interesting, too, that his new Albatros DIII's (789/17) wing had cracked during the combat!

Seven FEs had taken off from Lozinghem, between Auchel and Lillers, west of Bethune, at 0950 to fly a Photo Op over Vimy Ridge, to the south-east of Lens, the patrol line being Lens to Henin Liétard (There were in fact two camera planes.) At 1030 they had crossed the lines north of Arras, where one aircraft aborted, its place being filled by a reserve machine that had flown with the formation for just this sort of eventuality. Grieg, who was leading, got rather ahead of the others and was suddenly pounced upon by a hostile scout (thought to have been an Albatros) at 1120 (1220 German time). The others saw Greig with the enemy fighter on his tail, driven down and forced to land near Rouvroy. He was seen to make a good landing.

When MacLennon made his report upon his return from Germany at the start of 1919, he noted: 'On outward journey we were attacked by a hostile machine. Escort was in rear of me. Richthofen attacked us from the rear, shooting up engine and wounding pilot. Engine stopped – landed. 6997 burnt. We learnt we were his eighteenth victory. Our flying kit was commandeered and taken to his Squadron No.11. Flying kit was my own personal property and [he] would give no reason for taking it.'

Writing later to Floyd Gibbons in 1926, MacLennan explained the sortie as follows: 'Grieg and myself were sent up to take mosaic photographs of the Vimy Ridge. This entails great accuracy in the actual exposures, a stopwatch being used so as to entail a correct overlap of each exposure. It is further necessary to keep at an exact altitude and to fly in a direct line, otherwise results obtained are unsatisfactory. Thus the taking of photographs fully employs the attention of both pilot and observer. An escort of three machines was provided, these flying behind and at a slightly greater altitude. Owing to slight error of judgement, this escort at the time of the attack were too far behind.

'I was actually taking photos when a burst of machine gun fire from behind notified the attack. I looked round and perceived a red enemy machine diving away. In the first attack he shot through both oil and petrol tanks and splintered the propeller; Captain Grieg was also shot through both legs. As a result the machine could only glide and the manoeuvrability was greatly impaired through lack of any engine power. Von Richthofen attacked all the way down till the machine was but a few hundred feet from the ground. He attacked each time from below and behind, in which position we were unable to return fire. Only once did he get in front when we managed to get off two bursts from the front gun, but at longish range and without result.'

Meantime, two of the FEs attacked the enemy fighter, driving it down to 6,000 feet where it flew off. For their part, the escort were unable to dive to help the doomed FE, as they still had the second photo machine to protect. The other Jasta 11 pilots engaged this FE and the escort, causing the British aircraft to become scattered.

Interestingly, a nearby 16 Squadron BE2c crew watched as the enemy fighter, with an FE on its tail (Second Lieutenants W D Matheson and his gunner, E G Green, in 7007) headed down. As the BE pilot continued to watch, he saw the FE break off and shortly afterwards the German scout went into a spinning nose-dive, falling to within a short distance of the ground. He later reported that while he did not see it crash it must have done so. Whether Richthofen was spinning away to get out of trouble, or as a result of the wing cracking is unclear. If the former, then obviously the strain imposed on his DIII caused the wing to crack. The FE crew were credited with an 'out of control' victory, but as so often happened, the German aircraft did not crash, although von Richthofen was forced to land.

Greig had indeed been wounded in the legs but made a good landing, MacLennan helping him from the machine. Their fuel tank had been punctured by Richthofen's fire, hence their rapid descent and landing before the whole thing caught fire. Once down, MacLennan had no difficulty in torching the petrol-soaked aeroplane before the arrival of German soldiers, thereby destroying maps and photos.

Some years later, Greig recorded: 'When we got near the lines I asked Mac whether our escort were in position. He shook his head, so fired a green Verey light as the signal to close up. After some little time he nodded to me and I took course for our photo area. I was standing up on the rudder bar, looking from the map to the ground, getting the machine in exactly the right position and keeping it on an even keel, the camera being a fixed one. The observer was looking through the camera sights and just beginning to take the exposures. There had been a complete absence of AA shells, but I thought this was because they were waiting for us to get further from our lines. At this moment I heard a machine gun and saw several bullet holes appear in the left wing. I turned to the right in a steep bank, nearly upsetting my observer, hoping to get the enemy in front of me and also to get back to my escort, but on completion of half a circle, the enemy fired another burst from the right side, putting the engine out of action and hitting me in the right ankle, knocking that foot off the rudder bar.

'I continued in circles, endeavouring to get a sight of the enemy but he succeeded in keeping below and behind me ... I saw several tracer bullets pass through the instrument board between me and my observer ... The firing stopped and we made for the lines but at this turn the observer pointed behind the machine, indicating another attack. A second later a small scarlet biplane passed over us and went away to the right ... Tried everything to get the engine going but it only spluttered fitfully. There was nothing for it but to land, between Vimy and Fresnoy, gliding through a batch of about a dozen field telephone wires, breaking them with the machine and rolling through some more before the machine stopped.'

Once down himself, Richthofen trundled into some wire and overturned, slightly damaging his new Albatros further. However, he still took the opportunity of meeting his two former opponents, and securing the aircraft's number as a souvenir of their encounter. In his book *Der Rote Kampffleiger* (*The Red Air Fighter*) which was published in Germany later in 1917, Richthofen describes this encounter, but says he was forced down due to engine trouble. With the war still on, he was obviously unable to admit to the real cause in print. However, he wrote that he was greeted by the two British airmen like a sportsman, although they were a little surprised at his arrival. They confirmed they had been surprised by his attack, and had been unable to return fire, so they were even more curious, and amused, that while they had made a good landing, he had made a hash of his.

Richthofen also says that as these were the first Englishmen he had brought down alive and had met, it gave him great pleasure in being able to talk to them. Reference to his red aircraft is also of interest as Richthofen had only painted his aircraft red for just over a month. However, it will be recalled that at least one red aircraft had been seen earlier (see victory No.5).

Von Richthofen was flying Albatros DIII Nr.789/17.

MACLENNAN, JOHN ERIC

LIEUTENANT 25 SQUADRON; THE CAMERONIANS (SCOTTISH RIFLES)

BORN ON 11 November 1896, MacLennan was living with his parents at 'Solva', Bromley, in Kent when the war broke out. He offered his services and was commissioned into the 3rd (Reserve) Battalion of the Cameronians on 16 June 1915. Within months, his application for transfer to the Royal Flying Corps had been approved and, after training, he was sent to join 25 Squadron in France on 14 September 1916, at the age of nineteen. After their encounter with von Richthofen, MacLennan cursed his luck as he set fire to the FE2b, as he had been due to go home on leave immediately following their return from this reconnaissance. Instead, he had to wait until 2 January 1919 before he was finally repatriated and could return to England. MacLennan remained in the Royal Air Force after the end of the Great War, retiring his commission on 1 January 1924. He lived between the wars at 'Westwood', Leasingham, near Sleaford, Lincolnshire. When the Second World War came, he returned to the RAF and served as a Squadron Leader (General Duties). John MacLennan died on 10 November 1961, just one day short of completing his sixty-fifth year.

GREIG, OSCAR

CAPTAIN 25 SQUADRON

BORN ON 5 June 1889, Oscar Greig was brought up in Pensile, Nailsworth, near Stroud, Gloucestershire. When the war came, he immediately volunteered for the Royal Flying Corps, having begun to learn to fly at Larkhill and Brooklands in 1912. However, because the War Office could not cope with the numbers coming forward, he was obliged to join the Army Service Corps as a driver, still a comparatively rare skill in 1914. Believing, like so many others, that the war would be over by Christmas, he was impatient to get over to France to 'do his bit'. He was told that the Red Cross were short of ambulance drivers and promptly asked for an extended leave of absence from the ASC. Greig landed at Calais on 28 October 1914, part of a Red Cross unit seconded to help the Belgian Army. He remained with the Red Cross until April 1915, when he returned home to pursue his ambition to join the RFC. His persistence paid off and he received a Special Reserve commission on 24 May 1915. Four days later he was awarded the Royal Aero Club Aviators Certificate (No.1276) and was given his 'Wings'. His initial training completed, he was posted to Joyce Green to fly the Vickers Gunbus, the British aeroplane designed specifically for aerial fighting. In July 1915, Greig was asked to ferry a Gunbus to St Omer and, after doing so, went on to join 5 Squadron at Abeele. He served with 5 Squadron, flying 23 missions, until October 1915 when, returning to England, he helped to test wireless equipment at Brooklands. From Brooklands he was sent to Gosport and there trained on photographic reconnaissance. On 18 December 1916, Greig, now a Captain, returned to France, joining 25 Squadron at Auchel. A little more than a month later, slightly wounded in the right ankle, he stood watching as his observer, John MacLennan, set fire to their grounded FE2b. Greig, in need of medical attention, was soon separated from MacLennan who was unhurt. The wound, although not serious, took time to heal and prevented him from joining in a number of escape attempts from the various POW camps he was incarcerated in over the next twenty-two months. When, at last, the end of the war came, Greig, like the other prisoners, assumed repatriation would follow immediately. But Germany was in a state of near revolution; communications were disrupted, chaos reigned in the place of the Kaiser. Eventually, impatient of the continued delays, Greig and a fellow officer decided to take matters into their own hands and, against orders, walked out of their erstwhile prison and kept on walking until they crossed the German border into Austria. After ten days, and a circuitous route which took them through Vienna, Prague, Turin and Paris, they at last arrived in England on 22 December 1918, just in time to celebrate Christmas at home. He was demobilised early, on medical grounds, in April 1919. But Oscar Greig had not finished with flying: he took it up again in civilian life, obtaining an 'A' Licence in October 1929. He died on 11 February 1969, at his home, 'The Mill', South Zeal, Okehampton, Devon. He was in his eightieth year.

1 FEBRUARY 1917

VICTORY NO. 19

BE2D No.6742
16 SQUADRON RFC
ENGINE No.521 WD 1884
GUNS: E633; E17453

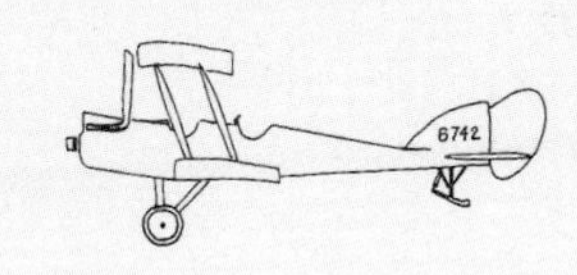

VON RICHTHOFEN'S Combat Report:
1600 hrs. BE two-seater No.6742.
Over trenches, one kilometre south-west of Thelus.
Occupants: Lieutenant Murray – Lieut McBar (sic), both wounded and died on 2 Feb.

About 1600 I spotted, flying with Leutnant Allmenröder, at 1,800 metres altitude, an artillery flyer. I managed to approach him within 50 yards apparently unnoticed, with my Halberstadter machine. From this distance, up to only the length of a plane, I fired 150 shots.

The enemy plane then went down in large, uncontrolled right-hand curves, pursued by Allmenröder and myself. The plane crashed into the barbed wire of our front lines. The occupants were both wounded and were made prisoners by the infantry. It is impossible to remove the plane.

BARON VON RICHTHOFEN

WEATHER: OVERCAST MORNING, BUT FINE FOR THE REMAINDER OF THE DAY.

This crew had taken off from Bruay airfield, west of Lens, at 1430 to fly, not an artillery spotting patrol, but a Photo Op to Thelus. At 1510 (British time) Canadian artillery reported a fight between three RFC and four enemy aircraft (sic). One BE was seen to land under control inside German lines, which was totally destroyed by shellfire 20 minutes later. A Forward Observation Officer also reported seeing an aircraft shot down by a hostile aeroplane at 1515, east of Neuville-St Vaast. Both Thelus and Mont Neuville-St Vaast are directly north of Arras – no more than six kilometres.

Significantly, von Richthofen was today flying a Halberstadt DII single-seat fighter. There had been two or three incidents of the new DIII model Albatros having wing problems, and with his own machine having a cracked wing the day before, the DIIIs were being withdrawn for modifications.

Von Richthofen was to fly Halberstadt machines for some weeks. *(cont.)*

MURRAY,
PERCIVAL WILLIAM
LIEUTENANT 16 SQUADRON; 6/DURHAM

THE SON OF tobacconists Mr and Mrs WA Murray of 10 Claremont Terrace, Norton on Tees, County Durham, Percy Murray was born in 1896. Educated at Armstrong College, Newcastle, and Durham University, Murray was studying for qualification as a mechanical engineer when the war intervened. Volunteering immediately, he was gazetted as Second Lieutenant to the 6th Battalion, Durham Light Infantry on 26 August 1914. Secondment to the Northumberland Division Cyclists Mounted Troops followed on 12 December 1914. He landed at Boulogne with the 6th Durhams on 17 April 1915 and was promoted Temporary Lieutenant on 5 November 1915. Murray survived the murderous fighting around Ypres when the 6th and 8th Battalions of the DLI both suffered so many casualties that they were forced to combine so as to remain a viable fighting unit. The amalgamation, now known as the 6/8th Battalion, fought on as a single entity for some time before sufficient reinforcements arrived and they could resume their original identities. Next, Murray successfully applied for transfer to the Royal Flying Corps and, after training, was appointed Flying Officer, RFC on 20 October 1916. He died from the effects of his wounds shortly after his machine was forced down behind German lines. He is buried alongside his Observer in Bois-Carre British Cemetery, Thelus, France (Fr.1321). He was twenty years of age.

McRAE,
DUNCAN JOHN
LIEUTENANT 16 SQUADRON; ALBERTA REGIMENT

BORN IN ALEXANDRIA, Ontario on 13 June 1892, the son of Andrew and Flora McRae of St Anne de Prescott, Ontario, Canada, McRae received his education in the local school system. After leaving school, he gained a position with a bank in Ottawa. A keen volunteer, he served in the 59th Regiment, Stormond Glengarry Highlanders from 1910 to 1912 when he joined the 43rd, Duke of Connaught's Own Rifles. He attested for overseas service with the 77th Battalion, Canadian Expeditionary Force, in August, 1915 and sailed with that unit from Halifax, Nova Scotia, aboard the SS *Missanabie* on 19 July 1916. Transferring to the 50th Btn (Alberta Regt) CEF, he went to France for the first time on 11 August 1916. He attended the usual subalterns' courses in 'Anti-gas' and 'Grenades' before successfully applying for transfer to the RFC on 19 December 1916, at the same time as one of his brothers was killed in the trenches. McRae was not Murray's usual observer but was 'filling in' on this occasion for the absent Lieutenant Lidsey. He was alive when he was extricated from the wreckage of his machine and from the German barbed-wire they were surrounded by, but died soon afterwards in enemy hands. He is buried, with his pilot, in Bois-Carre British Cemetery, Thelus, France (Fr.1321). He was twenty-four years of age.

14 FEBRUARY 1917

VICTORY NO.20

BE2D No.6231
2 SQUADRON RFC
ENGINE No.21996 WD 516
GUNS: 6098; 3913

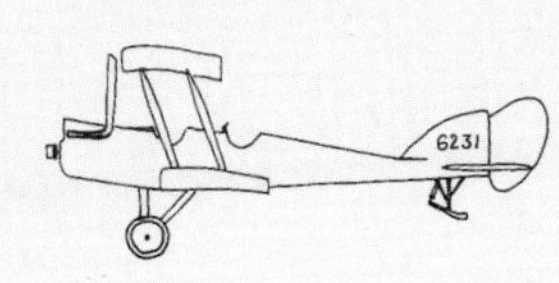

VON RICHTHOFEN'S combat report:
1200 hrs. BE two-seater.
Lens-Hulloch road, west of Loos. Occupants: one killed, the other severely wounded.
Name of pilot: Lieutenant Bonnet (sic) (died)
No details concerning plane, as wreckage landed in the fire zone.

After flying back from a conference with Jasta Boelcke, I spotted an enemy artillery flyer at a height of 2,000 metres, west of Loos.

I attacked the enemy and approached him unnoticed to some 50 metres. After several hundred shots, the plane dashed down, falling into our trenches.

The pilot was killed in the air, observer seriously injured when landing.

BARON VON RICHTHOFEN

WEATHER: FINE.

Again Richthofen was flying a Halberstadt, and, as stated, had been visiting his old Jasta 2 (Boelcke) at Lagnicourt and was on his way back to Brayelles, via the Front.

The BE crew had taken off from Hesdigneul, between Bethune and Bruay, at 0945 to fly an artillery observation sortie (Art Obs) to Lens. They had been at work for over an hour, successfully ranging for the 186th Siege Battery, before they were attacked. British observers saw the machine spiral down over Cité St Auguste at 1115.

The Lens-Hulloch road runs due north from Lens, a distance of no more than five kilometres, Cité St Auguste standing just to the east. The reason why Richthofen reported that the pilot had died in the air and the observer injured in the crash was no doubt due to the fact that the observer sits in the BE's front cockpit, the pilot in the rear, the only tractor aeroplane to have this cumbersome arrangement. When he returned from Germany, Bennett said that he recalled nothing of the action, the details being told him after his capture as he had suffered concussion of the brain for two days, and had no memory of the fight. When the BE crashed, Bennett said he'd 'put his leg out.'

Despite this, and the mis-spelling of the pilot's name, there is no dispute over this claim. *(cont.)*

BENNETT,
CYRIL DOUGLAS
SECOND LIEUTENANT 2 SQUADRON

CYRIL BENNETT was born in Moscow on 15 October 1897, the son of R H and Mrs Bennett who were in business and living in Riga in Imperial Russia. Educated at Malvern College (1912-16), Cyril 'joined up' and learnt to fly as soon as he left school, gaining the Royal Aero Club Aviators Certificate (No.3189) on 4 July 1916, at the age of eighteen. Given a commission in the Special Reserve, he received his Wings and was sent to 2 Squadron in France in August 1916. He was largely employed on photo-reconnaissance and artillery observation. Bennett suffered a fracture in the base of the skull and an injured hip in the crash and, after laying unconscious for fully two days in a German Field Hospital at Carvin, could never subsequently remember the details of his fight with von Richthofen. Shortly after his transfer to a hospital in Douai, he questioned his captors about the circumstances of his shooting down. He was told that his observer, whose identity the Germans had not yet established and whose name Bennett could not recall, had been shot in the air and had died soon after he was lifted from the wreckage. It was some time before it was finally established that the observer was, in fact, Herbert Arthur Croft. Still Bennett could not recall anything about the unfortunate Croft who, he was forced to conclude, he had met for the first time shortly before take-off. Bennett was detained in various camps at Ulm, Saarbrücken (where he shared quarters with D P McDonald, von Richthofen's 34th 'victory') Hannover and Holzminden, until he was finally repatriated on 6 December 1918. When Bennett returned to England, he learnt that his father's house in Moscow had been taken over by the Cheka (the forerunners of the KGB) after the 1917 revolution in Russia. He immediately requested the Air Ministry to send him to Russia to help in the fight against the Bolsheviks. His value as a Russian speaking pilot was obvious and although his health was less than perfect, his wish was granted and, at the end of March 1919, he crossed the English Channel again but this time he travelled to Marseille where he took ship for Constantinople. After a brief tour of the ancient city, he left to join 47 Squadron and the Intervention Force in the Caucasus. He remained with the Squadron, serving with Baron P Wrangel and General A Deniken's forces in the Volga region, until the final evacuation. After the war, Bennett entered the timber trade and, despite having to depend on a walking stick, travelled extensively. His facility with foreign languages also proved useful in his other capacity as an agent for Rolex Watches of Switzerland. During the Second World War, Bennett's talents were employed in a number of important posts including acting as the Chief Civil Censor in Asmara, Eritrea, and Liaison Officer with the Russians in Tehran.

CROFT,
HERBERT ARTHUR
SECOND LIEUTENANT 2 SQUADRON

KILLED IN THE air by von Richthofen's machine gun bullets, Croft's grave was marked by the German troops who recovered his body from the crashed machine. He is now buried in the Cabaret-Rouge British Cemetery, France (Fr.924).

14 FEBRUARY 1917

VICTORY NO.21

BE2c No.2543
2 Squadron RFC

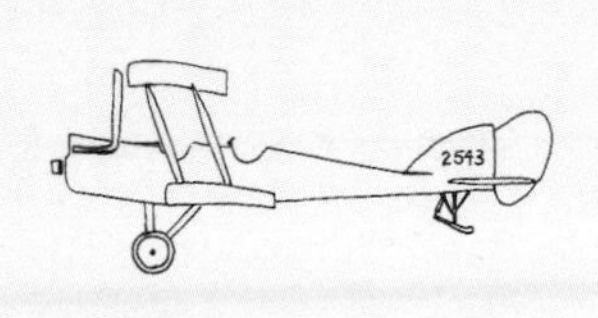

VON RICHTHOFEN'S Combat Report:
1645 hrs. BE two-seater.
Station, 1,500 metres south-west of Mazingarbe. No details, as plane landed on enemy's side.

About 1645 I attacked with my Staffel of five planes, artillery flyers, at low altitude near Lens. Whilst my gentlemen attacked a second BE, I attacked the one flying nearest to me. After the first 100 shots the observer stopped shooting. The plane began to smoke and twisted in uncontrolled curves to the right. As this result was not satisfactory to me, especially over the enemy's line, I shot at the falling plane until the left part of the wings came off.

As the wind was blowing at a velocity of 20 yards a second, I had been drifting far over to the enemy's side. Therefore, I could observe that the enemy plane touched the ground south-west of Mazingarbe. I could see a heavy cloud of smoke in the snow arising from where the plane was lying.

As it was foggy and already rather dark, I have no witnesses either from the air or from the ground.

Baron von Richthofen

Weather: fine, misty later.

This evening action is full of interest. For many years the victim of this encounter was thought to have been a Moranc Parasol (A266) of 3 Squadron RFC crewed by Lieutenant Thomas S Green and Second Lieutenant W K Carse who were both killed. Part of the reasoning is explained in the opening remarks of this book, ie: in trying to make evidence fit the situation.

Green and Carse were reported to have taken off at 1510, their aircraft being seen to fall and break-up at 1530 after an attack by a hostile aircraft at map reference M.29.d.55. This latter time would make it 1630 German time, which is 15 minutes before Richthofen made his claim. They were operating from Lavieville, west of Albert, and therefore would hardly be in combat more than 40 kilometres north of their section of the Front, where Mazingarbe is situated – six kilometres north-west of Lens. The biggest stumbling block, however, (and which people ignored for years) is that the RFC War Diary lists them as being lost on the 13th, the previous afternoon! In fact, they were shot down by Offizierstellvertreter Alfred Behling of Jasta 1 on the 13th near Le Transloy, almost opposite Albert. Jasta 1 were operating from Proville, on the south-west outskirts of Cambrai.

Despite Richthofen clearly stating that his victim was a BE, apart from this Morane other historians have even identified the machine either as a 20 Squadron FE2b (which fell to Paul Strähle of Jasta 18), or an 8 Squadron BE which returned with a wounded observer, although this action happened well before midday.

A study of the day's RFC combat reports shows that two 2 Squadron BE crews were in action with hostile aircraft at 1550 (ie: 1650 German time – and close enough to Jasta 11's action). Both British machines were engaged on Art Obs duty over Loos, working with the 24th Division's artillery; thus the area is exactly right. The hostile aircraft were described as three Halberstadt Scouts, one dark machine being very fast. With the night coming on, a red aircraft would have appeared 'dark'.

The crews were Bailey and Hampton (2543) at 6,800 feet above Loos, and nearby was Lieutenant H Fowler and Second Lieutenant E W Swann (6250), the latter at 7,000 feet just north of Loos. Fowler and Swann reported being attacked and turned to join the other BE. One Halberstadt came at them while another went for Bailey. Their gun jammed after 32 rounds, but it had been enough to deter the attacker, who turned away east as though hit.

Now free from immediate danger, Swann saw the other BE still being pursued with a third Halberstadt in attendance. Fowler nose-dived after the enemy aircraft, but before they could close, the two hostiles turned north-east, Swann sending a long burst after them but to no avail. Bailey, meantime, had quickly turned west when attacked, hoping to close with his companion, as Hampton manned his gun. However, in the initial attack by the leading Halberstadt, Bailey was hit in the knee. He put the BE into a spiral descent, still under fire, and then the rear gun mounting was hit and the gun fell overboard but not before it struck Bailey in the rear cockpit. It was this gun going over the back of the BE which Richthofen thought was a part of a wing coming off.

At this point, Bailey struggling and in pain, his BE in a steep spiral, the Halberstadts broke off and headed away. Low down, Bailey succeeded in righting the machine, got his bearings and headed for home, where he landed safely despite a badly shot-about BE, its fuselage, wings and his own seat having been shot through.

Everything fits the known facts with the exception that the BE did not '.. touch [hit?] the ground ..' and thus did not produce '.. a heavy cloud of smoke ... where [it] was lying.' We believe that this part of his report was again wishful thinking or auto-suggestion on Richthofen's part. He had, after all, made what he believed was a successful attack, had seen the BE fall in a manner which suggested it was uncontrolled (Bailey had been painfully wounded in the knee) and was going down in a steep spiral. What else could have happened other than the aircraft having hit the ground?

As he admits, he had no confirming witnesses, other than, one supposes, at least one of his pilots seeing the BE spinning down, and with the wind, for once blowing from east to west, he, like Hawker back in November, needed to get back to his own lines. It was also getting dark, and it would be even darker nearer the ground, so von Richthofen would have been less likely actually to see the BE land as he supposed. The smoke, of course, could have been anything, from a shell exploding to British soldiers having an early evening brew-up.

Von Richthofen was still flying a Halberstadt Scout.

Right: Albatros DIII 789/17 flown by von Richthofen early in 1917.

Painting opposite: Victory No.15

Painting overleaf: Victory No.33

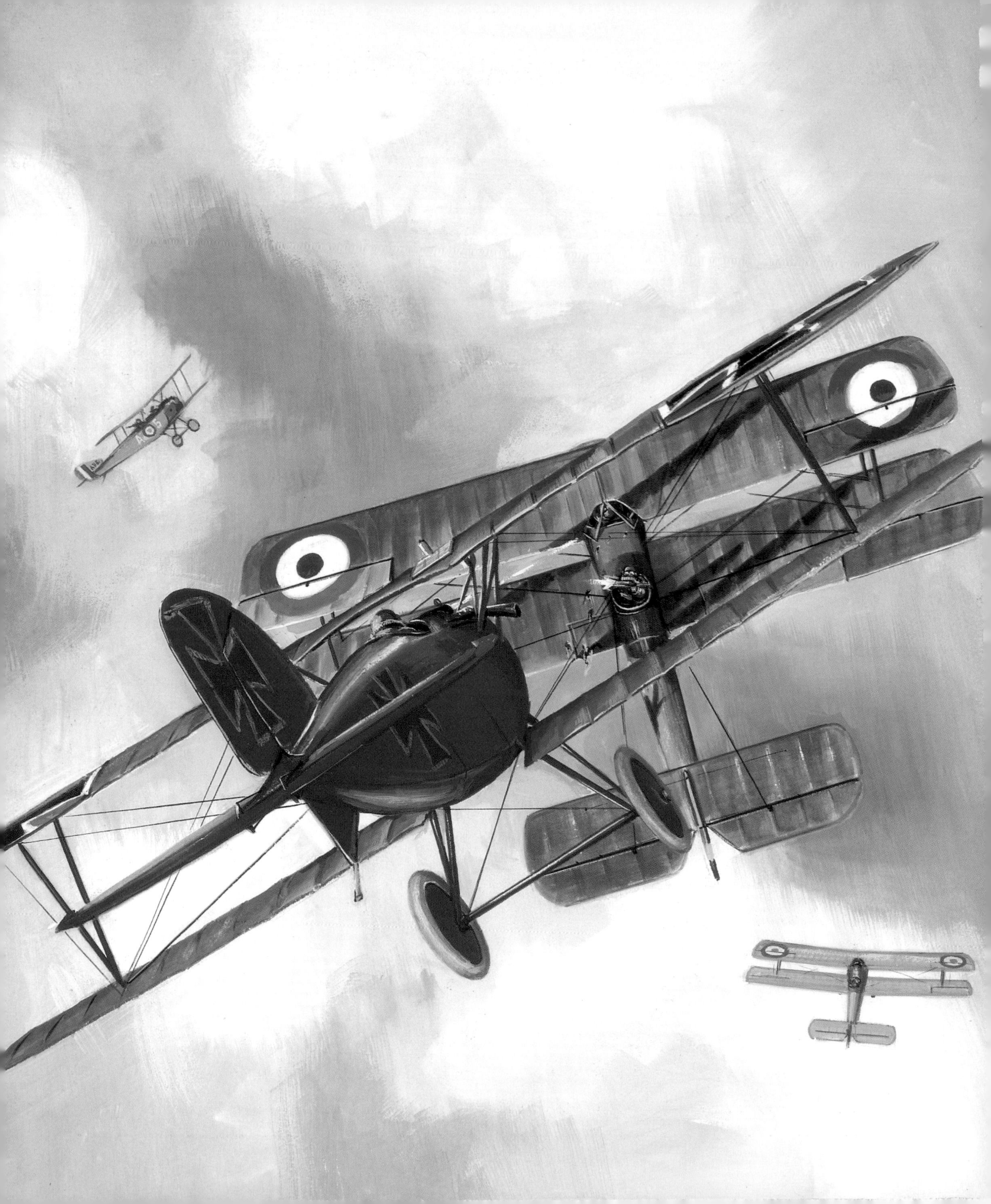

BAILEY,

GEORGE CYRIL

CAPTAIN 2 SQUADRON CB(1944) DSO

The son of Dr G H and Mrs Bailey of 'Marple Cottage', Marple, Cheshire, George Bailey was born on 15 July 1890. He was educated at the King Edward VII School, Stratford - upon - Avon (1902-06) at the same time as Reginald A J Warneford who, as a Sub-Lieutenant in 1 Squadron, Royal Naval Air Service, was later to win the Victoria Cross by bringing down a German airship in flames over Ghent in Belgium on 7 June 1915. Young Bailey showed a keen interest in photography, winning many prizes. Going on to the University of Manchester in 1907 to study civil engineering, he graduated BSc (Honours) three years later. Next came his formal apprenticeship with an engineering firm in Blackburn, Lancashire (1910-1913), followed by a year in Karlsruhe, Germany (1913-14) working on locomotive engineering. Now a qualified engineer, he gained a position with the Carriage Inspection Department of the Royal Arsenal in Woolwich in 1914. From Woolwich he was sent to Vickers in Barrow and worked on airship design. Returning to Woolwich, he was next engaged in gunsight testing. Bailey had volunteered immediately upon the outbreak of war but the Royal Arsenal refused to let him go until late in 1915 when he was, at last, allowed to take a commission in the RFC. His courage and outstanding ability as a pilot ensured his rapid promotion and he was awarded the Distinguished Service Order for his conduct in an action which occurred just prior to his brush with von Richthofen, *London Gazette*, 3/7/1917, page 2189:

'For conspicuous gallantry in action. He co-operated in an infantry raid by flying over the enemy's trenches at only 1,500 feet for more than an hour and a half in very adverse weather conditions. He attacked the enemy in the trenches with machine gun fire and located sixteen active enemy batteries during the fight. He has repeatedly done fine work'.

Bailey was wounded in the fight with the German ace but, nevertheless, managed to bring his machine and his Observer, Hampton, back home to safety. After he recovered from his wounds, Bailey was given command of No.57 Squadron in France, a Squadron he led from 9 September 1918 through to the Armistice and beyond, as part of the Army of Occupation in Cologne. Bailey married Phyllis, daughter of Sir John Foster Stevens, in 1918 and, deciding to remain in the Royal Air Force after the Great War, received a permanent commission in 1919. The couple had one son before Mrs Bailey died in 1927. Between the wars, Bailey served in India and Iraq, attended Staff College at Andover (1925) and advanced through the ranks before becoming Air Commodore in 1939. He was appointed Director of Equipment in the Air Ministry before his retirement in 1944, the year in which he also married for a second time, to Mary Ellen Goldney. In recognition of his services, Air Commodore George Cyril Bailey, DSO was appointed a Companion of the Most Honourable Order of the Bath (*London Gazette*, 8/6/1944, page 2568). He died at his home, 'Millhayes', Stockland, Honiton, Devon, on 1 June 1972 in his eighty-second year.

HAMPTON,

GEORGE WILLIAM BETTS

SECOND LIEUTENANT 2 SQUADRON; 3/5TH BTN SUFFOLK REGIMENT

Another of the 'oldies' – he was born in 1886 – George Hampton was a married man living with his wife, Violet, at 7 St Mary Road, Walthamstow, Essex when the war came. Volunteering immediately, he joined, as a private soldier (No.2139), the 1/4th Cameron Highlanders and accompanied that battalion to France on 19 February 1915. Selected for officer training, he was returned to England and was commissioned into the 3/5th, Suffolk Regiment on 31 August 1915. He soon became bored with life in a training/'feeder' battalion and successfully applied for transfer to the Royal Flying Corps. Shortly afterwards, he found himself on the Western Front with 2 Squadron. Although brought back safely by his pilot after their scrap with von Richthofen, Hampton, still flying with 2 Squadron, was to be killed less than a month later. On 11 March 1917, his BE2c (No.4541), piloted by 2/Lt. G C Hoskins, was shot down in flames over Loos – their adversary was probably Ltn Karl Schäfer of Jasta 11. Hampton is buried in Vermelles British Cemetery, France (Fr.423). He was thirty-one years old.

4 MARCH 1917

VICTORY NO.22

Once again the victim is unclear. In the past it was thought to have been Flight Sergeant R J Moody RFC and Second Lieutenant E E Horn (2nd Middlesex Regt & RFC) of 8 Squadron in BE2d No.6252. However, they took off on an Art Obs sortie at 0925 and fell in flames at 1030 (1130 German time), between Warlus and Dainville (20 km to the south of Loos), so the result, time and locality are all out. We now know that Leutnant Werner Voss of Jasta 2 got them, his 12th victory.

BE2D No.5785
2 SQUADRON RFC

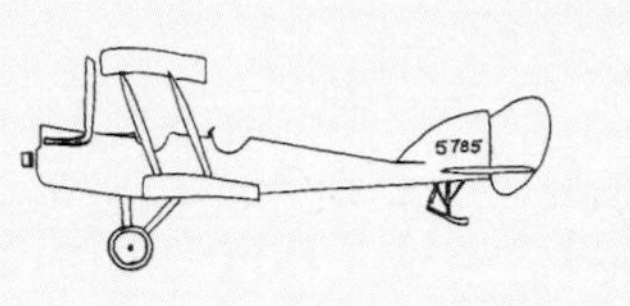

VON RICHTHOFEN'S Combat Report:
1250 hrs, one kilometre north of Loos. BE two-seater. Details unknown, plane fell on enemy's side.

I had started all by myself and was just looking for my Staffel when I spotted a single BE. My first attack was apparently a failure as my adversary tried to escape by curves and dives. After having forced my adversary downwards from 2,800 to 1,200 metres, he imagined himself safe and flew straight on once more. I took advantage of this, put myself behind him and fired some 500 shots at him. My adversary dived, but in such a steep way that I could not follow.

According to our infantry observations, the plane crashed to the ground in front of our trenches.

BARON VON RICHTHOFEN

WEATHER: FINE.

Right: Manfred von Richthofen showing his Pour le Mérite, Iron Cross 1st Class, Knight's Cross with Swords of the Royal House Order of Hohenzollern, Duke Carl Eduard Medal Saxe-Coburg-Gotha, Austro- Hungarian Military Merit Cross.

CROSBEE,
JAMES BENJAMIN EVELYN
LIEUTENANT 2 SQUADRON; 6TH BATTALION, WORCESTER REGIMENT

BORN IN NOTTINGHAM on 11 February 1897, Crosbee was the son of Walter A and Mrs Crosbee. His parents lived for a time at 30 Promenade, Cheltenham, Gloucestershire, where James received part of his education as a day-boy at nearby Cheltenham College. As soon as he was old enough, Crosbee volunteered and, late in 1915, was commissioned into the 6th (Reserve) Battalion of the Worcestershire Regiment. Learning to fly at his own expense, he gained the Royal Aero Club Aviators Certificate (No.2388) on 18 January 1916. His successful application for transfer to the RFC followed and 1917 saw him in France with 2 Squadron. After his encounter with von Richthofen, Crosbee managed to cross the lines and return safely to base. Although his observer, Prance, had been wounded in the air, Crosbee, fortunately, escaped injury. James Crosbee appears to have gone abroad after the war as, in 1927, his Great War medals (British War Medal and Allied Victory Medal) were returned to the Air Ministry by the London Postal Service, classified as 'undeliverable'. In later life, Mr Crosbee lived at 34 Rossetti Gardens, Chelsea, London SW3.

PRANCE,
JOHN EDWARD
SERGEANT (No.2008) 16 SQUADRON DCM ATTACHED 2 SQUADRON

BORN ON 3 November 1884, the eldest son of Sidney and Bessie Prance of Harbour House, Bideford, Devon. John's father was, for many years, the Harbourmaster of the north Devon port. The four Prance brothers volunteered their services early on in the war, John being accepted into the RFC as a Second Class Air Mechanic on 31 October 1914. Sent to join 9 Squadron in France in January 1915, he was promoted to 1AM on 1 March following. Later in that same month, at the height of the Battle of Neuve Chapelle, John was one of five ground crew who won the Distinguished Conduct Medal, *London Gazette*, 3/6/1915: *'For gallant conduct and valuable services on the night of 10/11 March 1915, in assisting to repair one of our aeroplanes which had been forced to descend near the firing line whilst being heavily shelled by the enemy. The machine was enabled to fly away by the following morning'.*
The machine concerned was a BE2c (No.1628, flown by Lt Blake and 2/Lt Meddlicott) of 2 Squadron which had landed damaged at Merris after being hit whilst performing Artillery Observation duties for 4th and 5th Siege Batteries. Prance was promoted Corporal and sent home on leave where he was fâted by the Mayor and citizens as the first Bidefordian to win the DCM. Promotion to Sergeant (1/12/15) was followed by training as an observer and further promotion to Flight Sergeant on 1 April 1916. On 4 January 1917, John married Miss Annie Wright of Bradford, Yorkshire in the United Methodist Church, Bideford. Service with 16 Squadron continued until that fateful day when he was 'loaned' to 2 Squadron who happened to be short of an observer for a photo-reconnaissance operation over Lens. Wounded in the leg, John Prance was returned to England for attention in a hospital in Nottingham. Following his recovery, he received training as an officer cadet, being commissioned Second Lieutenant on 28 November 1917, with a posting as an Equipment Officer to the No.1 School of Aeronautics, Reading. It seemed likely that John Prance would see out the rest of the war in this safe and relatively comfortable situation, but Fate was to deal him a different hand. Prance received a telegram from his wife with the dreadful news that their baby daughter, Monica Joan, had died on 16 June 1918. Grief-stricken, John Prance took the first available train home, the influenza he was suffering from intensifying with every mile. Arriving at last at his home at 26 Elm Grove, Bideford, he was so ill he was forced to take to his bed. So ill, in fact, that he was unable to attend his daughter's funeral. Tragically, John Prance died the following day, one of the earliest victims of the great influenza pandemic that was to claim tens of millions of lives around the world, far more than were lost in the Great War itself. He was buried with full military honours in Bideford Public Cemetery on 28 June 1918. He was thirty-three years of age.

All the other losses on the British side this day were Pups (3), 1½ Strutters (2), an RE8, an FE2b and an FE8 forced down inside British lines; and all are accounted for by known German pilots. One slight mystery is a 'Sopwith 4594' by Karl Emil Schäfer of Jasta 11, south-west of Haisnes, the serial 4594 being a BE number. However, this number may have concerned some other item aboard this aircraft, for it is fairly certain his victim was a 43 Squadron 1½ Strutter which he brought down at 1150 German time (A1109 crewed by Wood and Fenton). So who did von Richthofen engage?

Below: BE two-seater.

It is highly probable that his adversary was another 2 Squadron BE2d flying a Photo Op north of Lens. The type and area fits. This crew was attacked by a single-seat Halberstadt Scout with multi-coloured wings over a position given as N.8.b. Neither the pilot nor observer saw the attacking aeroplane as it came at them from out of a powerful sun's glare from almost head-on, the fourth or fifth shot hitting the observer in the leg just as he grabbed his gun. The Halberstadt then came in from astern, fired, dived below them, then swooped upwards and came at them again. Another attack tore away the left-hand ammunition rack, while a further attack punctured the fuel tank.

All the while the wounded observer kept up a return fire although he was beginning to weaken. The pilot went into a slow spiral, which steepened into a dive, the German fighter continuing to attack. When at 3,000 feet over the trenches, the hostile aircraft flattened out at 800 feet above the BE and, with a final burst from the observer, the Halberstadt made off towards Henin Liétard and became lost in the mist.

Certainly one could be forgiven for making a number of comparisons between both combat reports: the surprise attack, no other hostile aircraft observed/reported and von Richthofen was alone, the spiral (curves) and final dive, with the fighter following and firing; then the BE crew saying the fighter flattened out, Richthofen reporting the dive being too steep to follow.

The main problem is the report that a BE crashed behind the front line, whereas this 2 Squadron BE managed to get home and land without further damage. The fact, however, that von Richthofen lost sight of it and flew off, strongly suggests that as he did not see it crash, he or his adjutant obviously took the subsequent crash report on trust. A report having been received of an aeroplane crashing (or appearing to crash) – time and actual location not known – made a possible 2 and 2 come to a reasonable 4.

4 MARCH 1917

VICTORY NO.23

Sopwith 1½ Strutter
No.A1108
43 Squadron RFC
Engine No.R1169 WD 7782
Guns: 20024; 7500

VON RICHTHOFEN'S Combat Report:
1620 hrs, Acheville. Sopwith two-seater.
Occupants: Lieutenant W Reid and Lieutenant H Green, both killed, buried by local command at Bois Bernard.

Accompanied by five of my planes, I attacked an enemy squadron above Acheville. The Sopwith I had singled out flew for quite a while in my fire. After the 400th shot, plane lost a wing whilst making a curve. Machine hurtled downwards.

It is not worth while to have plane taken back, as parts are all over Acheville and surroundings. Two machine guns were seized by my Staffel. (One Lewis gun No.20024 and one Maxim [Vickers] gun L.7500).

Baron von Richthofen

Weather: fine.

The Sopwith two-seaters of 43 Squadron took off from Treizennes, just south of Aire, at 1340, to patrol south of Vimy. When the Jasta 11 pilots engaged the formation, this Sopwith was seen to leave the safety of the group and attack the fighters, three of which then proceeded to attack it, and it went down at 1525 (time agrees with the German 1620/1625 hrs).

Nearby was a patrol of 40 Squadron, engaged escorting the Sopwiths between Anneouelle and Oppy, Lieutenant K S Henderson (in FE8 6419) witnessing the fall of the Strutter. He and his companions were then engaged themselves, Henderson being shot up and having to land at 10 Squadron's base at Chocques, north-west of Bethune. Lieutenant C O Usborne went to the aid of the other Sopwiths over the La Bassée canal. He drove off a grey coloured Halberstadt, but was then hit himself by fire which damaged his rudder and holed his fuel tank. Henderson came to his aid and drove off this Halberstadt, but A4872 had to force-land behind the front line. Karl Emil Schäfer claimed an FE8 at this time but it was not confirmed.

Acheville is ten kilometres east of Vimy, with Bernard Wood four kilometres further east. Von Richthofen was flying a Halberstadt DII.

(cont.)

Right: Cabaret-Rouge British Cemetery, France.

GREEN,
HERBERT JOHN
SECOND LIEUTENANT 43 SQUADRON

'BERTIE' GREEN WAS born in East Rudham, Norfolk on 30 July 1897, the son of W S and Mrs Green. At the age of nine, he and the rest of his family moved north to 7 Springbank Road, Newcastle upon Tyne. Four years later he won a special scholarship to St Cuthbert's Grammar School where he distinguished himself, particularly in science subjects. From St Cuthbert's, Green passed into Armstrong College with the intention of taking a degree in science. He also joined the Durham University OTC. He broke off his studies to volunteer his services as soon as he was old enough to do so and was sent to the Officer Cadet Training Battalion at Oxford. From Oxford, he was gazetted Second Lieutenant to the Royal Flying Corps (SR) on 6 July 1916, so joining three of his brothers who were already with the flying service. He graduated from the Central Flying School, Upavon on 15 November 1916, and was then posted to Hemel Hempstead. The Christmas of 1916, his last, was spent at home. He crossed the Channel on 17 January 1917, and had been with his Squadron only a matter of weeks when he was killed. On the very day of Bertie's death, his brother Ernie, an observer with 16 Squadron, had arranged to call over on a visit from his own aerodrome at Auchy. Ernie went on to win an MC, before qualifying as a pilot and being shot down and taken prisoner on 3 February 1918. Ernie Green stayed on in the RAF after the war and was killed in a flying accident at Digby, Lincolnshire on 24 May 1922. Bertie Green is buried alongside his observer in Cabaret-Rouge British Cemetery, France (Fr.924). He was nineteen years old.

REID,
ALEXANDER WILLIAM
SECOND LIEUTENANT 43 SQUADRON; 1/6TH KING'S OWN SCOTTISH BORDERERS

ALEX REID, who was born in 1896, was the son of Captain J J and Mrs F E Reid of 'St Heliers', Denzil Avenue, Southampton. A keen volunteer, he joined the Hampshire Yeomanry (Carabiniers) as a trooper in 1913. He was amongst those who immediately volunteered for Imperial Service when war broke out and it was not long before he was commissioned, being gazetted to the King's Own Scottish Borderers on 28 December 1914. He was first sent to the Front as a replacement officer to the 6th Battalion of his regiment in November 1915, the 6th KOSB having been almost wiped out in the Battle of Loos in September 1915. Wounded in the trenches on 1 May 1916, Reid returned to England and following his recovery successfully applied for transfer to the RFC. He was sent for training at Reading on 26 January 1917, and then on to Hythe until 16 February 1917 before returning to France to join 43 Squadron on 23 February 1917. He lasted just nine days. Reid is buried alongside his pilot in Cabaret-Rouge British Cemetery, France (Fr.924). He was twenty years old.

BROUGHT DOWN

From top to bottom: Gregory and Benbow of 40 Squadron; Lübbert and Schäfer, Jasta 11.

While Manfred von Richthofen achieved his 24th victory on the afternoon of 6 March, he very nearly did not survive the morning. As he recorded in both his book and in a letter home, he was shot down at this time. The date has never been clear, some historians opting for 9 March, but it seems more feasible for the date to have been 6 March.

Both days and both actions involved the FE8s of 40 Squadron, but Richthofen mentions Lens as the area. 40 Squadron had a fight with enemy aircraft east of Loos on the ninth at 0930 hrs (1030 German time). However, their fight on the sixth (at 1050, 1150 German time) was above Givenchy-en-Gohelle on the other side of Lens, a more viable location.

On 6 March, Sopwiths of 43 Squadron were attacked by Jasta 11 and 40 Squadron came to their aid. Von Richthofen was in the thick of it and closed in on one opponent, but in doing so he momentarily failed to look behind. He suddenly heard a tremendous bang just after he had commenced firing. He knew at once his machine had been hit and then came a terrific stench of petrol – his tank had been shot through.

He dived away rapidly and shut off his engine, petrol squirting about his legs and feet. Looking back he saw he was leaving a white trail as the petrol vaporised. As he went down, the fight continued above and he then saw a British aircraft falling in flames, one of 43 Squadron going down (A978 shot down by Schäfer). Then he saw a German fighter spin down but the pilot righted his craft and made for a landing. Richthofen landed near Henin Liétard and took time to inspect the damage. Both fuel tanks had been drained of fuel and his engine had been damaged. He had been lucky the Halberstadt had not caught fire. The other Halberstadt he'd seen coming down was flown by Leutnant Eduard Lübbert, who'd been slightly wounded by a glancing shot to the chest but he got down safely. He would be killed on the 30th.

Who had shot down von Richthofen? Two 40 Squadron pilots put in combat reports, the same Lieutenant E L Benbow (A4871) who'd been in the fight of 23 January when John Hay had been killed, and Captain Robert Gregory (6384). Benbow had fired a burst at 50 to 20 yards into a machine painted mostly green. He had then zoomed and on looking back saw a machine go down in flames. However, he does not say it was his victim, and may have been the Strutter going down. Captain Bob Gregory, meanwhile, had attacked a Halberstadt and seen his bullets going into the enemy fighter which then dived vertically. Von Richthofen had certainly dived vertically – and fast. Obviously one of these had attacked von Richthofen. Benbow was credited with one hostile aircraft in flames, Gregory with an 'out of control' victory. If Benbow thought the Halberstadt trailing white smoke was a 'flamer' then that might have been von Richthofen, while Gregory had wounded Lübbert. There were no other Jasta 11 losses. Previous suggestions that it had been 9 March, a day 40 Squadron had lost three FE8s and had another pilot wounded, were wrong; it was not this action (fought at around 1020 German time) although it had been Jasta 11 who had got them: Schäfer two, Allmenröder and Wolff one each. It has also been said that von Richthofen had been brought down in this latter action, then rushed back to base, flown another aeroplane and shot down Pearson of 29 Squadron; these events do not conform to the fact that Richthofen clearly recorded that after he'd been brought down he had a sleep, then had lunch with the front line troops before going back to base. As Pearson was shot down at 1020 German time, this would not fit with von Richthofen's known movements.

6 MARCH 1917

VICTORY NO.24

BE2E No. A2785
16 SQUADRON RFC
ENGINE No.E1083 WD 5234
GUNS: 10487; 5393

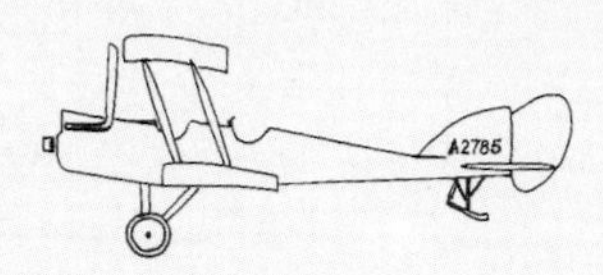

VON RICHTHOFEN'S Combat Report:
1700 hrs, BE two-seater, Souchez.
Details unknown, as plane landed on enemy's side.

Together with Leutnant Allmenröder, I attacked two enemy artillery flyers at a low altitude over the other side [of the lines]. The wings of the plane I attacked came off; it dashed down and smashed on the ground.

BARON VON RICHTHOFEN

WEATHER: FINE.

An initial problem for earlier researchers was that the combat report, or at least the translation, was dated 3 March. However, the correct date is 6 March, this 16 Squadron BE taking off from Bruay at 1350 to fly an Art Obs sortie over Vimy and seen to be shot down by a hostile aircraft in a position given as Sheet 36C.S.25.c. Souchez is on the Bethune to Arras road, opposite Givenchy and located just inside the British lines at that period, the area covered by Sheet (map) 36.

There was another 16 Squadron BE in the locality which saw A2785 shot down. The pilot was Flight Sergeant S H Quicke, flying with Captain L E Claremont as his observer. They were flying BE2d No.5834 above no-man's-land' at 1610 (1710 German time) on their way to their artillery observation area. Claremont pointed to the spinning BE and Quicke turned west, but at the same moment, Claremont heard the rattle of machine guns. Quicke then saw a white- coloured machine in front of them and a few moments later a bright red Halberstadt appeared directly above them. It had been out of sight of Claremont, obscured by the top wing centre section. As he saw it, the Halberstadt curved down and behind the BE and began firing but Claremont immediately returned fire with a burst of 70 rounds, whereupon the red machine turned away sharply to fly back across the German lines.

However, the upper left aileron had been hit and put out of action and one of the outer struts had also been broken. Quicke side-slipped the BE and landed it safely in a field near Camblain L'Abbée. Richthofen would shoot down Quicke on 21 March (see victory No.29).

Left: Karl Allmenröder, Jasta 11.

GOSSET–BIBBY,

GERALD MAURICE

SECOND LIEUTENANT 16 SQUADRON

The only son of the Reverend Arthur G and Mrs A Gosset-Bibby, Gerald was born on 9 April 1897 at Kimbolton, Huntingdonshire where his father was headmaster at the Grammar School. Following Prep School at Wells House, Malvern Wells, he was a boarder at Oundle School from 1911 to 1914. At the time of the outbreak of war, his father had retired and the family were living at 11 St. Augustine Road, Bedford. He enlisted in the RFC as soon as he was old enough to be accepted and served as an NCO observer during the first Battle of the Somme in July 1916. He impressed his superiors and was returned to England for pilot training and a commission. Gazetted a Flying Officer he returned to the Front in February 1917, joining 16 Squadron who were largely engaged in spotting for the Artillery. Days later, young Gosset-Bibby lay dead in a French field after a one-sided fight with von Richthofen over the Canadian trenches. He is buried in Barlin Cemetery, France (Fr.12). He was nineteen.

BRICHTA,

GEOFFREY JOSEPH OGLIVIE

LIEUTENANT 16 SQUADRON; 2/CANADIAN MOUNTED RIFLES

Although both of his parents were British, Geoffrey Brichta was born in Lundenburg, Austria on 6 July 1884. His father, a doctor, was in practice in Vienna at this time. Following his father's death some years later, his mother, Marina, returned to England with her young son, eventually settling at 'Eastburn House', Northwood, Middlesex. Musically gifted, he sang in the choir in Christchurch Cathedral. He emigrated to Canada in 1908, eventually settling four years later in North

Battleford, Saskatchewan, by then a married man with one daughter. Making practical use of his musical talents, he ran the North Battleford Piano Company and was also an enthusiastic member of a local militia unit, 22nd Btn, the Saskatchewan Light Horse. Like so many other Canadian patriots, Brichta, now the father of three children, left the comfort of hearth and home and volunteered to serve King and Empire, sailing for England with the 9th Canadian Mounted Rifles in November, 1915. He was eventually posted to France in March 1916, but only after transferring to the 2nd Btn Canadian Mounted Rifles. Next, he successfully sought a transfer to the RFC, being taken on strength as an observer in September, 1916. Brichta joined 16 Squadron on probation on 7 October 1916, as something of a rarity although there were many Canadian pilots in the RFC, there was only ever a handful of Canadian observers. Shortly after his arrival, on 20 October, Brichta was the observer in a BE2c (No.2546) which crashed on taking off from Bruay aerodrome. He and his pilot, 2/Lt Mitchell, were both unhurt but their machine was completely wrecked. Further training followed and his entry into the air war coincided with a heavy programme of flying during the early months of 1917. His Squadron was particularly hard worked and hard hit, losing 20 planes in a six-week period. Following his death, Britchta's wife, Mrs A G Brichta, who had been living at 'The Briars', Sutton West, Ontario, returned to live in Southbourne, Bournemouth, in England. Geoffrey Brichta is buried alongside his young pilot in Barlin Cemetery, France (Fr.12). He was thirty-two years old.

9 MARCH 1917

VICTORY NO.25

DH2 No.A2571
29 SQUADRON RFC
ENGINE No.30377 WD 4098
GUN: 6855

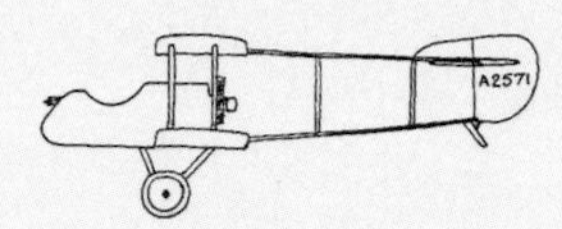

VON RICHTHOFEN'S Combat Report:
1155 hrs, Vickers one-seater. No. on tail AMC 3425a.
Between Roclincourt and Bailleul, this side of line, 500 metres behind trenches.
Occupant: Not recognisable, as completely burnt.

With three of my planes I attacked several enemy planes. The machine I had singled out soon caught fire and dashed downwards after firing 100 shots. The plane is lying on our side, but cannot be salvaged as it is nearly completely burned and too near the Front.

BARON VON RICHTHOFEN

WEATHER: LOW CLOUDS AND SNOWSTORMS ALL DAY.

On this occasion, von Richthofen was flying Leutnant Lübbert's Albatros DIII, another reason why his own shoot-down was on the sixth and not the ninth – as Lübbert was wounded on the former date.

The DH2s of 29 Squadron had flown a morning escort sortie, having taken off from Le Hameau at 0920. Little else is known other than that Pearson was seen falling in flames into the German front line area, which ties in with Richthofen's report. Apart from the 40 Squadron massacre one hour and twenty minutes earlier, these were the only losses suffered by the RFC on this date.

The initial patrol had been just three aircraft: Lieutenants Pearson, Blofeld (7858) and J G Aronson (A5024). Pearson and Blofeld had taken off at 0920, Aronson being delayed until 0940 with no indication he had caught up. He certainly saw nothing of enemy aircraft, and even Blofeld, who saw one, reported it was too far off to engage, so he could hardly have been in contact with Pearson when the latter was shot down. There must have been other British aircraft in the general area for Richthofen to report 'several' aircraft, but Pearson must have almost been on his own now, or perhaps he had tagged on to another bunch of aircraft. He would have known how dangerous it was to be swanning about alone.

Roclincourt and Bailleul (-Sir-Berthoult), not to be confused with the town of Bailleul north-west of Armentières up on the northern sector of the British front, is just north-east of Arras, to the south of Vimy Ridge.

The number quoted by von Richthofen has nothing to do with the actual serial number of this DH2 but rather it concerns the manufacturer, in this case the Aircraft Manufacturing Company (AMC).

Pearson had gained a brief moment of glory on 4 March 1917, sharing in bringing down an Albatros DII (902/16) in British lines, west of Arras. This was flown by Leutnant Max Böhme of Jasta 5, who was taken prisoner. Pearson shared it with an FE crew of 11 Squadron.

PEARSON,
ARTHUR JOHN
LIEUTENANT 29 SQUADRON MC; NORTHAMPTONSHIRE REGIMENT AND MACHINE GUN CORPS

BORN IN JULY 1887, the son of Charles W and Esther Pearson of 'Shenley House', Heath, Leighton Buzzard, Bedfordshire, Arthur Pearson was educated at the Royal Latin School, Buckingham. From school, he took a three-year course in Mechanical and Electrical Engineering at the City and Guilds Institute, London. After graduating, he joined the Western Electric Company, Woolwich. A specialist in the installation of telephone exchanges, his work took him to China, where he installed two new telephone exchanges for the Imperial Court in Peking, receiving a presentation of two fine Cloisonné vases in appreciation of his work. From Peking, he was sent to Durban in South Africa and then on to Australia. Returning from Australia in 1913, he was next directed to Antwerp and it was from that city that he hurried home as soon as he heard news of the outbreak of war. Arriving in England, Pearson joined the Royal Fusiliers as a private soldier in September 1914. It was not long before he was selected for officer training, subsequently receiving a commission in the 8th (Reserve) Battalion of the Northamptonshire Regiment on 27 March 1915, before being transferred, in 1916, to the newly formed Machine Gun Corps. He fought in the first battle of the Somme and was awarded the Military Cross for gallantry in the early days of that gory conflict, *London Gazette*, 19/8/1916, page 8230:

'For conspicuous gallantry during operations. When held up by the enemy's wire after an advance through heavy fire, he established himself in a shell hole and held on for five hours. He then withdrew bringing back his gun and a wounded man'.

The wounded man rescued by Arthur Pearson was, in fact, his own servant (batman). An exceptional marksman of undoubted and proven bravery, Pearson's application for transfer to the RFC was quickly approved. After pilot training at Upham, he returned to France to join 29 Squadron at Le Hameau in December 1916. Pearson's body was never found and he is commemorated on the Arras Memorial to the Missing, France.

11 MARCH 1917

VICTORY NO.26

BE2D No.6232
2 SQUADRON RFC
ENGINE No.23100 WD 2096
GUNS: 17458; 17352

VON RICHTHOFEN'S Combat Report:
1200 hrs, BE two-seater, south of La Folie Wood, near Vimy. Occupants: Lieutenant Byrne and Lieutenant Smythe (sic), 40 Squadron. Both killed. Plane No.6232, Details of motor not at hand, as motor dashed into earth; cannot be dug up as locality under heaviest artillery fire.

I had lost my squad, and was flying alone, and had been observing for some time an enemy artillery flyer. In a favourable moment I attacked the BE machine, and after 200 shots the body of the machine broke in half. The plane fell smoking into our lines.

The plane is lying near the forest of La Folie west of Vimy, only a few paces behind the trenches.

BARON VON RICHTHOFEN

WEATHER: FINE IN MORNING; CLOUDY IN AFTERNOON.

Although he got the name of the crew and the serial number right – he also had the number cut from the wreckage – reference to 40 Squadron is incorrect.

Smyth had been flying for some time with the Squadron, having had an indecisive combat with an Albatros Scout on 8 February in this same aircraft above Cité Colonne, with Second Lieutenant L S White as his observer. On this day he took off to fly a Photo Op and was seen to be attacked over Givenchy at 1045 and brought down on the German side of the lines. The BE was something of a veteran with over 224 hours on its flight record.

Givenchy is on the southern outskirts of Lens, the wood edging on to what had been La Folie Farm. Von Richthofen was flying a Halberstadt DII.

Right: Cabaret-Rouge Cemetery where Smyth and Byrne are buried; also Croft, Dunn, Green and Reid.

SMYTH,
JAMES
SECOND LIEUTENANT 2 SQUADRON

SMYTH, AN ULSTERMAN born in the Ballymacarrett district of Belfast, was brought to England as a boy by his father who was seeking work in the rope and hemp industry. In August 1914, Smyth was living with his wife, Ethel Martha, and their two children at 'Mossvale', 98 Chestnut Road, Plumstead, Kent. He worked with the Borough Engineering Company of London and his employers, anxious to retain his services, obtained exemption for him and dissuaded him from 'joining up'. Eventually, however, he insisted on enlisting and volunteered for the Royal Flying Corps. Because of his maturity and engineering abilities, he was quickly picked out as officer material. Following the usual training, he was sent to the Front as a pilot with 2 Squadron. He is buried in the Cabaret-Rouge British Cemetery, France (Fr.924).

BYRNE,
EDWARD
SECOND LIEUTENANT 2 SQUADRON; 4/GORDON HIGHLANDERS

BORN IN 1881, and therefore one of the oldest of von Richthofen's victims, Edward Byrne was brought up in orphanages in Edinburgh and educated at St Joseph's College, Dumfries. Like many other orphans, Byrne joined the Regular Army as soon as he was old enough. He spent twelve years in the Royal Army Medical Corps, serving in China, India and Africa. In 1914, having retired from the Army four years earlier, he had made his home in the Catholic Working Boys Home in Hartington Place, Edinburgh. He had also secured a trusted position in the Scottish capital, managing the home and estate of a prominent local businessman. The moment war was declared, Byrne volunteered without hesitation and was soon in France with the Australian Volunteer Hospital Corps, thus qualifying for the award of the 1914 Star. Bored with his duties in the Hospital Corps, he successfully applied for transfer to the Duke of Westminster's Armoured Car Squadron, then also in France. Because of the static nature of the war on the Western Front, it was decided to send the Squadron to the Middle East. Before he left for Egypt, the Duke of Westminster personally recommended Byrne for a commission. Gazetted to the 4/Gordon Highlanders, he served with that battalion in the trenches until he was severely wounded. After recovering his fitness, he was again successful with an application for transfer, this time to the Royal Flying Corps. After completing the appropriate training, he was sent as an observer to join 'C' Flight, No.2 Squadron, in France. Byrne had always kept in touch with the principal of his old orphanage and, in a letter sent to that gentleman shortly before his death, he confessed to a fear of being shot down in flames. He is buried in Cabaret-Rouge British Cemetery, France (Fr.924). He was thirty-six years old.

17 MARCH 1917

VICTORY NO.27

FE2B No.A5439
25 Squadron RFC
Engine No.854 WD 7464
Guns: 19901; 19633

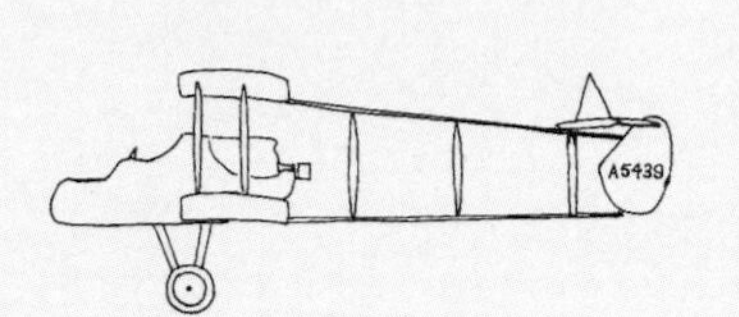

VON RICHTHOFEN'S Combat Report:
1130 hrs, Oppy. Vickers two-seater No.A3439. Motor No.854. Machine guns: 19633 and 19901

About 1130 I attacked with nine of my machines, an enemy squadron of 15 aircraft. During the fight I managed to force a Vickers two-seater aside, which I then, after 800 shots, brought down. In my machine gun fire the plane lost its open-work fuselage.

The occupants were killed and were taken for burial by the local commander at Oppy.

Baron von Richthofen

Weather: fine all day; ground mist early morning.

The serial number, gun numbers and engine number all check with the RFC loss report. 25 Squadron had flown out at 0900 in company with Sopwiths of 43 Squadron on a Photo Op between Annoeullin and Vitry. There were nine FEs, three being photo machines, led by Captain C H C Woolven, the nine 43 Squadron Strutters being led by Captain D C Rutter.

This formation was engaged by an estimated 15 to 20 hostile fighters. Initially there had been just eight fighters below them over Beaumont, but as they climbed they were joined by another dozen or so which came from the direction of Douai. The RFC aircraft kept a good and close formation as the air battle commenced.

The FEs claimed three fighters driven down out of control, and two others shot down in flames by Captain L L Richardson/Second Lieutenant D C Wollen, and Lieutenant H E Davies/2AM L Emsden, whilst a sixth was forced to land by Sergeant J H R Green/Second Lieutenant N W Morrison. However, Boultbee and King went down and 43 Squadron lost two of their number, Second Lieutenants J E Rimer/R H Lownds (A1111) and Second Lieutenants R A Constable/C D Knox (A1097), who all died.

No.43 Squadron later reported that they had seen about 15 enemy aircraft at 1045, manoeuvring into the sun before they dived to the attack. Captain Rutter followed the FEs whose leader had begun to circle. Seeing one fighter attack an FE, Rutter had stalled his machine up and fired several bursts with his front gun, claiming hits. His observer, Lieutenant Venn, meantime, drove off several fighters with his rear gun.

Lieutenant F M Kitto engaged another enemy fighter, firing from 30 yards to close range and it went down out of control. Major A S W Dore, the CO, was flying this sortie and was attacked by two fighters, but his observer, Sergeant Cubberley, drove them away. Of 43's two losses, one went down in flames, these falling to Allmenröder and Wolff either side of Athies, east of Arras. Oppy, where von Richthofen's victims came down, is further to the north-east, above Gavrelle. Jasta 11 suffered no losses. Von Richthofen was flying a Halberstadt DII.

BOULTBEE,
ARTHUR ELSDALE
LIEUTENANT 25 SQUADRON; 3/NORTHAMPTONSHIRE REGIMENT

ARTHUR BOULTBEE was born in Colne, St Ives, Huntingdonshire in 1897, the son of the Reverend Frederick Croxall Boultbee and his wife, Henrietta. By the time of the Great War, Arthur was living with his parents at the Rectory, Hargrave, Northamptonshire. Educated at St John's, Leatherhead, Surrey he was awarded an Exhibition in History (worth £25) and admittance to St Cathrine's College, Cambridge. However, anxious to emulate so many of his peers, he left Cambridge after only one term to 'join up'. He was given a commission in his county regiment, the Northamptonshires. A successful application to join the RFC was followed by flight training and eventual posting to 25 Squadron on New Year's Day, 1917. Ten weeks later, he was dead. A photograph of poor Boultbee's dead body was sent to von Richthofen with a message scrawled on the back: 'To Baron Manfred von Richthofen; Sir, I witnessed on 17 March 1917 your air fight, and took this photograph, which I send to you with hearty congratulations, because you seldom have the occasion to see your prey. Vivat Sequens! (Here's to the next!) With Fraternal Greetings, Baron von Riezenstein, Colonel and Commandant of the Eighty-seventh Reserve Regiment'. Boultbee is buried in Canadian Cemetery No.2, Neuville-St Vaast, France (Fr.1896). He was nineteen years old.

KING,
FREDERICK
2ND CLASS AIR MECHANIC (No.61783) 25 SQUADRON

THE SON OF Tim and Florence King of Deeping St Nicholas, Spalding, Lincolnshire, Fred King was born in his home village in 1894. He was educated at the local Middle Township School and had hardly ventured beyond the boundaries of his own community before volunteering for service with his county regiment, the Lincolnshires. Bright and keen, Fred King was picked out from a group of likely candidates and transferred for service in the Royal Flying Corps, going on to train as an observer. He continued to do well in the flying service and, following his death, his mother was told that he would have been offered a commission had he survived. Like his pilot, he is buried in Canadian Cemetery No.2, Neuville-St Vaast, France (Fr.1896). He was twenty-two years of age.

17 MARCH 1917

VICTORY NO.28

BE2g No.2814
16 Squadron RFC
Engine No.E640 WD 2989
Guns: 17440; 15754

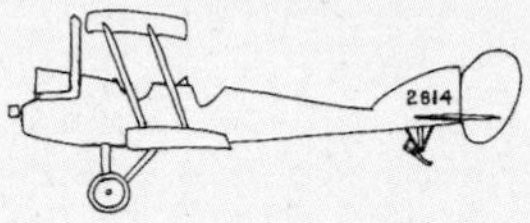

VON RICHTHOFEN'S Combat Report:
1700 hrs, above trenches west of Vimy. BE two- seater. No details, as plane landed between the lines.

I had spotted an enemy infantry flyer. Several attacks directed from above produced no results, especially as my adversary did not accept a fight and was protected from above by other machines. Therefore, I went down to 700 metres and attacked my adversary, who was flying at 900 metres, from below.

After a short fight my opponent's plane lost both wings and fell. The machine crashed into no-man's-land and was fired at by our infantry.

Baron von Richthofen

Weather: fine all day; ground mist early morning.

This 1st RFC Wing BE2g had taken off from its base at Bruay at 1525 hrs to fly an Art Obs sortie over Farbus. It was seen to be attacked by an enemy fighter, the machine breaking up at 1,000 feet, crashing in a position given as Sheet 27.a.5.9.

For some reason, Sergeant Howlett's name does not appear in surviving 16 Squadron records. Either he was very new to the Squadron or, as so often occurred, being an NCO these personnel records were not retained as were those of officers. Nor does his name appear on 16 Squadron's casualty list for this day although Watt's does.

Von Richthofen was flying Halberstadt DII.

While it is true that by this time von Richthofen's red fighter was becoming well known in France – although a number of Jasta 11's other pilots had parts of their aircraft similarly painted red – there is no doubt that he was not unique in flying a red aeroplane, which obviously led to it being thought he was everywhere on the Front. Evidence of this can be seen by the presence of another red scout engaged that same afternoon, above Bihucourt, at 1525 (1635 German time), which is just north-west of Bapaume, some 25 kilometres south of the Farbus area.

A 4 Squadron BE2 crew, also engaged on Art Obs work, was attacked by six Halberstadt scouts, one of which was painted bright red. The BE pilot, Second Lieutenant N H Colson, was hit in the shoulder and the machine riddled with machine gun bullets. The observer, Second Lieutenant H Bagshaw Mann, kept up a steady return fire, and saw his bullets smash the propeller of their attacker, which glided away in the direction of Sapignies. Among others, this was Jasta 2's area, so did at least one of its pilots fly a red aircraft? It will be recalled that way back in October 1916, at least one Jasta 2 pilot had a red machine before von Richthofen.

WATT,
GEORGE MACDONALD
SECOND LIEUTENANT 16 SQUADRON

GEORGE WATT was born at 5 Circus Gardens, Edinburgh on 8 January 1890, the second son of George Watt, KC, Sheriff of Inverness, Elgin and Nairn, and his wife, Jessie. He was educated at Fettes College, leaving in July 1907 to attend Edinburgh University. A keen rugby footballer, he played to a very high standard with the Edinburgh Institute. In 1912 he secured a position with a British timber company operating in Burma. In July 1916, like many thousands of others before him, he returned from abroad to fight for King and Empire. He joined the Royal Flying Corps and was trained at Turnhouse, near Edinburgh and at Montrose, gaining his 'Wings' on 6 January 1917. Soon afterwards, he was sent to the Front, arriving for active service with 16 Squadron on 17 January 1917. He is buried in Bruay Cemetery, France (Fr.32). He was twenty-seven years of age.

HOWLETT,
ERNEST ADAM
SERGEANT (No.L8861) 16 SQUADRON

A LONDONER, ERNEST Howlett was living with his widowed mother, Rosina Howlett, at 39 Amersham Road, New Cross, SE, when he volunteered for service with the East Kent Regiment (The 'Buffs') at the outbreak of war. An outstanding soldier, he was promoted to Sergeant in the trenches before returning home for transfer into the Royal Flying Corps and, after being awarded his observer's 'Wing', he was sent to join 16 Squadron at St Omer, France. He is buried, along with his pilot, 2/Lt G MacD Watt, in Bruay Cemetery, France (Fr.32). He was twenty-six.

21 MARCH 1917

VICTORY NO.29

BE2F No.A3154
16 SQUADRON
ENGINE No.2021 WD 1704
GUNS: E10689; E2173

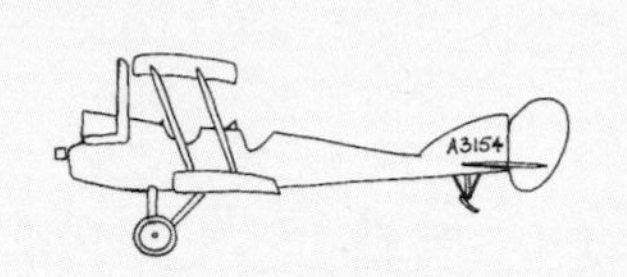

VON RICHTHOFEN'S Combat Report:
1730 hrs, BE two-seater. Hill 123, north of Neuville. Plane details unknown, as plane came down on enemy's territory.

Message came through that enemy planes had been seen at 1,000 metres altitude in spite of bad weather and strong east wind. I went up by myself intending to bring down an infantry or artillery flyer.

After one hour I spotted at 800 metres a large number of enemy artillery flyers beyond the lines. They sometimes approached our front, but never passed it. After several vain attempts I managed, half hidden by clouds, to take one of these BEs by surprise and to attack him at 600 metres, one kilometre beyond our lines.

The adversary made the mistake of flying in a straight line when he tried to evade me, and thus he was just a wink too long in my fire (500 shots). Suddenly he made two uncontrolled curves and dashed, smoking, to the ground. The plane was completely ruined; it fell in section F.3.

BARON VON RICHTHOFEN

WEATHER: LOW CLOUDS AND RAIN DURING MORNING; CLEARING IN PLACES IN THE AFTERNOON.

Flight Sergeant Quicke and Second Lieutenant Lidsey had left their base at Bruay, south-west of Bethune, at 1500 to do artillery observation work. Caught by Richthofen, the BE fell into the British lines, with Quicke dead and Lidsey mortally wounded.

By one of those strange coincidences, Quicke had, possibly unknown to him, had a brush with von Richthofen before but flying with a different observer, on 6 March (see victory No.24). Lidsey too may well have believed he had had an encounter with von Richthofen a month earlier on 4 February 1917. However, von Richthofen was on a visit home, showing off his Ordre Pour le Mérite to his mother at Schweidnitz on that date.

Again it was an afternoon show, Lidsey taking off with Lieutenant Morris, but Morris then became sick and had to return. Lidsey got another pilot, Captain Neale, and, after a false start, they took off in BE No.4592 to take photographs in the Bailleul area (Bailleul-Sir-Berthoult, just to the north-east of Arras, not the more well known town 45 kilometres further north – a common mistake by historians as men on the Arras front referred to 'their' Ballieul-Sir-Berthoult as plain Bailleul.)

At 1625 they were attacked by a German fighter which, interestingly, the crew referred to in their subsequent report, as being the '... Halberstadt Destroyer painted red'. The fighter dived on their tail, Lidsey firing 100 rounds from his Lewis gun whereupon the Halberstadt cleared away without firing. Later, Lidsey wrote in his diary: 'Flew with Lt Morris – sick. 1420 took off with Neale. Forced to return 10 minutes later. 1520 took off on Photo Recce to Bailleul. Attacked by two Huns three miles behind the lines, one being the man with the machine painted red who has done us so much damage. Opened fire with my gun and they cleared off.'

So, even at this stage some RFC units were only too aware of a red aircraft (or to be correct, a number of red aircraft) operating on their front and being successful in bringing down RFC machines. Even in his absence, the British airmen could believe that in seeing a red fighter over the Front von Richthofen was present. Little did Lidsey know that he would fall to the 'real' Halberstadt Destroyer a few weeks later. Von Richthofen was flying a Halberstadt Scout.

QUICKE,
SIDNEY HERBERT
FLIGHT SERGEANT (No.711) 16 SQUADRON

IN 1913, QUICKE was amongst the first direct entrants into the embryonic Royal Flying Corps which had been formed in the previous year. He was a Londoner who lived with his widowed mother, who had re-married and was now Mrs. A M Rea, at 36 Straun Villas, East Finchley, London N2. He was also amongst the first to go overseas, accompanying 4 Squadron as a First Class Mechanic when that unit left for France on 12 August 1914, just eight days after the declaration of war, thus qualifying him for the award of the 1914 Star and 'Underfire' clasp, the so-called 'Mons Star'. He did well in his chosen profession and promotion followed. He qualified as an observer on 31 March 1916, and went on to obtain his Royal Aero Club Aviators Certificate (No.3890) on 27 November 1916, the award of his pilot's 'Wings' following shortly afterwards. Quicke and his observer, Second Lieutenant Lidsey, were on their second patrol of the day when they encountered von Richthofen. Quicke is buried in the Bruay Cemetery, France (Fr.32).

LIDSEY,
WILLIAM JOHN
SECOND LIEUTENANT 16 SQUADRON; 1/4 (TA) OXFORDSHIRE & BUCKINGHAMSHIRE LIGHT INFANTRY

BORN IN JUNE 1895, William Lidsey was the son of Councillor William I R and Mrs Emily Crosier Lidsey of 'Hardwick House', Banbury, Oxfordshire. He was educated at Magdalen College School, Brackley, and had not long embarked on his business career (training as an auctioneer and valuer) when war broke out. With many of his friends, he helped to form the Banbury detachment of volunteers who joined the 1/4th (Territorial) Battalion of the Oxfordshire and Buckinghamshire Light Infantry. The Battalion landed at Boulogne on 30 March 1915, and moved forward to the Front. After a period in the trenches, he was sent home for officer training and was commissioned Second Lieutenant into his own Battalion on 2 February 1916. Returning to France in June 1916, he again served in the trenches until November 1916, when he joined the RFC. Shot down on his second patrol of the day, Lidsey was barely alive when he was extricated from the wreck of the BE2f. With the brutal honesty of the day, Lidsey's parents received the following message: *'Your son was admitted on the evening of Wednesday, 21st, mortally wounded in the head and legs and an operation was impossible, he was partly conscious when he was brought in but passed away 3 o'clock Thursday morning'.* He is buried in Aubigny Communal Cemetery Extension (Fr.95). He was twenty-one.

24 MARCH 1917

VICTORY NO.30

SPAD SVII NO.A6706
19 SQUADRON RFC
ENGINE NO.5687
GUN: L4810

VON RICHTHOFEN'S Combat Report:
1155 hrs, Givenchy.
Spad No.6607, with Hispano Suiza 140 hp motor. The first encountered here. Machine gun No.4810. Occupant: Lieutenant Baker.

I was flying with several of my gentlemen when I observed an enemy squadron passing our Front. Aside from this squadron, two new one-seaters which I did not know were flying nearby. They were extremely fast and handy.

I attacked one of them and ascertained that my machine was the better one. After a long fight I managed to hit the adversary's tank. The propeller stopped running. The plane had to go down.

As the fight had taken place above the trenches, my adversary tried to escape, but I managed to force him to land behind our lines near Givenchy. The plane turned over, in a shell hole, upside down, and was taken by our troops.

BARON VON RICHTHOFEN

WEATHER: FINE ALL DAY.

The French Spad had been taken on the strength of 19 Squadron at the end of 1916, replacing the awful BE12s, and they were a much better prospect for the pilots in air combat. Why von Richthofen had not come across them before must have been pure chance, for they had been operating from Fienvillers, opposite the Bapaume sector of the Front for some weeks.

However, the Squadron had flown an Offensive Patrol to the Lens-Harmes-Bailleul area strength unknown, but certainly there were two of them, Baker and Second Lieutenant F L Harding in A263. At 1050 they had become engaged with ten hostile aircraft – the exact number according to von Richthofen – but Harding had suffered a gun stoppage and had to break off. Baker was not so lucky and was picked off, Harding reporting him down near Cretien. When he returned from Germany just before Christmas 1918, Baker reported that he had been having engine trouble, and had been attacked while trying to remedy this, and hit in the right knee.

The Spad's serial number on von Richthofen's combat was either a reporting error or a subsequent typing error, but the gun number was almost correct, the actual number being L4810, while the engine number had been 5687.

Von Richthofen was flying a Halberstadt DII.

BAKER,
RICHARD PLUNKETT
LIEUTENANT 19 SQUADRON 11/CANADIAN MOUNTED RIFLES

'DICK' BAKER was born in British Columbia on 18 October 1888, the son of Frederick and Mrs Baker of 1991 Nelson Street, Vancouver, BC. He was privately educated in Vancouver and in Victoria, BC before joining the Bank of Montreal in 1905. After some seven years with the bank, he left their employ and became a sales manager with a local company. He joined the 11th Battalion, Canadian Mounted Rifles early in 1915 and served in the trenches in France, receiving shrapnel wounds to the head. The wounds were slight but some small pieces of the shrapnel remained lodged in his skull. It was many years later before he was troubled by his wounds but in later life they caused him considerable discomfort. After recovering in England, he transferred to the RFC in September 1916, and graduated from the Central Flying School on 3 January 1917. He recrossed the Channel early in February, 1917, joining 19 Squadron on the 28th of that month. He had had precious little experience in flying a Spad (1 hour, 22 minutes) when he was sent over the lines on his last patrol, easy prey for von Richthofen. Wounded in the knee and taken prisoner, he spent the rest of the war in a variety of PoW camps including Karlsruhe, Crefeld, Gefangenenlager Strohern Korcis, Sulingen Suligan and Bad Colberg. Finally, he was repatriated on 12 December 1918. Returning to Vancouver, Baker worked in import and export and was involved in the management of the Medical-Dental centre in the city. He died in April 1954 at the age of sixty-six.

Right: Richthofen's trophy room at Schweidnitz.

25 MARCH 1917

VICTORY NO.31

Nieuport XVII No.A6689
29 Squadron RFC
Engine No.T7401 J
Gun: 6632

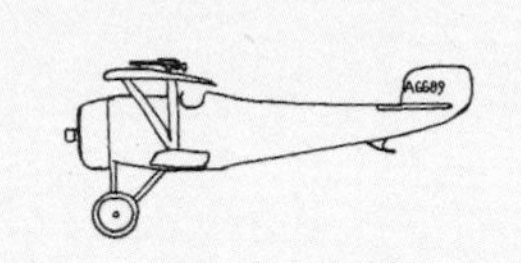

VON RICHTHOFEN'S Combat Report:
0820 hrs, Tilloy.
Nieuport one-seater – burnt.
Occupant: Lieutenant Grivert (sic) – English.

An enemy squadron had passed our lines. I went up, overtaking their last machine. After only a very few shots, the enemy's propeller stopped turning. The adversary landed near Tilloy, upsetting his plane. I observed that some moments later the plane began to burn.

Baron von Richthofen

NB. From this date, German and British times became the same, and would continue so until 16 April, so on the next few reports, the times should coincide.

Weather: clear in the morning with occasional clouds.

This action follows the not unusual pattern of a German staffel taking off once an Allied formation had been reported crossing the front lines. This was a good tactic, for it allowed the German aircraft to know exactly where the enemy was; they had not used fuel in patrolling, and could position themselves to advantage, often placing themselves between the Allied aircraft and the lines, knowing their adversaries would have to get by them in order to reach home, fighting not only their fighters but the wind and with emptying petrol tanks.

No.29 Squadron's Nieuport scouts were now perhaps the RFC's – and the French Air Service's – main fighter at this stage and were more than a match for the Halberstadt and Albatros scouts. They still only had one gun – a Lewis on the top wing, set to fire over the propeller (the French often had a machine-gun on the engine cowling, firing through the propeller arc with an interruptor gear) – as opposed to the twin Spandau of the German fighters, but they were nimble enough to have a good scrap with the enemy scouts and win.

Gilbert – the Germans again having trouble with the English spelling – was not as fortunate as a more experienced pilot and was quickly and easily picked off by the experienced leader of Jasta 11. 29 Squadron, according to its record book, had mounted a number of two-man escort patrols this morning, Gilbert and Lieutenant T J Owen (A6721) taking the first slot, taking off from their base at Le Hameau at 0705. In view of Gilbert's later remarks, perhaps the two-man patrols had been scheduled differently.

They had not long had their Nieuports and no doubt even the more senior pilots were still getting used to them. Owen landed back at base at 0800, having had carburetor problems. Gilbert obviously stayed out to continue the assigned task and paid for being alone over the Front, which is why Richthofen thought he had picked the last machine.

However, it seems that some of the other Nieuports later got off, for the next two-man element had been airborne at 0730 and had seen enemy aircraft, four being engaged at 0830, by which time Gilbert was having his first moments of gratitude for being alive even if a prisoner. His machine, when lost, had less than nine hours flying time on its record sheet.

All this might be explained in Gilbert's report made when he returned from prison camp in late 1918. He recalled that there should have been five Nieuports accompanying the photo-machine. As the other four had failed to get off the ground (at least altogether) he had carried on alone. He said: 'Escort to 11 Squadron FE's on photo op. I was surrounded and cut off by Richthofen's squadron over Douai and shot down; petrol tank hit, controls shot away. Nieuport 15A crashed and burnt, totally destroyed.'

The Squadron was to lose another pilot before these morning duties were over, Lieutenant John George Will being killed in not dissimilar circumstances. He and another pilot had taken off at 0825, but his partner had had to return with rev counter problems. Although the other pilot changed planes and headed back to the front, Will (in A6751) failed to return. He had played rugby for Cambridge and Scotland and had been wounded with his regiment (Leinsters) earlier in the war.

Von Richthofen was flying a Halberstadt DII, and Tilloy is just south-east of Arras.

GILBERT, CHRISTOPHER GUY

LIEUTENANT 29 SQUADRON; AIR EFFICIENCY MEDAL (1951); 6/DORSETSHIRE REGIMENT

One of eight brothers who served in the Great War (two were killed), Guy Gilbert was commissioned Second Lieutenant into the 1/6th (Service) Battalion, Dorsetshire

Regiment, on 2 December 1914. He, and coincidentally another future 'victim' of the Red Baron, 2/Lt Waldemar Franklin (Number 46), accompanied the 1/6th Dorsets to France on 13 July 1915. His service in the trenches was followed by a transfer to the Royal Flying Corps. His flying career, however, was brought to an abrupt halt on that cold morning in March 1917, a morning he was to recall many years later when, in 1970, he wrote a letter to the film company United Artists who, he knew, were making a film based on the von Richthofen story entitled *'The Red Baron'* (US title: *'Von Richthofen and Roy Brown'*): *'I was flying a Nieuport Scout, a new aircraft to me, as fighter escort to a big FE2b plane which was in a dawn photographic reconnaissance mission. It was only a short flight and I thought I would be back for breakfast. So I rolled out of bed, threw a greatcoat over my pyjamas and took off!'* So it was that Guy Gilbert was pulled from the flaming wreck by German troops and taken prisoner in his pyjamas! Over the next twenty-two months he was held in a number of camps including Crefeld, Schwarmstedt, Holzminden and Graudenz, and made several unsuccessful attempts to escape. He was finally re-patriated on 2 December 1918. Six years later he married Gay from Southsea and for many years they ran the Royal Ascot Hotel near the famous racecourse. A member of the RAFVR, he was called back to the service in 1939. During the Second World War, he received the appointment, 'Officer Commanding Troop Ships', and despite being on the wrong end of a number of U-boat attacks, he survived the war unscathed. He was awarded the Air Efficiency Medal in 1951 and finally retired from the RAFVR in 1954, with the rank of Wing Commander. Guy Gilbert died in his home at 176 Milton Road, Waterlooville in 1973. He was eighty years old.

This ended von Richthofen's March scoring. He had downed ten Allied aircraft during the month but the killing time of April was only days away.

There is another report of a red fighter being encountered, this one on 30 March. A BE2d No.5875 of 13 Squadron, with Lieutenants Bell and J W S Clark, was flying an Art Obs sortie at 1740 hrs above Roclincourt. Clark was alert and spotted two Albatros Scouts, one, painted red, manoeuvring to attack, but Clark opened fire, whereupon the red machine wheeled about and flew off towards Bailleul-Sir-Berthoult. Was this Richthofen? It could be for he was no fool. Why attack an aircraft with an alert gunner? There were plenty more targets around, and if he could surprise one of them, so much the better.

Below: Menu Card for a Dinner held at Gravenz PoW Camp, Germany to celebrate the Armistice. The Menu is signed by the host and organiser, Lt C G Gilbert and many of his fellow prisoners.

GRAUDENZ GERMANY

NOVEMBER 12TH 18

MENU

SOUP
MOBILOIL

MEAT
CURRIED STEW
BRAISED SHOCK ABSORBER
CRASHED POTATOES
SPLIT ARSE BEANS

SWEET
FRUIT SALAD
PASSENGERS IN A FLAT SPIN (CUSTARD)

SAVORY
FIRST SOLOISTS

MONOCOQUE COFFEE

PETROL.

LT C G GILBERT

2 APRIL 1917

VICTORY NO.32

BE2D NO.5841
13 SQUADRON RFC
ENGINE NO.21962 WD 278
GUNS: 19594; 2966

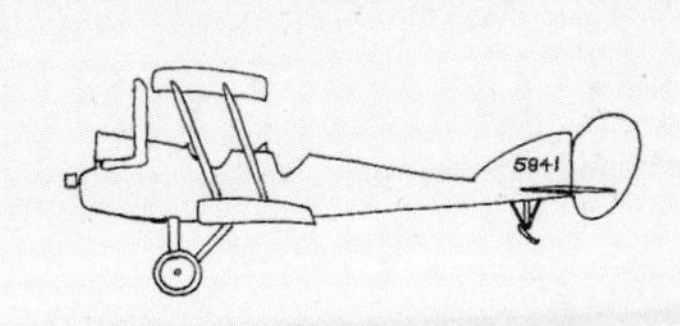

VON RICHTHOFEN'S Combat Report:
0835 hrs, Farbus village.
BE two-seater No.5841. Motor: PD 1345/80. Occupants: Both killed. Name of one – Lieutenant Powell. The second occupant had no documents or identification.

I attacked an enemy artillery flyer. After a long fight I managed to force adversary nearly to the ground, but without putting him out of action. The strong and gusty wind had driven the enemy plane over our lines. My adversary tried to escape by jumping over trees and other objects. Then I forced him to land in the village of Farbus where the machine was smashed against a house. The observer kept shooting until the machine hit the ground.

BARON VON RICHTHOFEN

WEATHER: WIND, RAIN, AND LOW CLOUDS.

Little wonder Powell gave von Richthofen a run for his money; he had been in France for several months and knew his business. The gallant observer had also been in France since 1915 and had gained experience, so it was not surprising he kept up a spirited return fire until the end.

They had taken off from Savy, 16 kilometres north-west of Arras, at 0747 to carrry out a Photo Op (they carried an 8" camera with an F/4.5 lens) and had been out less than an hour. Farbus village is to the east of Vimy, seven kilometres north-east of Arras.

The discrepancy in the engine number from von Richthofen's report and the RFC casualty report is unresolved.

Von Richthofen was now back permanently on the modified Albatros DIII, having taken over 2253/17. Eventually this machine had a red spinner, fuselage, tailfin, rudder, and struts. Its Patee crosses to wings and tailplane were overpainted although the black crosses showed up faintly. The Albatros Company logo on the tail was not overpainted.

Sometime after the end of March the fuselage cross was crudely repainted with a white outline. Contrary to some suggestions, this machine had the usual camouflage top wing markings of standard mauve/dark green segments while the undersurfaces were turqouise blue. *(cont.)*

POWELL,
PATRICK JOHN GORDON
LIEUTENANT 13 SQUADRON; ARMY SERVICE CORPS

BORN ON 20 September 1896, Powell's family home was at 18 Indow Road, Upper Norwood, London. He received part of his education at Dulwich College (1911-12) before joining the Connaught Coach Works in Long Acre, London WC2. In September 1914, he joined the University and Public Schools Battalion, Royal Fusiliers. Just two months later he was selected for, and passed into, the Royal Military College, Sandhurst, whence he was gazetted as Second Lieutenant, to the Army Service Corps on 17 March 1915. He served in the Armentières sector in northern France and was promoted Lieutenant in April 1916. Returning home, he applied for transfer and was posted for training with the RFC at Christchurch. He was awarded the Royal Aero Club Aviators Certificate (No.3686) on 16 June 1916, receiving his 'Wings' shortly afterwards. Sent first to 12 Squadron in November, 1916, he transferred to 13 Squadron on 19 December 1916 reputedly 'by far the best photographer in the Squadron'. Powell had returned from a two-week leave only five days before he was killed. His remains were lost and he is commemorated on the Arras Memorial to the Missing, France. He was in his twenty-first year.

BONNER,
PERCY
1ST CLASS AIR MECHANIC (No.1897) 13 SQUADRON

THE SON OF Henry and Mrs Bonner of 'Luscombe', 68 Woodbridge Road, Guildford, Surrey, Percy Bonner (noted as 'having a ready grasp of mechanics') joined the RFC in 1914, leaving behind his job in the Reading Department of the *Surrey Advertiser*. Apart from a brief period of leave in November 1915, his parents were never to see him again. The crash site was visited by the von Richthofen brothers, Manfred and Lothar. Afterwards, Lothar wrote:

'It was a sad sight which we saw. Half of the machine was hanging from a roof, the other half was on the ground. After inspecting the remnants, we went home. The soldiers around the place had in the meantime recognised my brother and cheered us madly'.

Bonner's remains were lost and he is therefore commemorated on the Arras Memorial to the Missing, France. He was twenty-three years old.

2 APRIL 1917

VICTORY NO.33

SOPWITH 1½ STRUTTER
NO.A2401
43 SQUADRON RFC
ENGINE NO.R1072 WD 6283
GUNS: 21341; L7765

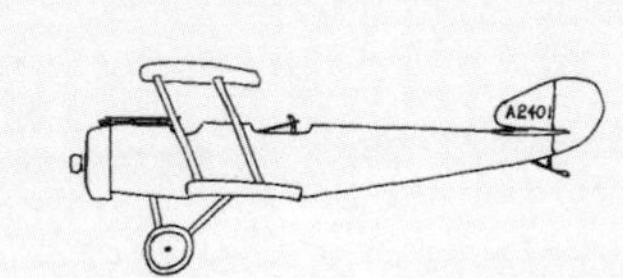

VON RICHTHOFEN'S Combat Report:
1115 hrs, Givenchy.
Sopwith two-seater A2401. Motor: Clerget Blin without number, Type 2. Occupants: Sergeant Dunn and Lieutenant Warrens (sic).

Together with Leutnants Voss and Lothar von Richthofen, I attacked an enemy squadron of eight Sopwiths above the closed cloud cover on the enemy's side. The plane I had singled out was driven away from its squad and gradually came over to our side. The enemy plane tried to escape and hide in the clouds after I had holed its benzine tank. Below the clouds I immediately attacked him again, thereby forcing him to land 300 metres east of Givenchy.

But as yet my adversary would not surrender and even as his machine was on the ground, he kept shooting at me, thereby hitting my machine very severely at an altitude of five metres. I once more attacked him, while on the ground, and killed one of the occupants.

BARON VON RICHTHOFEN

WEATHER: WIND, RAIN, SNOW FLURRIES AND LOW CLOUDS.

Six Sopwiths of 43 Squadron had flown out on a Photo Op to the east of Vimy, taking off at 1030, led by Captain Donald Campbell Rutter (3rd Sussex Regt & RFC who would be killed on 7 June). They were engaged by enemy aircraft at about 1100 hrs and Warren was last seen spiralling down into clouds.

Second Lieutenant Charles Etienne deBerigny with 2AM Enrys Bowen reported seeing five Albatros Scouts which followed the formation and then one attacked Warren (one of the two camera machines), who was flying to his left. Bowen emptied a drum of Lewis at the German fighter without result. As far as deBerigny could see, Warren's machine appeared undamaged at the time but then went into cloud. Another fighter then attacked their Sopwith from behind and the observer, having reloaded, fired and claimed the fighter went down in flames on the British side, witnessed by several of the other crews. The German fighters then dived away through the clouds.

As it happens, Dunn, according to Peter Warren after the war, was mortally wounded in the abdomen in Richthofen's first attack. Warren immediately dived for the clouds but these proved too thin to conceal themselves in, allowing Richthofen to follow quickly and make a further attack. This time Warren's instrument panel was smashed, the fuel tank was holed and the engine stopped; the front gun belt was also severed. Finding his elevator controls also damaged, Warren found it difficult to glide down, especially as Richthofen was still firing into the Strutter.

Bullets went all round Warren, ripping both his shoes and the sleeves of his flying suit but without hitting him. He finally managed to crash-land and helped his wounded observer from the rear cockpit, the latter mumbling, 'Think I'm done.' Richthofen came down again and shot them up, Warren later insisting that neither he, and certainly not his badly wounded observer, had any desire or thought of firing at the red fighter above them. Whether Richthofen's machine came under someone else's fire, or his explanation was just an excuse to strafe the two-seater, is now conjecture. Dunn died six hours later in a German dressing station, while Warren was taken to Douai; Richthofen received the serial number to add to his growing collection.

Surprisingly, in his book Richthofen refers to being hit by the downed gunner, and when talking to Voss, the latter had said that if that had happened to him, he would have shot them up on the ground. Ricthofen then says: 'As a matter of fact I should have done so, for he had not surrendered.' This is obviously a matter of book editing so that the hero of Germany would not look bad in the eyes of his worshippers, nor give his country's enemies cause for a more serious charge to be brought against him.

When Warren had initially reported the action on his return from prison camp, he said one of the Germans was flying a red machine, and that his observer had died six hours after they had come down. He had not been able to burn the Sopwith, for Dunn had been unconscious so he had been unable to extricate him from the cockpit before German troops arrived, and he stated that they had come down near Avion.

It had been Dunn's first sortie with Warren. He'd earlier flown with Second Lieutenant C P Thornton (3rd King's Liverpool Regt & RFC), and on 4 March 1917, they had claimed a German two-seater shot down in flames north of Vermelles (NE Vimy) flying A961. Thornton was taken prisoner on 5 April. It had not been Dunn's first success for while with 70 Squadron he had shot up and forced an Albatros two-seater to land on 25 January 1917, flying with Lieutenant D G A Allan.

Charles deBerigny and 2AM Bowen, who had witnessed the Richthofen fight, would themselves be killed in a crash at the end of the month. Who they had claimed shot down on 2 April is a mystery, for Jasta 11 certainly suffered no losses.

Von Richthofen was flying Albatros DIII No.2253/17. His two companions – there is no mention of five Albatros Scouts – were his younger brother Lothar, who had recently joined the Jasta and had downed his own first victory on 28 March, and Leutnant Werner Voss of Jasta 2 (Boelcke), who had 23 victories. Voss had been on a visit to Jasta 11's airfield, and flying off to return home Manfred took off to accompany him. Once in the air, the younger Richthofen had recognised the red fighter and joined them. Voss was Manfred's closest rival in air victories and was about to receive the Pour le Mérite, although he would then go on leave and miss the April blood letting.

Below: Manfred and Ltn Hans Klein of Jasta 4.

WARREN,
ALGERNON PETER
SECOND LIEUTENANT 43 SQUADRON

THE SON OF Edward P Warren, FRIBA, and Margaret Warren of 'Breach House', Cholsey, Wallingford, Oxfordshire and 20 Bedford Street, London, WC1, Peter Warren was born on 21 January 1898. Educated at Westminster School (1911-15) and Magdalen College, Oxford, he interrupted his education to join the RFC on 8 July 1916. He trained first as an observer with 57 Squadron from 15 August 1916, before transferring to No.34 Reserve Squadron on 20 November 1916 for pilot training. He graduated as a pilot on 3 February 1917, and three weeks later was sent to the Front to join 43 Squadron. Captured and taken prisoner after his fight with von Richthofen, he spent most of his captivity in the Offiziersgefangenenlager, Schwarmstedt, in the Province of Hannover before being repatriated, at last, on 17 December 1918. Returning to Oxford, he graduated BA in 1921, winning the Beit Prize in Colonial History. Subsequently he qualified and practised as an architect, becoming MA (Oxon) in 1936. Married Doris Hicking, a widow with five daughters, in 1935. Served as a Captain in the Royal Engineers in the Second World War. Died on 7 October 1979 at the age of eighty-one, still resident in the family home in Cholsey.

DUNN,
REUEL
SERGEANT (No.6396) 43 SQUADRON

THE SON OF John and Susan Dunn, Reuel was born in 1893. At the outbreak of war, the family home was at 88 Harrington Road, Workington, Cumberland, but Reuel was living in lodgings in Newcastle upon Tyne, near to his job as a ship's architect with the shipbuilders Swan, Hunter and Whitworth. He enlisted in the ASC in 1915 and was sent to France as a motorcycle despatch rider in January 1916. Next, he was transferred to general duties with a Transport column but, bored with the routine, he successfully applied for another transfer, this time to the RFC. After the usual period of training he was awarded his observer's 'Wing', serving first with 70 Squadron in 1916 before being posted on to 43 Squadron. Shot in the abdomen, Dunn was unconscious during most of the fight with von Richthofen, dying just six hours after his pilot had crash-landed their machine. Reuel Dunn is buried in Cabaret-Rouge British Cemetery, France (Fr.924). He was twenty-four years of age.

3 APRIL 1917

VICTORY NO.34

FE2D No.A6382
25 SQUADRON RFC
ENGINE No.127573 WD 13896
GUNS: 26751; 24934

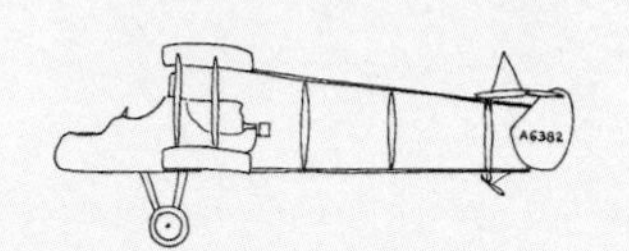

VON RICHTHOFEN'S Combat Report:
1615 hrs, between Lens and Lieven.
Vickers two- seater, No.A6382. Motor unrecognisable.
Occupants: Pilot (sic): Lieutenant O'Beirne , killed.
Observer (sic): McDonald.

Together with Leutnant Schäfer and Leutnant Lothar von Richthofen, I attacked three enemy planes. The plane I myself attacked was forced to land near Lieven. After a short fight the motor began to smoke and the observer ceased shooting. I followed adversary to the ground.

BARON VON RICHTHOFEN

WEATHER: STORM AND LOW CLOUDS.

Despite mixing up their positions in the aircraft, these were Richthofen's victims. The FEs had taken off at 1512 to fly a Photo Op between Mericourt and Gavrelle. At about 1630 they were engaged by six Albatros Scouts, British AA batteries seeing two FEs fall. The other one brought down was A6371, flown by Lieutenant L Dodson MC (S Staffs Regt & RFC), made PoW and Second Lieutenant Henry Scott Richards (15th Notts & Derby Regt & RFC) who died of wounds. They were shot down by Schäfer at La Coulotte for his ninth victory.

Jasta 11 gives the actual location of Richthofen's victory as Cité St Pierre which is more in keeping with his report, so the FEs were probably on their way back to their base at Lozinghem. Both FEs were virtually brand new; A6382 had flown for just eight and a half hours, A6371 for three and three-quarter hours.

Some time after the war, McDonald said they had been asked by the CO to fly a volunteer Photo Sortie to Vimy Ridge. He also says they were engaged by three enemy fighters, two of whom the FEs shot down, but they seemed to be decoys as they were then attacked from above by up to sixteen German fighters. (When he returned from Germany in 1918 he said there were 11 enemy fighters and that his engine and controls were hit and damaged.) He also said that his observer, after downing one of the first three, was hit in the head and died instantly, whereas in fact he seems to have died of his wound shortly afterwards. McDonald does confirm that they had taken their photos, so they must have been heading north-west for home. Jasta 11 had no losses.

Von Richthofen was flying Albatros DIII No.2253/17.

McDONALD, DONALD PETER

SECOND LIEUTENANT 25 SQUADRON; 2/1 LOVAT SCOUTS

BORN IN BRITAIN in 1895, McDonald was, in 1914, living at his parents' home in Somerset West, Cape Province, South Africa where his father was a farmer and stock-breeder. In the early months of the war, he served with the colonial forces who opposed the German aggression in southern Africa. (Photographs show McDonald wearing the ribbon of the African General Service Medal, athough a search through the medal rolls has not, so far, revealed his entitlement.) Returning to Britain, he first joined the 2/1 Lovat Scouts and then was attached to the Cameron Highlanders before finally transferring into the RFC and qualifying as a pilot. He crossed to France on 23 March 1917, joining 25 Squadron. *The Times* of 19 May 1917 reported that, *'a postcard dated 11 April has been received from 2/Lt D P McDonald, Cameron Highlanders and Royal Flying Corps, who was reported 'missing' on April 3, stating that he is a prisoner at Karlsruhe and is not wounded'.* Later in 1917, McDonald was transferred to the Offiziersgefangenenlager at Saarbrücken where, coincidentally, he shared quarters with Cyril Douglas Bennett, von Richthofen's 20th 'victory'. He was finally repatriated in December 1918, first visiting the McDonald family home in England, 'Orchard Lodge', Avon Dasset, near Leamington, before losing no time in returning to the family's other home in South Africa. D P McDonald was killed in a car accident in SW Africa (now Namibia) in 1946, aged 51.

O'BEIRNE, JOHN INGRAM MULLANIFFE

SECOND LIEUTENANT 25 SQUADRON; 2/ROYAL WARWICKSHIRE REGIMENT

THE YOUNGER OF Major Arthur and Gertrude O'Beirne's sons, 'Jack' O'Beirne was born in Leamington, Warwickshire on 24 April 1893. The family had homes at 'Astrop Grange', Banbury, Oxfordshire and at Augherea, County Longford, Ireland. He was educated at Summerfields, Oxford, Radley College and had just finished a three-year course at the School of Mining, Cambourne, Cornwall when the war broke out in Europe. He volunteered immediately and obtained a commission in the Reserve Battalion of his father's old regiment, the Royal Warwicks, on 25 August 1914. After training, he was sent to the Front to join the 2nd Battalion of his regiment, then heavily involved in the First Battle of Ypres. Taken ill through drinking poisoned water, he was invalided home in November 1914. After regaining his health, he was sent to the Royal Military College, Sandhurst from where he graduated on 19 October 1915, again being gazetted to the Royal Warwickshire Regiment. He next successfully applied for transfer to the Royal Flying Corps, which occurred in February 1916. After training, he was awarded his 'Wing' and was sent to France as an observer in May 1916. Following a further period of illness, which lasted from August to November 1916, and forced his return to 'Blighty', he recrossed the Channel for the last time with orders to join 25 Squadron by 20 December 1916. Jack's elder brother, Arthur (Queen's Own Oxfordshire Hussars and 57 Squadron, RFC) was also shot down whilst piloting a DH4 (No.A7467) on a bomb raid against Heule aerodrome on 27 July 1917, dying from his wounds the following day. Jack O'Beirne's body was never recovered and he is commemorated on the Arras Memorial to the Missing, France. He was in his twenty-fourth year.

5 APRIL 1917

VICTORY NO.35

BF2A No.A3340
48 Squadron RFC
Engine No.1/190/30 WD 10443
Guns: 22089; A1194

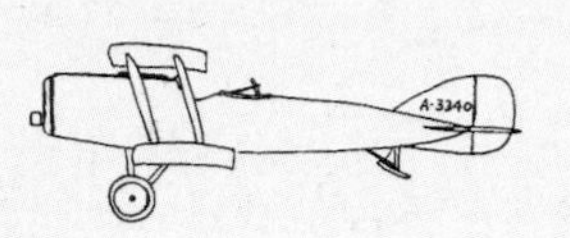

VON RICHTHOFEN'S Combat Report:
1115 hrs, Lewarde, south of Douai.
Bristol two-seater No.3340. Motor No.10443.
Occupants: Lieutenant McLickler (sic) and Lieutenant George; both seriously wounded.

It was foggy and altogether very bad weather when I attacked an enemy squad flying between Douai and Valenciennes. Up to this point it had managed to advance without being fired upon.

I attacked with four planes of my Staffel. I personally singled out the last machine which I forced to land after a short fight near Lewarde. The occupants burnt their machine.

It was a new type of plane which we had not seen as yet; it appears to be quick and rather handy. A powerful motor, V-shaped, 12 cylinder; its name could not be recognisable.

The DIII, both in speed and in ability to climb, is undoubtedly superior. Of the enemy squad which consisted of six planes, four were forced to land on our side by my Staffel.

Baron von Richthofen

Weather: misty and cloudy.

Painting opposite: Victory No.44.

Painting overleaf: Victory No.52.

With the continued build-up towards the coming Arras Battle, the RFC, despite the poor weather, continued to fly over the Vimy area. No.48 Squadron with its new Bristol F2a two-seat fighters, had arrived in France on 8 March 1917, being based at Bertangles, just to the north of Amiens. It began a period of preparation, the men getting used to both France and their new aeroplane.

On 5 April it finally felt ready to begin operations, and led by its senior Flight Commander, Captain William Leefe Robinson, VC (A3337), with Lieutenant E D Warburton in the back seat, six Bristols headed into hostile territory – von Richthofen's hostile territory.

Although a new and superior type of aeroplane, the new squadron had not realised its potential and in any event, had decided to use the usual defensive tactic if attacked, that of closing up and keeping the opposition at bay with their rear gunners' Lewis fire. Unhappily, this failed to save them from the assault of Jasta 11, and four of the new aircraft were quite quickly picked off.

They were engaged at between 1045 and 1100, and Robinson was among those brought down, claimed by Vizefeldwebel Sebastian Festner, his 4th victory, coming down at Aniche to be taken prisoner. Second Lieutenant H B Griffiths, in the same formation, later reported seeing a machine diving and smoking over Douai, while three other Bristols were heavily engaged by superior (sic) numbers of hostile aircraft.

For his part, Lechler later stated that his observer's gun had failed during the course of the action when Richthofen was behind them and then the man was wounded. Before Lechler could do anything, both fuel tanks were pierced and he was wounded too, in the head and leg. However, he got his fighter down, pulled the wounded George from the rear cockpit and then set fire to the machine. George died six days later in a German hospital.

Robinson had won his Victoria Cross for shooting down the German airship SL11 over Cuffley, north of London, on the night of 2/3 September 1916. He survived captivity only to die in the influenza epidemic on 31 December 1918.

Von Richthofen was flying Albatros DIII No.2253/17.

A6796

LECHLER,
ARTHUR NORMAN
SECOND LIEUTENANT 48 SQUADRON; MANCHESTER REGIMENT

THE YOUNGEST OF four brothers, Arthur Lechler was born on 13 February 1890, the son of W I A and Mrs Lechler, a coffee planter living and working in Yercaud, Madras Presidency, India. He was educated at St Lawrence College, Ramsgate (1906-08), Finsbury Technical College and Edinburgh University (1912-14 and 1918-19), from where he finally graduated BSc in 1919 after an enforced break in his degree course due to the war, before going on to become a chartered civil engineer (AMICE). When war broke out, Lechler was living and studying in Edinburgh and so, in September 1914, he volunteered along with many of his friends into the 9th Battalion of The Royal Scots, known locally as 'The Dandy Ninth', so-called because it was the only 'kilted' battalion of the regiment, the others wearing the less flamboyant 'trews'. Selected for officer training, he was commissioned into the 15th (Service) Battalion, Manchester Regiment, on 3 March 1915. Lechler succeeded in his application for a transfer to the RFC and, after pilot training, was sent with 48 Squadron to France. Wounded and taken prisoner by the Germans, he was eventually released into internment in neutral Holland on 9 April 1918 to enable his wounds to receive the appropriate treatment. He was finally repatriated on 7 September 1918. After qualifying as a civil engineer, he worked mainly in India in the years between the two world wars. Served as a major in the Royal Engineers in the second war, based at Edinburgh Castle with HQ Scottish Command. Died suddenly and unexpectedly on 7 June 1949, at the age of fifty-nine.

GEORGE,
HERBERT DUNCAN KING
SECOND LIEUTENANT 48 SQUADRON; 2/ROYAL DUBLIN FUSILIERS

HERBERT GEORGE was born in Satara, India on 23 July 1897, the son of Duncan and Florence George, whose home in England was at 7 Stanhope Terrace, Hyde Park, London. He spent his early years with his family in India and, like his father before him, returned to England to be educated at Clifton College (1910-14). After Clifton, he entered the Royal Military College, Sandhurst whence he was commissioned into the Royal Dublin Fusiliers on 12 May 1915, while still only seventeen years of age. Because of his youth, he was kept at the regimental depot in Cork in southern Ireland until 1916, when he was sent to join the 2nd Battalion of his regiment in the trenches. Soon after his arrival in France, he successfully applied for transfer to the Royal Flying Corps and was returned to England in July 1916 for training. George, now an observer, accompanied 48 Squadron to Flez, in France, on 8 March, 1917. Wounded in the leg and back, he was taken by the Germans to St Clothilde's Hospital in nearby Douai, where he died the following day. He is buried in Douai Cemetery, France (Fr.1276). He was nineteen years old.

Below: Burnt out Bristol Fighter.

5 APRIL 1917

VICTORY NO.36

BF2A No.A3343
48 Squadron RFC
Engine No.1/190/22/ WD 1046
Guns: 21294; A1194

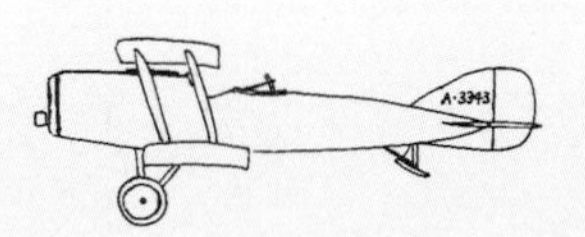

VON RICHTHOFEN'S Combat Report:
1130 hrs, Cuincy. Bristol two-seater.
Occupants: Pilot: Lieutenant Adams,
Observer: Lieutenant Steward (sic) – unwounded. Plane details not at hand as machine was burned.

After having put the first adversary near Lewarde out of action, I pursued the remaining part of the enemy squadron and overtook the last plane above Douai. I forced him to land near Cuincy. The occupants burnt their machine to ashes.

Baron von Richthofen

As the battle continued after victory No.35, Richthofen caught and downed a second Bristol Fighter, while the fourth loss fell to the guns of Leutnant Simon, Georg Simon, his first and only WW1 victory. His victim, Lieutenant H A Cooper (1/10 London Regt & RFC) and Second Lieutenant Alan Boldison (in A3320) were both wounded (Cooper severely) and taken prisoner. They came down north of Monchecourt.

Cuincy is situated on the outskirts of Douai, although the spelling of the location was originally Quincy. Lewarde, where the first of Richthofen's victims came down, is six kilometres to the south-east of Douai, so it can be seen that 48 Squadron, despite this being their first patrol, were way beyond the front line – something like 25 kilometres over, which seems a trifle foolhardy. Monchecourt is even further to the south-east by another five kilometres while Aniche is five kilometres to the north-east of this location, which was 32 kilometres beyond the Front! It certainly seems amazing they flew so far over, especially as they would have known that Jasta 11's airfield was at Douai, with Jasta 3, 4 and 33 all in the vicinity too.

Once again the Germans had the observer's name spelt wrongly, as they had for the pilot of the previous Bristol, noted as McLicker rather than Leckler.

Upon his return from Germany in December 1918, Adams reported that his Vickers gun had developed a No.3 stoppage in the first clash and he had been unable to free it. As the fight continued his main fuel tank had been hit and he became separated from the others whilst changing over to the other tank. Attacked by two German fighters he had then been shot down. His observer's Lewis gun was also giving trouble, Adams saying that it never fired more than three shots consecutively.

In Stewart's report at the end of 1918, he confirms his gun problems: 'In formation of six machines we were attacking Richthofen's squadron of six machines. My guns were either frozen or jammed – so much so that I could fire only single shots. After fighting about ten minutes the petrol tanks were pierced and the pilot put the machine into a spin. We were followed down to the ground.'

Von Richthofen, of course, was still in 2253/17.

Note that the gun number for this machine and the previous A3340 are recorded as the same. (Note too that Stewart is occasionally referred to as Stuart – even the typed repatriation report shows Stuart, but Stewart is correct, the same as noted in Richthofen's report – almost!)

In the late afternoon of 5 April, 60 Squadron were flying an OP over Reincourt at 1845. Jasta 11 appeared on the scene, Second Lieutenant G A H Pidock (Nieuport A6770) reporting, 'Two Albatros Scouts, one was red – there appear to be several of these now.' He then saw the red machine attack one of 60's machines and Pidcock attacked it, firing three-quarters of a drum of Lewis at it. Second Lieutenant T Longwill then attacked the red machine and it went spinning down out of control. At 1900 Second Lieutenant D N Robertson (A311) attacked another red Albatros which had red and green wings, south-east of Croisilles. His fire was seen to hit in the vicinity of the pilot's seat whereupon the Albatros dived steeply. So once more the red Albatros machines were well advertised.

ADAMS,
ALFRED TERENCE
LIEUTENANT 48 SQUADRON MID; 3/WILTSHIRE REGIMENT

BORN ON 1 June 1896, the son of stockbroker Percy C D Adams and his wife of 14 Vernon Road, Edgbaston, Warwickshire, he received his education at Marlborough (1910-14). Amongst the very first to volunteer, he was commissioned into the Wiltshire Regiment on 15 August 1914. Adams successfully applied for transfer to the Royal Flying Corps and was eventually awarded his 'Wings'. After his encounter with the Red Baron, he was taken prisoner, and not until 14 December 1918 was he repatriated. With the war over, he could now resume his education and, on 21 October 1921, he was admitted to be a member of the Middle Temple (Inns of Court), subsequently being called to the Bar on 28 January 1924. He practised as a barrister on the Oxford circuit from 1916 to 1938, taking cases in the Oxford, Worcester, Hereford, Gloucester, Monmouth, Salop and Staffordshire sessions. Adams lived at Hurlesmere, Belbroughton, Worcestershire for most of his adult life. Died in 1958 at the age of sixty-two.

STEWART,
DONALD JAMES
LIEUTENANT 48 SQUADRON; 2/YORK AND LANCASTER REGIMENT

DONALD STEWART, who lived all of his life in Sheffield, was commissioned Second Lieutenant into the regiment most closely associated with that city, the York and Lancaster Regiment, on 24 November 1915. Like so many other young men, he was attracted by the undoubted 'glamour' identified with the Royal Flying Corps and soon sought transfer to that over subscribed service. To his delight, his application was successful and, after the appropriate training, he was given his 'Wing' and sent to join 48 Squadron in France. He was unhurt in the encounter with von Richthofen but remained a prisoner of the Germans until finally repatriated on the last day of 1918. D J Stewart died at his home, 490 Firshill Crescent, Sheffield on 18 December, 1981.

Above: The BF2a (A3343) flown by Adams and Stewart before it went to France.

7 APRIL 1917

VICTORY NO.37

NIEUPORT XVII NO.A6645
60 SQUADRON RFC
ENGINE NO.T3557
GUN: 5868

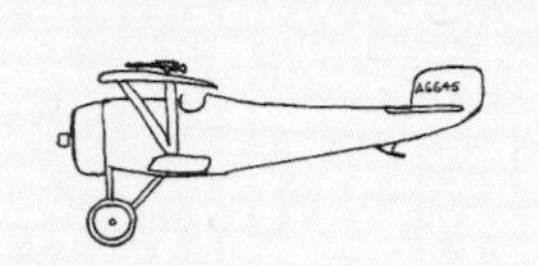

VON RICHTHOFEN'S Combat Report:
1745 hrs, Mercatel, other side of our lines.
Nieuport one-seater, English; details not at hand.

I attacked, together with four of my gentlemen, an enemy squadron of six Nieuport machines, south of Arras and behind the enemy lines. The plane I had singled out tried to escape six times by various manoeuvres. When he was doing this for the seventh time, I managed to hit him, whereupon, the engine began to smoke and the plane itself went down head first, twisting and twisting. At first I thought it was another manoeuvre, but then I saw that the plane dashed, without catching itself, to the ground near Mercatel.

BARON VON RICHTHOFEN

WEATHER: LOW CLOUDS AND RAIN.

The start of the Arras Offensive was just two days off, not that the ordinary squadron pilot or observer knew that. A prerequisite of any attack was photographs, needed by the Generals and planners, which is why so much aerial activity had been present over the Vimy Ridge sector, as well as other parts, of late.

The German fighter pilots had been reasonably successful in hindering photographic sorties and so it was decided, in order to gain what was said to be vital photos to the south of Arras, that a patrol of Nieuport Scouts, one equipped with a camera, should make the attempt. Perhaps, they thought, there would be less chance of German fighters attacking British scouts.

At 1640, a small section of 60 Squadron Nieuports headed for the Front for this 'special mission', having taken off from their base at Filscamp Farm, west of Arras. This is the reason the Nieuports were flying above the Front rather than inside German territory, when Jasta 11 attacked.

In the fight, two Nieuports were shot down, the other falling to Kurt Wolff (his seventh victory); this also crashed in British lines north of Mercatel. Karl Emil Schäfer was also credited with a Nieuport in British lines, but only two were lost. (60 Squadron did lose a third Nieuport – A6773, Captain M B Knowles, PoW – this day, but this loss occurred at 1925, claimed by Leutnant Wilhelm Frankl of Jasta 4, his 20th and final victory. Frankl was killed the next day.) Mercatel is five kilometres due south of Arras. The second loss in the Jasta 11 fight was Second Lieutenant Charles Sidney Hall RFC, aged 18, from Northumberland (A6766). His brother, Captain L W Hall, was also in the RFC. Another brother was in the REs.

George Smart fell at Sheet 53.M.7.d., having been burned to death in the crash. He was buried in a shell hole close to the wreck by front line troops that evening. A cross, made from the broken propeller, was placed at the head of the grave by some members of the Squadron who came to the spot. This area was later torn up by shelling and the grave site lost. Smart, like Hall, also had a brother in the RFC, Captain Charles D Smart, originally with 5 Squadron but in April 1917 on detachment to 16 Squadron at Bruay.

(He would be awarded the MC in September.) Ten days after his brother had been shot down, Charles tried to find the grave but by then it had totally disappeared.

Some time after the burial, the smashed wreckage was found at position N.14a, Sheet 51B. The grave was identified by a rough iron cross to which was attached a Field Service card bearing the number of the machine – A6645 – and the words 'British Airman, name unknown'. As the map references appear to refer to different locations, the latter position seems more positive due to the Nieuport's serial number being noted. Unless the broken propeller had been replaced by this rough iron cross, perhaps the first one had been another grave. In any event George Smart is only remembered on the Arras Memorial of those with no known graves. Smart had, on 24 March, flown A6646 on an OP, but on landing at 1700 hrs, had banked to avoid some barbed wire, hit the ground and turned over, badly damaging his Nieuport, but he had been unhurt.

Von Richthofen was flying Albatros DIII Nr.2253/17.

SMART,
GEORGE ORME
SECOND LIEUTENANT 60 SQUADRON

THE SON OF cotton mill owner Gerald Arthur Smart and his wife, Edith, of 'Farley Hill', 468 Bury New Road, Kersal, Lancashire, George was born on 17 August 1886. Educated privately and at Shrewsbury (1901-03), he joined the family firm, 'Rockliffe Mill' (Cotton Manufacturers) of James Street, Manchester, immediately after leaving school. Intent on flying, he joined the RFC as a 'ranker' aeroplane mechanic in 1915. Subsequently, Smart learned to pilot an aeroplane at his own expense, being awarded the Royal Aero Club Aviators Certificate (No.3707) on 20 October 1916. Given his 'Wings', he was sent to 60 Squadron in France as a Sergeant Pilot. The Squadron history describes Smart as 'originally an NCO pilot who had lately been commissioned for gallantry in the field'. His brother, Charles, also a pilot in the RFC, flew first with 5 Squadron and then with 13 Squadron, gaining the award of an MC later in 1917. George Smart's body was never found and he is commemorated on the Arras Memorial to the Missing, France, and on the family grave in St Paul's Churchyard, Kersal. He was thirty-one years old.

8 APRIL 1917

VICTORY NO.38

Sopwith 1½ Strutter
No.A2406
43 Squadron RFC
Engine No.1154 WD 7767
Guns: 28517; L690

VON RICHTHOFEN'S Combat Report:
1140 hrs, near Farbus. Sopwith two-seater. Occupants: Lieutenant Heagerty, wounded; Lieutenant Heath-Cantle, killed.
Details of plane not to hand, as plane is lying in shellfire and is also dashed to pieces.

With three of my planes I attacked three Sopwiths above Farbus. The plane I singled out soon made a right-hand curve downwards. The observer ceased shooting. I followed the adversary to the ground where he dashed to pieces.

Baron von Richthofen

Weather: fine but cloudy.

The three Sopwiths were on a Line Patrol to the southern part of the 1st Army area, leaving their airfield at Treizennes at 1030. The other two pilots were Lieutenants James Collier and F M Kitto (in A7804), the latter's observer being 2AM Arthur William Cant.

They were north-east of Vimy at 1130, patrolling between Lens and Arras, when they were attacked by eight (sic) enemy fighters. Five of these got on Kitto's tail and he put his Strutter into a spinning nose-dive, pulling out 2,000 feet below, but the fighters had followed him down. Kitto spun again and this time shook them off. Meantime, despite the gyrations, Cant had fired back and claimed one fighter had spun into the clouds out of control. There were no Jasta 11 losses.

Heagerty and Cantle were last seen gliding down through clouds after this combat, at 1135. Richthofen was later surprised to learn that the pilot had survived the final plunge; Cantle's body was found a week later by advancing British Third Corps troops as they over ran the crash site. They gave the position as B.13.d.7.4., which is near to where they buried him.

When interviewed by Floyd Gibbons after the war, Heagerty too thought that there were more than three enemy fighters after them. He recalls fighting the red fighter, although he had no idea who the pilot had been. He heard Cantle firing back at their attacker but then this stopped abruptly, in the same instant that his controls went limp. The Strutter fell headlong, the red fighter following them down, still firing. Heagerty was unable to do anything about it until near the ground. In desperation he stood on the rudder bar which turned the machine for a wing-first crash, but that is all he knew until he came round at midnight in a German dugout. He had a bad gash above one eye, which was later stitched up without anaesthetic, and with three of the doctor's assistants sitting on him and holding him down!

Earlier, however, in his repatriation report in December 1918, Heagerty had noted that he had been attacked by two enemy aircraft, had his controls shot away and been forced to come down out of control. He had not been wounded but had been injured in the crash. Von Richthofen was flying Albatros DIII Nr.2253/17.

CANTLE,
LEONARD HEATH
LIEUTENANT 43 SQUADRON 2/1 SURREY YEOMANRY

BORN ON 10 August 1895, Leonard was the first son of journalist George Heath Cantle of 'Cornerways', Partmore Park, Weybridge, Surrey. He was educated at Shields Court, Westgate-on-Sea, Charterhouse (1910-12) and at Trinity Hall, Cambridge. He interrupted his Cambridge degree course and joined the Surrey Yeomanry, into whose 2/1st Line Regiment he was commissioned on 1 December 1914. The 2/1st Surrey Yeomanry provided reinforcements and replacements for Line Regiments and, on 3 December 1916, Cantle was among 186 officers and men sent to join the 11th Battalion of the Queen's Regiment, then in the trenches alongside the Ypres-Comines canal in Flanders. He soon found himself disenchanted with life in the trenches and successfully applied for transfer to the RFC, which was achieved on 20 February 1917. Cantle trained for his observer's 'Wing' at Reading and Hythe before being sent to 43 Squadron in France on 20 March following. His body was never found and he is commemorated on the Arras Memorial to the Missing, France. He was twenty-one years old.

Left: Lt Heagerty (bottom left) in PoW camp cricket team. Third from left standing is Capt W L Robinson VC, shot down by Jasta 11 on 5 April.

HEAGERTY,
JOHN SEYMOUR
SECOND LIEUTENANT 43 SQUADRON EAST KENT REGIMENT (THE BUFFS)

AT THE OUTBREAK of war, John Heagerty was living with his widowed mother, Mrs N M Heagerty, at 'Cobo', Harvard Hill, Gunnersby, London W4. Commissioned on 12 May 1915, he was sent to join the 3rd (Special Reserve) Battalion of the East Kent Regiment (The Buffs) at the Citadel, Dover on 10 June 1915. He embarked for the Dardanelles on HMS *Olympic*, arriving at Mudros on 22 November 1915, just in time for the start of the general evacuation of the Gallipoli Peninsula and consequently was redirected to Egypt. Heagerty returned from Egypt on 18 September 1916, and joined the RFC at Oxford on 1 October following. Graduating as a pilot on 13 March 1917, his first posting was to 34 Reserve Squadron, Ternhill. From Ternhill he was posted, in tandem, with his observer, Leonard Heath Cantle, to 43 Squadron in France on 23 March 1917. Sixteen days later, the twenty-year-old Heagerty was forced down and wounded by von Richthofen. Taken prisoner, Heagerty received excellent medical attention on the front line before being sent to the rear and confinement for the rest of the war. It was 17 December 1918, before he was finally repatriated.

8 APRIL 1917

VICTORY NO.39

BE2G No.A2815
16 SQUADRON RFC
ENGINE No.1707 WD 2644
GUNS: 17031; 17446

VON RICHTHOFEN'S Combat Report:
1640 hrs, Vimy, this side of the lines. BE2 No.A2815
Occupants: Both killed, name of one – Davidson (sic).
Remnants distributed over more than one kilometre.

I was flying and surprised an English artillery flyer. After a very few shots the plane broke to pieces and fell near Vimy, on this side of the lines.

BARON VON RICHTHOFEN

Richthofen gained this, his second kill of the day, by encountering the 16 Squadron crew who were engaged on making a photo mosaic of the village of Farbus, just hours before the British offensive was due to begin. They had taken off at 1500 hrs and British ground observers witnessed their BE shot down by a hostile aircraft at 1640, 1,000 yards west of Vimy.

There was a report that they fell on the British side and were buried by British troops, but Richthofen not only claims they fell inside the German lines, but he also secured the serial number for his trophy wall. Where he got the name Davidson from is not known; perhaps once again, one of the flyers was wearing someone else's coat or gloves, or perhaps carried a map with this name on it.

Due to them falling in the battle area, the two men were not buried immediately, but a week later by British soldiers, near the Bois de Bonval, after their bodies were discovered by advancing Allied troops during the Battle of Arras.

Guy Everingham's mother received the terrible news of his loss by telegram, but nobody thought to inform his wife Gladys, who had to learn it from her mother-in-law.

Von Richthofen was flying Albatros DIII Nr.2253/17.

Despite two patrols and two victories, Richthofen was apparently out again that evening. A BE crew of 16 Squadron reported seeing seven hostile aircraft patrolling the line near Farbus, led by a red machine. The hunting area was proving a good one, but he had achieved all he was going to this April day.

Richthofen was obviously keen to equal Boelcke's score of 40 but he would have to wait a few days yet. The Battle of Arras began on the morning of 9 April, despite low clouds and strong wind. This, of course, kept the aerial activity down, frustrating Richthofen and making him wait three further days to achieve the 40th.

MacKENZIE, KEITH INGLEBY

SECOND LIEUTENANT 16 SQUADRON; ARGYLL AND SUTHERLAND HIGHLANDERS

ALONG WITH CORPORAL Alfred Beebee, MacKenzie, who was born on 26 June 1898, the son of K W I and Florence MacKenzie of 'Lansdowne House', Ryde, Isle of Wight, was the youngest of von Richthofen's victims. He was gazetted Second Lieutenant to the Argyll and Sutherland Highlanders in April 1916 whilst still only seventeen years old. He was awarded the Royal Aero Club Aviators Certificate (No.2906) on 17 May 1916, becoming attached to the Royal Flying Corps shortly afterwards. He is buried in Bois-Carre British Cemetery, Thelus, France (Fr.1321). He was aged 18.

EVERINGHAM, GUY

SECOND LIEUTENANT 16 SQUADRON; ROYAL WELSH FUSILIERS

THE ELDER SON of William and Patricia Florence Everingham, Guy was born in Barry, Glamorgan, South Wales, on 28 June 1894. Privately educated, he was living at 'Vaenor', Hawarden Road, Colwyn Bay, Denbighshire, North Wales when war broke out in August 1914. He enlisted as a private soldier in the 13th (1st North Wales) Battalion of the Royal Welsh Fusiliers in October 1914. Soon picked out as 'officer material', he was gazetted Second Lieutenant to the same battalion on 25 February 1915. His younger brother, Robin, was killed while serving as a Trooper with the Welsh Horse in Gallipoli on 10 December 1915. Sent to France in March 1916, Guy served first as a Line Officer in the trenches but was later sent for more specialised work as a Bombing Officer in the 113th Trench Mortar Battery. A successful application for transfer to the RFC followed in September 1916. His training as an observer was briefly interrupted when he married Gladys Annie Brown at Holy Trinity Church, Llandudno on 19 February 1917. The couple set up home at 'Lynwood', St David's Place, Llandudno, North Wales. After a short period of leave, he returned to France for duty with 16 Squadron. Guy Everingham is buried alongside his young pilot in Bois-Carre British Cemetery, Thelus, France (Fr.1321). He was twenty-two.

11 APRIL 1917

VICTORY NO.40

BE2c No.2501
13 Squadron RFC
Engine No.22930 WD 853
Guns: 2170; 17353

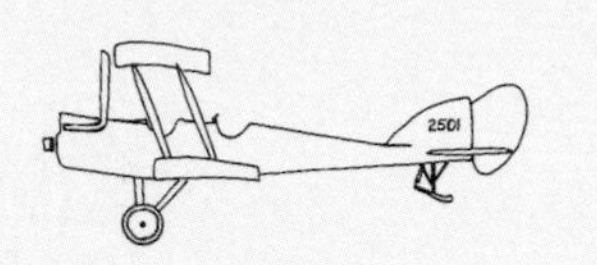

VON RICHTHOFEN'S Combat Report:
0925 hrs, Willerval, this side of lines. BE two-seater; details cannot be given, as English attacked this part of the Front, thus making communication with front lines impossible.Occupants: No details.

Flying with Leutnant Wolff, I attacked English infantry flyer at low height. After a short fight the enemy plane fell into a shell hole. When dashing to the ground, the wings of the plane broke off.

Baron von Richthofen

Weather: high wind, low clouds and snow.

There is a good chance that Gunner Pierson had already survived an attack by von Richthofen three days earlier, on 8 April. Flying with Captain T Macleod, they were engaged by a red Albatros Scout, one of two hostile machines they encountered over Farbus between 0730 and 0810. They were trying to do an Artillery Observation job, but each time they tried to cross the lines these two fighters would approach, forcing Macleod to head back. They tried several times, but on each occasion the red Albatros would attack, and finally they gave up and went home.

Today, Richthofen was more successful. The BE crew took off at 0805, from the airfield at Savy to fly their sortie over the advancing 17th Corps front. Richthofen surprised them, bringing them down in the battle area. Despite being wounded, both men managed to crawl from the wreckage and reached the comparative safety of a recently abandoned German dugout until found by advancing British soldiers.

Von Richthofen was flying Albatros DIII Nr.2253/17. He had now equalled the total scored by his former friend, commander and mentor Oswald Boelcke. This made him not only the highest living German ace but the equal highest, living or dead. Richthofen the hunter now set his sights on being THE highest with his 41st victory.

DERWIN, EDWARD CLAUDE ENGLAND

LIEUTENANT 13 SQUADRON

BORN IN 1894, Claude Derwin lived with his foster mother, Mrs M Andrews, at 22 Phillimore Street, Stoke, Devonport, Plymouth. A keen church-goer, he regularly attended St James the Great Church, Keyham. He volunteered for service with the Royal Flying Corps in 1915, gaining his Royal Aero Club Aviators Certificate (No.1484) on 29 July 1915. After his fight with von Richthofen, and his subsequent rescue by British troops, he was sent home to recover from his wounds in an English hospital. Back to fitness and cleared to fly, Derwin was next posted to 26 Training Depot Squadron based in Edzell, Scotland where he met and became engaged to Mabel Tamblin of Scotstounskill, Glasgow. Tragically, with less than a month to go before the Armistice, he was killed on 14 October 1918 in a flying accident over the aerodrome. Derwin's Camel (No.C6752) stalled in a turn, spun in and crashed to the ground. His body was brought home to Plymouth and his burial was accorded full military honours with a band and firing party from the Devon Regiment, as well as a group of RAF officers, in attendance. He is buried in Western Mill Cemetery, Plymouth, Devon. He was twenty-four years old. The carefully chosen quotation inscribed on his grave, reads: *"Give us the wings of faith to rise Within the veil and see The Saints above, how great their joys how bright their glories be."*

PIERSON, H

GUNNER 13 SQUADRON

Rescued by British troops after his encounter with von Richthofen, Pierson was sent home to England to recover from his wounds. He survived the war and is said to have emigrated to Australia in the early twenties.

Far left: Manfred in his Albatros DIII coming in to land.
Below: Claude Derwin and the BE2.

13 APRIL 1917

VICTORY NO.41

RE8 No.A3190
59 Squadron
Engine No.643 WD 3759
Guns: 23593; A111

VON RICHTHOFEN'S Combat Report:
0858 hrs, between Vitry and Brebières. New Body DD; plane burnt. Occupants: Lieutenant M A Woat (sic) and Steward (Thomas) (sic) both killed. Motor No.3759; fixed Motor V-shaped, 12 cylinders.

With six planes of my Staffel I attacked an enemy squadron of the same force. The plane I had singled out fell to the ground between Vitry and Brebières, after a short fight. On touching down both occupants and machine burned to ashes.

Baron von Richthofen

Weather: fine but cloudy.

This was a special day for Baron Manfred von Richthofen. Not only did he finally exceed Boelcke's score of 40, but by the end of this day he had downed three British aircraft, the first time he had scored a triple.

His first victory was, once again, achieved due to the tactics of his opponents, the British Royal Flying Corps. Engaged in a bitter struggle of air supremacy over the Arras battle front, they were taking a hammering from the nimble Jasta aircraft. Although quite often schemes were tried, which sometimes worked, that would put fighter aircraft in direct escort of Corps or bombing aeroplanes, this was still the era well before air-to-air radio communication, or air-to-ground control. Therefore, once in the air, either the escort or the escortees were liable to miss each other in the skies over France. All too often the escortless machines would, in the fast growing tradition of the flying service, press on alone.

This is why, generally, the RFC had a policy of merely putting up Line or Offensive Patrols in the general area of known or planned air activity, in the hope that they would be around when the Art Obs or Photo Op or bombing aircraft were operating and be able to engage or ward off hostile depredations against the slower and more vulnerable aircraft. Sometimes, these same Corps or bombing units, tired of being left to the mercy of the Albatros or Halberstadt Scouts, tried to enhance their chances of survival by other means. 59 Squadron tried it today.

The Squadron was new to the Front, although they had brought their new type, the RE8, to France in February. This new type began its baptism during April. Known as the 'Harry Tate' – an early rhyming slang which was derived from the music hall singer and entertainer of the period – it was meant to be a successor to the BE2 variants. It did become so, but in many ways it was just as vulnerable as the poor BE to air attack.

Left: RE8.

On this morning, six crews of 59 were assigned a photo job to Etaing, 15 kilometres east of Arras. As they took off from their base at La Bellevue, situated 12 kilometres north-east of Doullens on the straight Doullens-Arras road, one carried a camera – A3203 – crewed by two Scotsmen, Lieutenant Philip Bentinck Boyd (Gordon Highlanders & RFC) and Second Lieutenant Philip Oliphant Ray (6th Cameron Highlanders & RFC). The other five machines would provide escort.

In the planning of this operation, the RE8s should have met up and been escorted by a Flight of Spads from 19 Squadron and a Flight of FE2d pushers of 57 Squadron, but they failed to make rendezvous.

Having taken off at between 0810 and 0815, it was 36 kilometres (in a straight line) to Etaing, but they must have either drifted further north or been chased in that direction to have been shot down north of their objective. Vitry and Brebières, where Richthofen's victim came down, is six kilometres due north, by the Scarpe River. The other RE8s – all downed by Jasta 11 – fell to Lothar von Richthofen (two, victories four and five) at north-east of Biache-St-Vaast and at Pelves; Festner got one down north of Dury (his ninth kill) while Wolff brought his down north of Vitry, to bring his score to ten. Biache and Pelves further to the south-west are also along the Scarpe, which indicates that the surviving REs followed the river westwards and were picked off as they did so.

Only Dury is south of Etaing, Festner gaining the first kill, either near the REs' objective or he chased one south while the others headed north. The sixth RE8 was shot down by a Jasta 4 pilot, who joined in the mayhem – Leutnant Hans Klein, his sixth victory – which crashed between Biache and Hamblain-les-Près.

Thus the Squadron at La Bellevue waited in vain for its six crews to return, only a silent and empty sky rewarding those watching for their return. All twelve men were killed. In addition to those mentioned, the others were: Captain George Bailey Hodgson RFC (GL)/Lieutenant Charles Herbert Morris (Royal Welsh Fusiliers & RFC) in A3216; Lieutenant Arthur Horace Tanfield (3rd Warwicks & RFC)/Lieutenant Andrew Ormerod RFC in A3225; Lieutenant Herbert George McMillan Horne (19th London & RFC)/Lieutenant W J Chalk RFC, in A4191; Lieutenant A Watson RFC (GL)/ Lieutenant E R Law RFC, in A3199.

Von Richthofen was flying Albatros DIII Nr.2253/17, and despite the incorrect name spelling, A3190 was definitely his 41st victim.

(cont.)

Below: Manfred's red Albatros DIII

STUART,
JAMES MAITLAND
CAPTAIN 59 SQUADRON; 1/ROYAL INNISKILLING FUSILIERS

ALTHOUGH THE FAMILY had homes in Ireland at 'Stranocum House', Stranocum, County Antrim and at Somerset, Coleraine, County Londonderry, James Stuart was born in Queensland, Australia on 16 September 1896 where his father, James Stuart Senior, also owned large station properties. He was educated at King's School, Parramatta, New South Wales, Cheltenham College and the Royal Military College, Sandhurst. Graduating from Sandhurst, he was gazetted into the First Battalion, Royal Inniskilling Fusiliers. Almost immediately, he successfully sought attachment to the RFC which followed on 22 September 1915, when he was sent to Farnborough. Having completed his pilot training on 15 November 1915, he was sent to France the following month. He served in France until September 1916, when he was posted to the Home Establishment for a comparatively restful four months. Promoted to Captain and Flight Commander in November 1916, he returned finally to France on 13 January 1917, going on to join 59 Squadron upon its arrival at the Front on the 23rd of the following month. General Trenchard wrote of him: 'He has done exceptionally well and his record of 440 hours war flying is a very fine one'. His body was never recovered and he is commemorated on the Arras Memorial to the Missing, France. He was twenty years old.

WOOD,
MAURICE HERBERT
LIEUTENANT 59 SQUADRON MID; 4/LINCOLNSHIRE REGIMENT

BORN ON 25 June 1893, the son of watchmaker Arthur William Wood and his wife, Julia Mary, of 'Eversley', Grove Hill, Woodford, Essex. He was educated at Bancroft's School, Woodford and University College, London, from where he graduated BA with Honours in History in 1912 and again, in French, in 1913. He was also awarded prizes for academic excellence in 1912. After leaving University College, London he joined the staff at Stamford Grammar School, Lincolnshire. A member of the Officer Training Corps from 1911, he was gazetted as Second Lieutenant to the 4th (Territorial) Battalion, Lincolnshire Regiment, on 13 August 1913, with further promotion to Lieutenant following on 17 May 1915. As Battalion Bombing Officer, he accompanied the 4th Lincolns to France on 1 March 1915. After service in the trenches, he was next appointed second in command of the Grenade School, 2nd Army Headquarters, and was mentioned in Sir Douglas Haig's despatches of 30 April 1916. He returned home in July 1916, and married Hilda Newman. Transfer to the RFC followed and he joined 59 Squadron as an observer on 15 January 1917. His body was never recovered and he is commemorated on the Arras Memorial to the Missing, France. He was aged 23.

13 APRIL 1917

VICTORY NO.42

FE2B NO.A831
11 SQUADRON RFC
ENGINE NO.985 WD 7595
GUNS: 19776; 19554

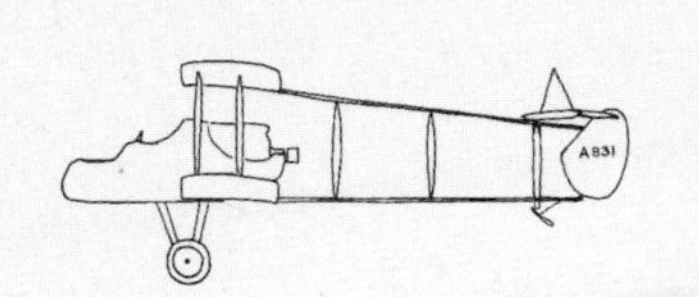

VON RICHTHOFEN'S Combat Report;
1245 hrs, between Monchy and Feuchy.
Vickers two-seater, details unknown, as plane downed beyond enemy lines.

Together with Leutnant Simon, I attacked a Vickers two-seater, coming back from German territory. After rather a long fight, during which I manoeuvred in such a way that my adversary could not fire one shot, the enemy plane plunged down to the ground between Monchy and Feuchy.

BARON VON RICHTHOFEN

WEATHER: FINE, BUT CLOUDY.

This FE2 had left its base at Izel-le-Hameau at 1125, part of an Offensive Patrol. When Richthofen attacked it, it was near to the lines, so came down on the British side where it was wrecked and shelled. A second FE, flown by Lieutenant Charles Eric Robertson and Second Lieutenant H D Duncan, also came down and was forced to land, following an attack by Kurt Wolff, timed ten minutes prior to von Richthofen's claim (1235). Wolff reported his target had come down south of Bailleul-Sir-Berthoult, noted by the British as at Sheet 51B.b.27.a., which is 1,000 yards west of Bailleul.

The area where Richthofen's FE came down is just below the Scarpe, about four kilometres south-east of Arras, whereas Bailleul is five km to the north-east of Arras. As there has been some suggestion that Cunniffe may have been downed by Wolff, and Robertson by Richthofen, the precise locations, recorded by Jasta 11, are worth noting. This, together with the fact that Richthofen reports his FE as crashing and then shelled, whereas the other FE (A827) did not feature as a loss, merely as a 'forced to land' inside Allied lines, makes it pretty certain that Cunniffe and Batten were the victims. Robertson, by then a Captain, was killed in action on 12 July, brought down by AA fire in a Bristol Fighter.

Recovering from his wound, Sergeant Cunniffe later received the Italian Bronze Medal for Military Valor, gazetted on 22 May 1917. This was no doubt awarded for his continued good work not the least of which was an earlier fight he'd been in on 3 April. In FE2b 4897, with 2AM J T Mackie as his observer, they had flown an afternoon photo escort. Attacked by German fighters, the aircraft had been damaged, the observer's gun mounting shot through, and Mackie himself wounded, but Cunniffe had got them back.

Von Richthofen was flying Albatros DIII Nr.2253/17.

Of interest while Cunniffe was with 23 Squadron was a crash during a flight in

FE2b No.A5479 on 10 February, with Private (Rifleman) C Upson as observer. They were on a Line Patrol between Rossignol Wood and Warlencourt soon after mid-day. Landing at No.7 Squadron's base, presumably with a mechanical problem, they crashed. Cunniffe was not hurt but Upson was thrown out and suffered a cut face. Poor Upson had been in the wars the previous day too, flying with Second Lieutenant A Holden, in FE2b 4886, on a gun practice sortie. Upson, in changing a drum on his Lewis gun, dropped it and it flew back, hit the propeller and smashed it, causing them to force-land. They got down safely but the machine was damaged.

On 25 February, Cunniffe took off at 1349 hrs in 4970 to fly a recce sortie north-east of Bapaume. Again he had a mechanical problem, recorded for certain this time as engine failure. He tried to get into Vert Galant aerodrome but had to come down in an adjacent field. The FE was only slightly damaged in the forced landing, and his observer, Second Lieutenant R Law, was only a little bruised.

CUNNIFFE, JAMES ALLEN

SERGEANT (No.11820) 11 SQUADRON; BRONZE MEDAL FOR MILITARY VALOUR (ITALY) BRITISH EMPIRE MEDAL (CIVIL DIVISION) 1950

THE SON OF W E and Mrs C Cunniffe of 'British House', Port Tenant, Swansea, James Cunniffe was born in 1895. His father was the manager of the British Wagon Works in Port Tenant. James volunteered for service with the Royal Flying Corps and served as an observer with 23 Squadron for six months, in the meantime learning to fly at his own expense and gaining the Royal Aero Club Aviators Certificate (No.3698) on 15 October 1916. He returned to 23 Squadron as a pilot in January 1917, but was subsequently transferred to 11 Squadron on 6 April 1917. Cunniffe was awarded the Bronze Medal for Military Valour by the King of Italy (*London Gazette*, 26/5/1917, page 5199) for gallantry during a fight which took place on 3 April 1917, when Cuniffe's observer, 2AM J T Mackie, was wounded and Cunniffe had a small part of his nose blown away when the machine gun exploded in his face. After their fight with von Richthofen, Cunniffe and his observer, Batten, slowly regained consciousness to find themselves trapped inside the mangled wreck of their FE 2b. Both were totally disorientated but knew that wherever they were, they were attracting shelling from both sides. An observer in a nearby balloon had seen the crash and, making a rapid descent, made his way over to them, pulled them out of the debris and guided them to safety. The 'Balloonatic', Robert Page, still then an officer in the RAF, visited Cunniffe's home in Swansea in the thirties, and again received his thanks for saving his life. Cunniffe spent two years in a hospital in Spalding, Lincolnshire before returning to his job in the Public Analyst Laboratory in Swansea. Two years later, now married to Lillian May, he secured a position with the Swansea Gas Light and Coke Company for whom he worked until his retirement in 1956. He was awarded the British Empire Medal (*London Gazette*,

18/6/1950, page 2802) for, amongst other meritorious services, maintaining the supply of gas to Swansea, under the most difficult and dangerous conditions throughout the German air raids on that city. He retired to Bosherston, Pembrokeshire where he died on 8 January 1959, at the age of 64.

BATTEN, W J

2ND CLASS AIR MECHANIC
(No.46731) 11 SQUADRON

Batten joined the Royal Flying Corps on 8 February 1917.

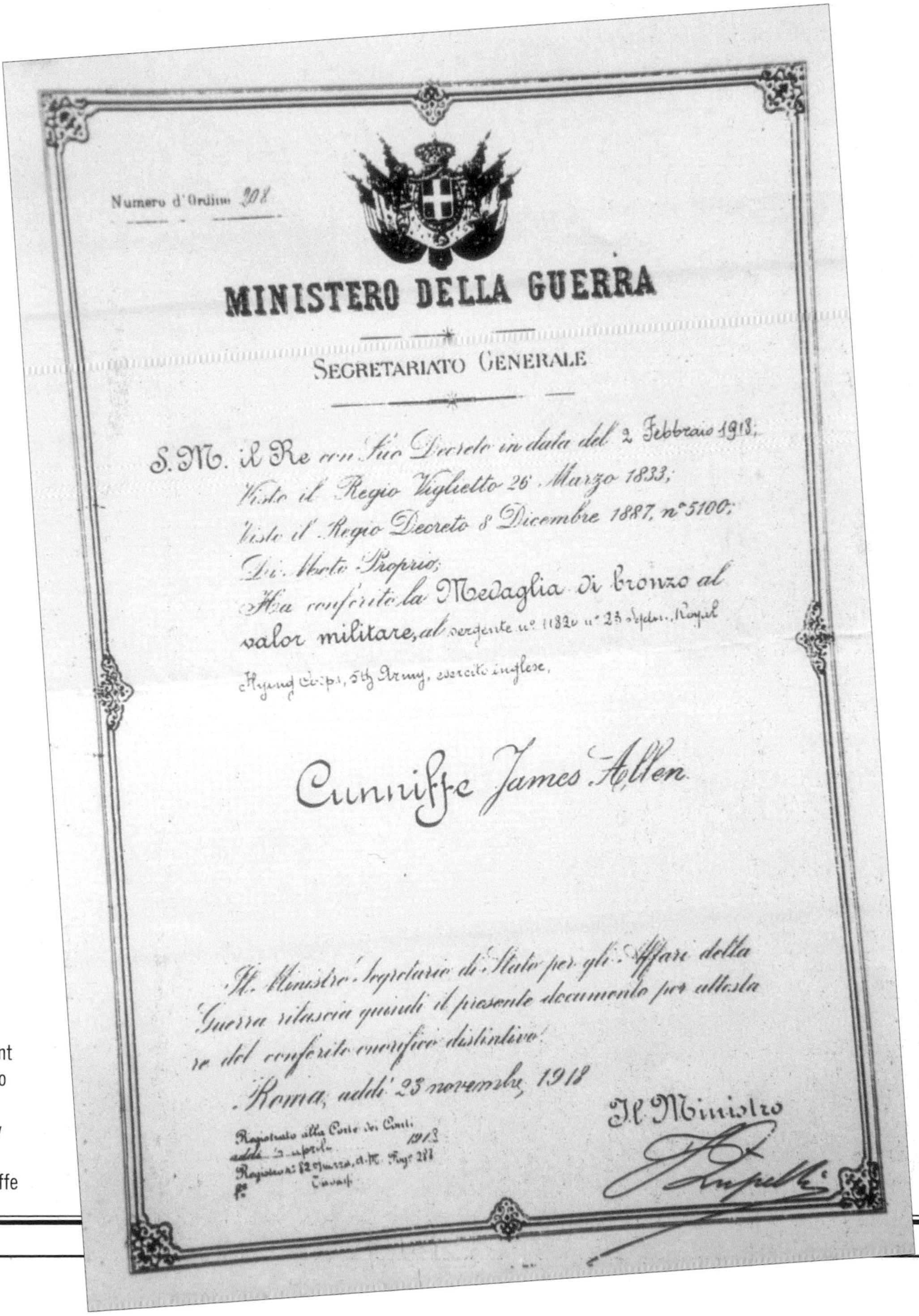

Numero d'Ordine 208

MINISTERO DELLA GUERRA

SEGRETARIATO GENERALE

S.M. il Re con Suo Decreto in data del 2 Febbraio 1918;
Visto il Regio Viglietto 26 Marzo 1833;
Visto il Regio Decreto 8 Dicembre 1887, n° 5100;
Di Moto Proprio;
Ha conferito la Medaglia di bronzo al valor militare, al sergente n° 11820 n° 23 Squadr., Royal Flying Corps, 5th Army, esercito inglese,

Cunniffe James Allen

Il Ministro Segretario di Stato per gli Affari della Guerra rilascia quindi il presente documento per attestazione del conferito onorifico distintivo.

Roma, addì 23 novembre 1918

Il Ministro

Registrato alla Corte dei Conti addì 3 aprile 1919
Registro n° 82 Guerra, ... Fog° 281

Right: Bestowal document for 'la Medaglia di bronzo al valor militare' (the Bronze Medal for Military Valour, Italy) conferred upon Sergeant J A Cunniffe

13 APRIL 1917

VICTORY NO.43

FE2B NO.4997 (BARODA NO.17)
25 SQUADRON RFC
ENGINE NO.917 WD 7527
GUNS: 23118; 26632

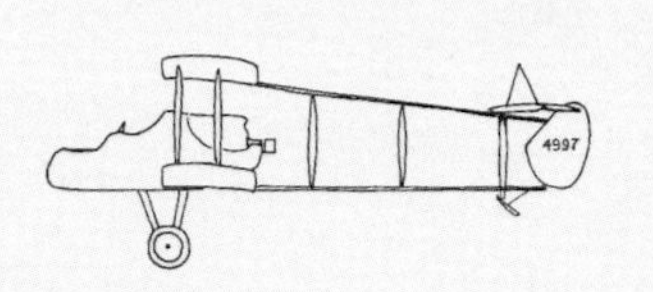

VON RICHTHOFEN'S Combat Report:
1935 hrs, Noyelles-Godault, near Henin Liétard. Vickers two-seater, No.4997. Motor No.917, 8 cylinder stand. motor. Occupants: Lieutenants Bates and Barnes, both killed.

With three planes of my Staffel, I attacked an enemy bombing squadron consisting of Vickers (old type) above Henin Liétard. After a short fight, my adversary began to glide down and finally plunged into a house near Noyelles-Godault. The occupants were both killed and the machine destroyed.

BARON VON RICHTHOFEN

The FE Squadron had indeed been on a bomb raid against an ammunition dump and the railway junction between Henin Liétard and Lens. Captain J L Leith (Hampshire Regt & RFC), who was about to receive the MC, had led six FEs out at 1840. Soon after they had bombed, they saw five hostile scouts approaching. They looked like Nieuports, and having been advised that a Nieuport patrol would be in the locality to give them some protection, they did not open fire.

Suddenly the scouts dived at two of the FEs, taking them by surprise. The engine of Bates/Barnes' aircraft, and that of Sergeant J Dempsey and Second Lieutenant W H Green's (A784) were hit and both machines began to drop down. Captain Leith, with Lieutenant G M A Hobart-Hampden (A6383) and Sergeant W J Burtenshaw/Sergeant J H Brown (A7003), immediately turned to help and Leith claimed one fighter shot down, crashing near Sallaumines, confirmed by British AA guns. Burtenshaw and Brown also claimed one destroyed, as did Second Lieutenants R G Malcolm and J B Weir (A6373), but neither Jastas 11 or 4 suffered any losses in personnel. The other fighters veered off and did not approach again.

When last seen, both damaged FEs were seen to be under control, so it was thought that both crews may well have survived as prisoners. In the event, and unseen by the other FE crews, Bates and Barnes crashed into a house and were killed. The other two, shot down by Sebastian Festner, did get down east of Harnes and were taken prisoner, Green having been wounded. Harnes is just north of a line Henin-Lens.

In fact the Squadron lost a third FE, timed a little earlier than 1930, at 1910, credited to Hans Klein of Jasta 4 who had shared in the 59 Squadron massacre that morning. Klein brought down a minor ace of the RFC, Captain Lancelot Lytton Richardson RFC and his observer Lieutenant Douglas Charles Wollen RFC, who were both killed; they were downed over the Front at Vimy and may have been on another job. Richardson had seven victories and was also about to receive the MC. This was Klein's own seventh victory.

Von Richthofen was flying Albatros DIII Nr.2253/17. The day's events had brought his score to an impressive 43, and he also had the serial number trophy to confirm that 4997 was his.

BATES,
ALLAN HAROLD
SECOND LIEUTENANT 25 SQUADRON

THE SON OF Archibald and Harriet Elizabeth Bates of the 'Utility Stores', 44 St Helens Road, Swansea, Allan was born in May 1896. He received his early education at the local municipal school near to the Bates' combined home and shop which sold hardware and electrical goods. From school, Bates went to the Technical College in Swansea and was showing great promise as a student of engineering when the war came. He worked for a while in an aeroplane factory before successfully seeking entrance into the Royal Flying Corps. Initially, he was sent to an Officer Cadet Training Battalion based at Lincoln College, Oxford, from where he was gazetted Second Lieutenant into the RFC. Following further training, he was awarded his 'Wings' and his first work as a pilot was ferrying aeroplanes to St Omer. He was eventually sent to join 25 Squadron at the Front on 6 April 1917. Exactly one week later, he was dead; his machine crashed against the wall of a house in the village where he and his observer now lie buried. Their graves, along with those of three other British dead, lie under the shadow of a slag heap, the headstones framed by a boxed hedge of laurel in a remote, difficult-to-find, corner of the Noyelles-Godault Communal Cemetery (south end), France (Fr.1314). He was in his twenty-first year.

Above: The graves of 2/Lt A H Bates and Sgt W A Barnes, Noyelles-Godault Communal Cemetery, France. 'In some corner of a foreign field'.

BARNES,
WILLIAM ALFRED
SERGEANT (No.61925) 25 SQUADRON MSM

BORN IN 1885, Bill Barnes was the son of Chief Warder William Barnes and his wife, Edith. Mr Barnes, senior, had been a professional soldier before entering the 'Convict Service' and his son, William, followed in his footsteps by joining the Army Service Corps (No.5/18094) on 10 April 1901. Young Barnes served in Egypt and in Khartoum, in the Sudan, for some years before returning to England where he was stationed when war broke out in August 1914. He was sent to France on 5 October 1914, his unit forming part of 7th Division, and qualified for the award of the 1914 Star. His excellent work and valuable service were further recognised by the award of the Meritorious Service Medal (*London Gazette*, 18/10/1916, page 10041). After several attempts, the now Sergeant Barnes finally succeeded in securing a transfer into the Royal Flying Corps. After the appropriate training, he was given his observer's 'Wing' in November 1916. He next enjoyed a brief leave at home, visiting his two brothers and his sister as well as his parents, who were then living at Avenue Lodge, Parkhurst Prison, on the Isle of Wight. Finally, Barnes was sent to join 25 Squadron in France on 1 April 1917. He lasted less than two weeks. Sergeant Barnes, MSM, is buried in a remote corner of the equally remote Noyelles-Godault Cemetery (south end), France (Fr.1314). He was thirty-one years old.

14 APRIL 1917

VICTORY NO.44

NIEUPORT XVII NO.A6796
60 SQUADRON RFC
ENGINE NO.T8341
GUN: 15104

VON RICHTHOFEN'S Combat Report:
0915 hrs, one kilometre south of Bois Bernard, this side of lines. Nieuport one-seater, No.6796; Motor: No.8341/IB Rotary.
Occupant: Lieutenant W O Russell, made prisoner.

Above Harlex, one of our observer planes was attacked by several Nieuports. I hurried to the place of action, attacked one of the planes and forced it to land one kilometre south of Bois Bernard.

BARON VON RICHTHOFEN

WEATHER: FINE MORNING; CLOUDY IN THE AFTERNOON.

Left: Nieuport Scouts.

The Nieuport Scouts of 60 Squadron were once more about to be cruelly treated by Jasta 11. 'A' Flight had taken off at 0830, five machines led by Captain Alan Binnie, to fly an Offensive Patrol to the east of Douai and spotted the German two-seater at 0915, which tallies with von Richthofen's report. Binnie led the attack, but as only one pilot of the formation returned to base, it was his report alone which gave any indication of how the other four pilots met their end.

Second Lieutenant G C Young, in B1509, saw Binnie wing over and dive on two hostile machines, and the others all followed him down. While one of the two-seaters was being engaged, Young saw two other hostile machines to his right, so turned off to attack them. He opened fire but his gun jammed after about five rounds, so pulling round quickly he got into a spin. Struggling to regain control, when he did so he looked about but could see no sign of the others, so remained for some time over Arras before finally heading back.

Seeing and attacking those two enemy aircraft, then spinning down probably saved his life, for the others were all engaged by Jasta 11 and wiped out. For Russell, it was only his second patrol – the first, a Line Patrol, had been flown on the 12th – so he was no match for von Richthofen. In any event, Russell later reported that in attacking the two-seater with Binnie his engine had been hit by the German observer and also his fuel tank as petrol was running into the cockpit. Knowingly or unknowingly, Richthofen obviously took advantage of the situation and finished him off, and with such an adversary pumping Spandau bullets into his petrol-soaked machine, Russell was lucky to survive.

Russell's report following his return from prison camp is virtually the same: 'While on OP with formation of six machines, followed flight commander on several EA scouts. After firing half a drum I flattened out but engine [cut and] failed to start. One EA scout followed on my tail, when I turned towards the lines, shooting all the way. Could not reach the lines and turned over on landing. Machine considerably shot about. Unable to get out before Germans surrounded me. Patrol tank probably hit as fuel continued to stream out even after the Germans righted the machine.'

The others were downed by brother Lothar (east of Fouquières for his sixth victory), Wolff (south-east of Drocourt for his fourteenth) and Festner (at Gavrelle in the front line, for his eleventh) between 0915 and 0923, so they made short work of them. The pilots brought down were: Captain A Binnie MC (A6772), an Australian, who had to have his left arm amputated, and was repatriated in January 1918; Second Lieutenant Lewis Charlton Chapman RFC (B1523), from London, who died of wounds two days later; Second Lieutenant J H Cook RFC (B1511), from New Zealand, killed, and credited to Wolff, south-east of Drocourt. All locations are over a wide triangular area Lens-Henin-Gavrelle.

Von Richthofen was flying Albatros DIII Nr.2253/17.

RUSSELL,
WILLIAM OSWALD
LIEUTENANT 60 SQUADRON

BORN IN LONDON on 11 June 1892, Bill Russell was living with his parents at 676 Commercial Road, Limehouse in the capital city when the war came. He learnt to fly at his own expense and gained the Royal Aero Club Aviators Certificate (No.1738) on 12 September 1915. Formal pilot training followed and he was awarded his 'Wings', shortly afterwards. Taken prisoner by the Germans, Bill Russell had to wait until 2 January 1919 before he was repatriated. After leaving the Royal Air Force, Russell moved south and adopted a lifestyle far removed from the London docklands, living at Hilliers Farm, St Mary Bourne, Andover, Hampshire.

16 APRIL 1917

VICTORY NO.45

BE2E No.3156
13 Squadron RFC
Engine No.1742 WD 2679
Guns: 13040; 18976

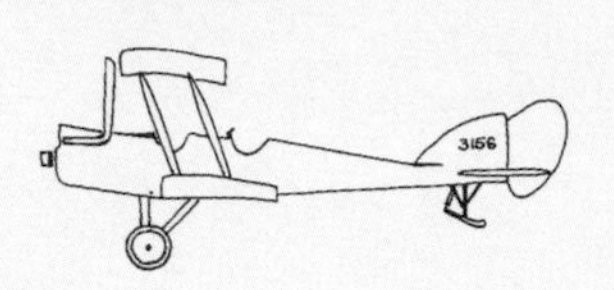

VON RICHTHOFEN'S Combat Report:
1730 hrs, between Bailleul and Gavrelle. BE two-seater. No details as plane fell on other side.

When pursuit-flying (height of clouds 1,000 metres) I observed an artillery flyer at 800 metres altitude; approached him unnoticed, and attacked him, whereupon he fell down, smoking. The pilot caught the machine once more, but then lost control at 100 metres. The plane plunged down between Bailleul and Gavrelle.

Baron von Richthofen

NB – the clocks had changed again on the Western Front, German time from this date being once more ahead of Allied time by one hour. This would continue until 9 March 1918.

Weather: rain and low clouds all day.

Two things are significant: firstly von Richthofen does not actually say that he saw his victim crash, which he normally did when he saw it; and secondly the time of the action.

There had been few combats this day, due to the bad weather. It hadn't stopped 60 Squadron receiving another mauling from Lothar, Wolff and Festner at 1030 that morning, but this action of Manfred's was the last recorded of the day, and the first since shortly after lunch.

No.13 Squadron had sent out 3156 at 1450, to fly an Art Obs sortie over XVII Corp's front. They were reported shot down in position B.27.C or D, and appear to have got down reasonably well in a forced landing. However, the machine was then blown over by a strong wind, and then heavily shelled, having to be Struck off Charge. Both men had, however, been wounded, Andrews dying on 29 April in a hospital at Le Touquet.

In the past this victory had been identified as a No.4 Squadron BE2, 5869, crewed by Lieutenant Willie Green (Black Watch & RFC) and Lieutenant Cecil Eustace Wilson RFC (SR), the latter being killed, Green having a fractured skull and a broken leg. However, their take-off time is recorded as 1305, which would have them in the air for three hours 20 minutes if Richthofen had shot them down at 1730 German time, 1630 British.

Also there is a British report that they were brought down by AA fire over Savy. No.7 Squadron were operating from Matigny, south-west of St Quentin, so they should be working a good deal further south than the Arras front. The more well known Savy, is the airfield location 16 kilometres north-west of Arras, so they couldn't have been shot down there, more than 22 kilometres due west of the Vimy battle front. THE Savy is located six kilometres west of St Quentin, well over 50 kilometres from where von Richthofen sent his victim down. In fact, it seems certain Green and Wilson were brought down by Kflak 93.

PASCOE,
ALPHONSO
LIEUTENANT 13 SQUADRON

THE SON OF Edward and Jane Pascoe of 'Fernleigh', Goetolphin Road, Helston, Cornwall. Like so many others, he learnt to fly at his own expense, gaining the Royal Aero Club Aviators Certificate (No.3664) on 28 September 1916. After pilot training he was awarded his 'Wings' and was first posted to 53 Squadron in January 1917, where he met his 'Springbok' observer, Fred Andrews. He and Andrews were then posted, in tandem, to 13 Squadron on 18 March 1917. Pascoe was luckier than his observer; he survived von Richthofen's attentions and was eventually sent home to the 3rd London General Hospital in Wandsworth, London SW18 to recover from his wounds. Andrews never left France.

ANDREWS,
FREDERICK SEYMOUR
SECOND LIEUTENANT 13 SQUADRON

THE SON OF Thomas Frederick and Louisa G Andrews of Warden Street, Harrismith, Orange Free State, South Africa, Fred Andrews was born in 1889. He was educated locally at Mercheston College and School in Harrismith. Like so many others, he came over from South Africa in 1915 to volunteer his services. His first duty when he arrived in England was to visit his father's brother (after whom he was named) at his uncle's home at Handsworth Wood Road, Handsworth, Birmingham. Uncle Frederick ran the engineering company, F Andrews & Company, Brunswick Works, Cheston Street, Aston, Birmingham. Joining the Royal Flying Corps, Andrews initially served in the ranks with 1 Squadron; setting foot in France for the first time on 9 August 1916 and reporting for duty six days later. Selected for a commission, he was gazetted Second Lieutenant to the General List in March 1917, and posted to 53 Squadron where he met his pilot, Pascoe. He and Pascoe were sent, in tandem, to 13 Squadron on 18 March 1917. Desperately wounded after their clash with von Richthofen, Andrews was lifted from the smashed and overturned BE2e and passed through a series of dressing and casualty stations until finally reaching Le Touquet Hospital, where he died, thirteen days later, on 29 April 1917. He is buried in Etaples Cemetery (UK Graves), France (Fr.40). He was twenty-eight years old.

22 APRIL 1917

VICTORY NO.46

FE2B No.7020
11 SQUADRON RFC
ENGINE No.1049 WD 7659
GUNS: 22247; 21893

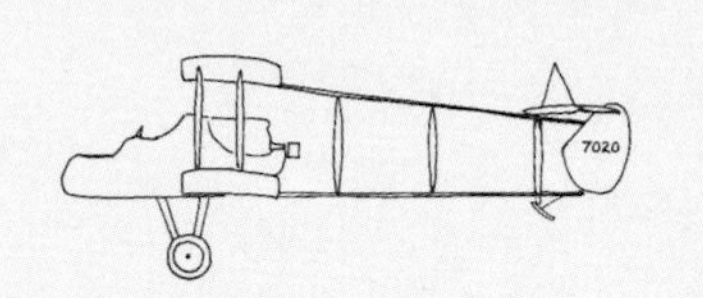

VON RICHTHOFEN'S Combat Report:
1710 hrs, near Lagnicourt. Vickers two-seater.
No details, as plane fell on the other side of line.

When my Staffel was attacking an enemy squadron, I personally attacked the last of the enemy planes. Immediately after I had discharged my first shots, the plane began to smoke. After 500 shots the plane plunged down and crashed to splinters on the ground. The fight had begun above our side, but the prevailing east wind had drifted the planes to the west.

BARON VON RICHTHOFEN

WEATHER: FINE BUT CLOUDY.

Six FE2s of 11 Squadron were assigned to a Photo Op on this afternoon, taking off between 1430 and 1445, and were found by Jasta 11 over an hour later, north-east of Bapaume. For once, however, although Jasta 11 did a great deal of damage to the British machines, they received credit for only two definite kills – one by Richthofen, another by Kurt Wolff (his 19th victory).

Wolff claimed his came down at Hendecourt, on the German side, whilst Richthofen's, as stated, came down at Lagnicourt, which Jasta 11 noted was in the British lines. 11 Squadron lost A5501, Sergeant T K Hollid/Lieutenant Bernard Joseph Tolhurst (11th West Riding Regt & RFC), the former being wounded and taken prisoner but dying of his wounds, Tolhurst being killed. One must assume this to have been Wolff's victory.

Richthofen recorded his victim as crashing to splinters. 7020 – one of the camera - carrying machines, was indeed a total wreck, coming down at position 57C.03.c. On hitting the ground it turned over three times, everything being smashed to pieces, the radiator and engine also having been shot through; Richthofen had said the FE had begun to smoke. When front line troops got the two men out, they found the pilot badly wounded with a bullet wound to his head and arm. The observer had been shot in the left leg. Both were dispatched to No.3 CCS near Bapaume.

Meantime, A5500, Second Lieutenants J J Paine RFC (SR) and J Rothwell (8th Manchester Regt & RFC), were both injured as Paine force-landed their shot-up FE, but well inside British lines (position given as 57C.I16.d), while A820 (another camera machine), Lieutenant C A Parker RFC (SR) and Second Lieutenant James Ernest Bytheway Hesketh RFC (GL) came down on fire in position 57C.D25.c. Parker's controls had been partly shot away and Hesketh seriously wounded, slumped over the side of his front cockpit. Parker held on to him as he put the FE down, then got him out of the now burning machine, carrying him to safety while under

Left: FE2b.

shell fire, but he later died of his injuries. There does not appear to be a claimant for this FE, and perhaps it was not known to have been lost by the Germans, despite it being near enough to the lines to be shelled.

Two other FEs returned to base with wounded observers, Second Lieutenant P A de Escofet, and 2AM J F Carr. In a later sortie, 11 Squadron's woes continued, with Captain E R Manning and Corporal R Tollerfield being shot-about and forced to land, Tollerfield being wounded also.

Von Richthofen was flying Albatros DIII Nr.2253/17.

Richthofen, or at least Jasta 11, seem to have been in evidence between 1845 and 1915 pm, during a bomb raid to Cambrai by FEs of 18 Squadron. Second Lieutenant R W Reid and Lieutenant K A Feranside-Speed (A5481) were over the target as four enemy aircraft attacked, one being an all red Albatros. They later reported what they said was a red Spad carrying a red circle on its wings, on which was a black cross in its centre. Reid would meet these aircraft again on 29 April (see later). It is well known that the Germans had a number of captured Spads, but whether they were used by them in combat is not certain.

FRANKLIN, WALDEMAR

LIEUTENANT 11 SQUADRON; 6/DORSETSHIRE REGIMENT

THE SON OF Mr and Mrs F J Franklin of 'Abbotsbury', Nelson Road, Bournemouth, Hampshire, Waldemar was born on 29 December 1896. He was educated at Marlborough (1910-13) and had just gone up to Cambridge when the war started. He volunteered immediately and was gazetted Second Lieutenant to the 6th (Service) Battalion of the Dorset Regiment on 22 September 1914 where, no doubt, he met Christopher Guy Gilbert, another of von Richthofen's victims-to-be (Number 31). Certainly, he embarked for Flanders with Gilbert and the rest of the 6/Dorsets when that Battalion went overseas for the first time on 13 July 1915. He served in the trenches alongside the Ypres-Comines canal and is mentioned in the Regimental History as 'engaged in bringing up supplies to the front line' during a calamitous frontal attack on a German position called 'The Bluff'. Franklin was one of the few officers to survive. He successfully applied for transfer to the Royal Flying Corps, becoming a Flying Officer early in 1917. Despite falling under the guns of the Red Baron and taking home a bullet in the leg as a souvenir of the encounter, Franklin survived the war and took up his education once again. He became a Member of the Mineralogical Society of Great Britain and Ireland and worked as a geologist for Anglo Iranian Oil in 1922, Shell Oil in 1937 and for Burma Oil until his retirement. With his wife, Catherine, he lived at 4 Great Quarry, Guildford, Surrey. Franklin died in Ewhurst, Surrey on 13 May 1972 at the age of seventy-six.

FLETCHER, WILLIAM FRED

LIEUTENANT 11 SQUADRON; LEICESTERSHIRE REGIMENT, MACHINE GUN CORPS

BORN ON 6 December 1894, Fletcher was living with his parents at 242 Osmaston Road, Derby and attending the University of Nottingham when the war came. His earlier education was at the Mundella Secondary School (1907-11) where he passed the Oxford Senior and London Matriculation in 1912. He acquired teaching experience as a student teacher for one year (1912-13) at Huntingdon Street School, Nottingham before going on to the University where he studied Science, Chemistry, Physics, Geology and Maths. He withdrew from his University course to join up and was gazetted Second Lieutenant into the 10th (Reserve) Battalion of the Leicesters. Promoted Lieutenant on 1 December 1914, he next transferred into the newly formed Machine Gun Corps on 14 June 1916. Still not content, he successfully applied for yet another transfer, this time into the RFC on 29 November 1916. First sent to 18 Squadron on 7 December 1916, he was then posted to 11 Squadron early in 1917. Fletcher was badly injured in the head and arm when his FE2b smashed into the ground but, thankfully, survived the war. He took up his education where he left off and, after qualifying, returned to teaching. After a long career, he died in Sheffield in December 1961 at the age of sixty-seven.

23 APRIL 1917

VICTORY NO.47

BE2F NO.A3168
16 SQUADRON RFC
ENGINE NO.E2167 WD 10718
GUNS: 19782; 19783

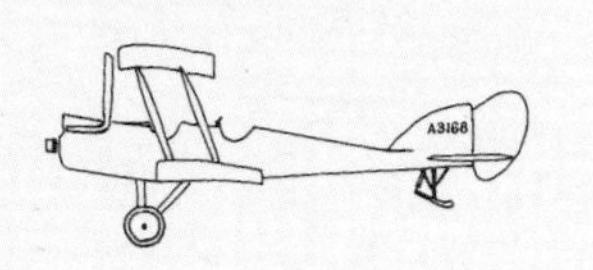

VON RICHTHOFEN'S Combat Report: 1205 hrs, Mericourt, this side of the lines. BE two-seater. No details, as plane broke in the air and was scattered in falling.

I observed an artillery flyer, approached him unnoticed, and shot at him from the closest range, until his left wing came off. The machine broke to pieces and fell near Mericourt.

BARON VON RICHTHOFEN

WEATHER: FINE.

Both Richthofen brothers were out hunting with the Staffel on this occasion and at the same time, came upon two 16 Squadron machines that were on a Photo Op to the east of Vimy, having taken off at 0925 and 0945 that morning.

Manfred brought his down at Mericourt, ground troops seeing them fall at position 36c.T.16.a, during an attack by five hostile aircraft. Lothar finished off the other five minutes later, at 1210, this going down into Allied territory north of Vimy for his tenth victory. The second crew were Second Lieutenants Charles Maurice Crow RFC, who was killed, and E T Turner (ASC & RFC), who survived wounded (A2875).

Von Richthofen was flying Albatros DIII Nr.2253/17.

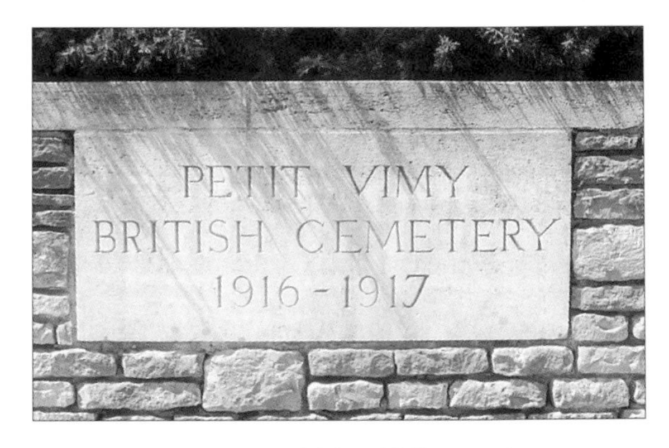

Above: The cemetery where Welch and Tollervey rest.
Below: BE2f A3168, before it became Richthofen's 47th victory.

WELCH,
ERIC ARTHUR
SECOND LIEUTENANT 16 SQUADRON; 7/KING'S OWN ROYAL LANCASTER REGIMENT

ALTHOUGH BORN IN London in 1894, Eric Welch was living with his parents, Mr and Mrs A T Welsh, at 1 Belle Vue Terrace, Lancaster when the war broke out. He had received part of his education at Lancaster Royal Grammar School before going on to become an apprentice motor engineer with a firm in Bedford, and later with the lorry manufacturers; Atkinson & Sons. Volunteering immediately the war broke out, he served in the ranks before being gazetted Second Lieutenant to the 10th (Reserve) Battalion, King's Own, on 12 May 1915. Sent next to join the 7th Battalion of his regiment, he became restless with the relative inactivity of the posting and successfully applied for transfer to the RFC. Following pilot training, Welch was first posted to 53 Squadron in France. From 53 Squadron he was transferred to 16 Squadron only a matter of days before his BE2f was shot to pieces by von Richthofen. Welch is buried in Petit Vimy British Cemetery, Vimy, France (Fr.269). He was twenty-three years old.

TOLLERVEY,
AMOS GEORGE
SERGEANT (No.3284) 16 SQUADRON

BORN ON 9 March 1896, Amos Tollervey was educated at the municipal school close to his family's home at 19 Bawtry Road, New Cross, Clifton Hill, London SE14. A distinct aptitude for engineering helped him secure his first job in a gun shop in the City of London. When war broke out, he was anxious to emulate his brother, Alfred, who was already in the Royal Navy. The Navy, however, was already over-subscribed in recruiting terms and so Tollervey opted for the flying service and, in January 1915, joined the Royal Flying Corps as a mechanic. He did very well in the service, showing a particular flair for photography. Within months of joining, he had been promoted through the various ranks and was already a Sergeant Observer. He was once wounded slightly in the arm but the wound was not serious enough to count as a 'Blighty' one and he was not sent home. Ironically, he should have been at home on leave at the time of his death but had, instead, deferred to a fellow Sergeant Observer whose wife was about to give birth to a baby. Tollervey is buried alongside his pilot, Eric Welch, in Petit Vimy British Cemetery, Vimy, France (Fr.269).

28 APRIL 1917

VICTORY NO.48

BE2E No.7221
13 Squadron RFC
Engine No.E1017 WD 5168
Guns: 27330; 6327

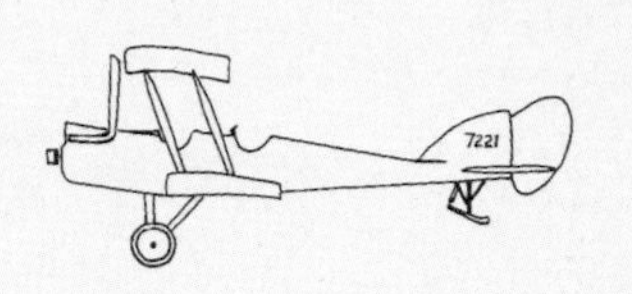

VON RICHTHOFEN'S Combat Report:
0930 hrs. Wood east of Pelves, south-east corner of Square 6998, this side of line. BE2. Pilot: Lieutenant Follitt, killed; Observer, F I Kirckham (sic), slightly injured.

While on pursuit-flying, about 0930, I attacked an enemy infantry or artillery flyer at 600 metres above the trenches. Above the wood of Pelves I caused the enemy plane to fall. The adversary, from the beginning to the end of the fight, was never able to get out of range of my guns.

Baron von Richthofen

Weather: low clouds.

This crew had taken off from Savy, north-west of Arras, at 0720, and for an hour had been happily ranging for the guns along the XVII Corp front. So intent had Kirkham been on his work, sending Morse messages down to the gun battery, that the first sign of attack was the sound of machine gun fire as Richthofen swooped down on the BE.

In the first pass, Follit was hit in the back and collapsed over the stick. Kirkham manned his rear gun, firing back steadily, despite knowing that he was sure to die in an imminent crash, but he could neither hit nor deter the red Albatros that followed them down, firing all the while. It was a case, yet again, of Richthofen continuing to fire at a doomed machine although he must have known it was finished. For his part, as he related to Floyd Gibbons in 1927, Kirkham decided to fight it out with the German pilot rather than attempt any kind of auxiliary control from his front cockpit, as this would have put his back to the assailant.

Coming down into the wood south of the Scarpe saved Kirkham, having already survived several bullets through his flying coat and another hitting his gun. The BE smashed into some trees near a gun battery and the next thing he knew he was being cut out of the wreckage. Petrol was everywhere, but there was no fire, despite the wireless key not having been switched off.

Follit, severely wounded and raving, was carried to an aid station near Vitry, along with Kirkham, Follit dying a few minutes after reaching it. Follit had only been married the previous year, but the Germans gave the observer a ring from the dead man's hand, which Kirkham was later to give to his widow.

As he was led into captivity, Kirkham was taken to Jasta 11's airfield, but the Baron was absent, so failed to meet his recent antagonist.

Upon his return to England, Kirkham said he knew he had been attacked by Richthofen, flying one of four Albatros Scouts that engaged them over Biache St Vaast, because of the invitation to the airfield.

Von Richthofen was flying Albatros DIII Nr.2253/17.

Left: R W Follit with his fiancée Lilian T Watkins – autumn 1914.

FOLLIT,
REGINALD WILLIAM
LIEUTENANT 13 SQUADRON; ROYAL FIELD ARTILLERY

THE YOUNGER SON of slate merchant William Follit and Mrs Follit of 'Avenue House', Clapham Park, London SW, Reg Follit was born on 3 September 1890. He was educated at St Lawrence College, Ramsgate (1900-07). A fine sportsman and a keen volunteer, he first joined the Honourable Artillery Company ('B' Battery) on 5 July 1909 but then allowed his membership to lapse. Immediately upon the outbreak of war, he again presented himself at the HAC Barracks and was accepted into '2/B Bty' on 6 August 1914. An obvious candidate, he was selected for officer cadet training and subsequently commissioned into the Royal Field Artillery on 17 July 1915. In the autumn of 1915, he married his fiancée, Lilian T Watkins. Within months they were parted, Follit being sent to join a battery in France in February, 1916. The autumn of 1916 saw the birth of a son, William, and a transfer to the Royal Flying Corps. Following flying training, he was parted from his wife and son for the last time, being ordered to join 13 Squadron at Savy in France. Terribly wounded after his machine crashed, Follit died less than an hour later in a German dressing station. His remains were lost in the subsequent battles over his grave and he is commemorated on the Arras Memorial to the Missing, France. He was twenty-six years old. After the war, his widow and son lived at 9 Glendower Place, South Kensington, London SW7.

KIRKHAM,
FREDERICK JAMES
SECOND LIEUTENANT 13 SQUADRON; ROYAL FIELD ARTILLERY

BORN IN 1894, Kirkham was living with his parents at 8 The Terrace, Brydges Road, Stratford, London E15 when war was declared. Commissioned into the Royal Field Artillery on 31 January 1916, he was first sent to the Front on 7 May 1916. Transfer to the RFC and training as an observer followed before, having been awarded his 'Wing', he was posted to 13 Squadron for Artillery liaison duties. Wounded and taken prisoner, Kirkham had to endure shelling from his own side as the German medics dressed his injured hands and face. He was even invited to write a reassuring note to his mother which the Germans promised to drop behind British lines. They kept the promise. His wounds bandaged, Kirkham was escorted to imprisonment in Douai, a long ten-mile walk away. Bedraggled and bloody, his ordeal was ameliorated by the kindness of some concerned French girls who pressed cigarettes into his bandaged hands. It was the last day of 1918 before Kirkham was finally repatriated. After the Great War, Kirkham lived at 193 Beehive Lane, Ilford, Essex.

29 APRIL 1917

VICTORY NO.49

SPAD VII No.B1573
19 SQUADRON RFC
ENGINE No.5768
GUN: L8479

VON RICHTHOFEN'S Combat Report:
1205 hrs. Swamps near Lecluse, this side of the lines. Spad one-seater. No details concerning plane, at it vanished in a swamp.

With several of my gentlemen, I attacked an English Spad group consisting of three machines. The plane I had singled out broke to pieces whilst curving and plunged, burning, into the swamp near Lecluse.

BARON VON RICHTHOFEN

WEATHER: FINE.

Richthofen was fast approaching a score of 50 victories, at which time he had promised both himself and his mother a rest. It is certain too, that the German High Command would have wanted their flying hero out of danger. On this day he would achieve no fewer than four victories, taking his total over the magic 50 mark.

The three Spads had taken off from Vert Galant shortly before midday, led by the CO, Major H D Harvey-Kelly DSO (A6681). Harvey-Kelly was a man long on experience. A pre-war airman, he had transferred to the RFC from the Royal Irish Regiment, and it has long been known that he became the very first British pilot to land in France after the beginning of the war in August 1914.

Like most of the squadron commanders in France by 1917, he was not permitted, ordinarily, to fly on operational duties, but like many of his fellow COs, he did. Today he chose once more to fly.

According to the sole survivor of this expedition – and perhaps to folk lore too – they had received a call saying that von Richthofen and his men had been reported over the Front, and a request to go up after him. The story may be true, but it seems strange that even someone as experienced in flying, if not in current front line combat, as Harvey-Kelly, should have then gone aloft with just two others, neither of whom were over-experienced, to seek out and knock out the Red Baron and some of his Jasta! If this was to be done, surely he would have gone 'mob-handed', to use a modern phrase.

Whatever the truth, it will not surprise anyone that Jasta 11 knocked down all three Spads in short order. Harvey-Kelly went down under the guns of Kurt Wolff, Lieutenant W N Hamilton (A6753) to Lothar von Richthofen, and Applin to the Master himself. Only Hamilton survived, as a prisoner. Harvey-Kelly fell at Sailly-en-Ostrevent, Hamilton at Izel (Oppy) and Applin east of Lecluse.

Applin had been the first to fall, so the others had been harried to the north-west, Hamilton obviously not being able to escape due west to the front lines, and finally forced

APPLIN, RICHARD

LIEUTENANT 19 SQUADRON

Born on 3 June 1894 in Clevedon, Somerset, Richard Applin was the only child of school teacher Charles Ernest and Mrs Applin. Richard was educated at Taunton School, Southampton, from where, following family tradition, he went on to teacher training. As soon as he was able, he volunteered and was accepted into the Inns of Court Officers Training Corps (Private, Number 6/2/6804) at Lincoln's Inn on 14 October 1915. Following basic training he was sent to No. 11 Officers Cadet Battalion at Camberley on 7 May 1916, before being commissioned Second Lieutenant (General List) on 4 September 1916. Keen to fly, he volunteered for the Royal Flying Corps and joined 7 Reserve Squadron ('B' Flight) in October 1916. His first experience of flying was as a passenger in a Maurice Farman 'Longhorn' (No.358) on 4 November. Applin's first solo flight, again in a 'Longhorn', was completed on 6 December 1916. At this time, Richard married his fiancée, Margaret Hannah Brown and they set up their home at 27 Westridge Road, Southampton. The new year found him flying Martinsyde Scouts at the Central Flying School and, by the time he joined 19 Squadron in France on 14 March 1917, he had 55 hours, 55 minutes flying time, of which 45 hours 45 minutes was solo. With 19 Squadron, he initially 'cut his teeth' on a BE2c before he was allowed to take off in his first Spad on 3 April 1917. His serious patrolling duties began on 21 April 1917 and by the time he met von Richthofen he had accumulated a mere 75 hours of flying, training and operational. Initially reported as 'Missing', the first notification of his death came from the enemy, a note being dropped from a German aeroplane in September, 1917. His body was never recovered and he is commemorated on the Arras Memorial to the Missing, France.

Left: Manfred with the mercurial Ltn Werner Voss.

down a mile or so inside the lines. After the war he thought that he and Harvey-Kelly had shot down five of their attackers. Jasta 11 had no losses.

When Hamilton returned from his period of captivity, he reported: 'OP between Douai and Cambrai. Major Harvey-Kelly leading, sighted and attacked Richthofen's circus (sic) 14-strong, over Epinoy. Lieutenant Applin was shot down at once and killed. Circus split up, half on the Major, half of me. My guns gave repeated No.4's, eventually a No.2 [stoppage]; I had shot down one HA but then gun jammed hopelessly over Douai, so made for the line, having lost the Major who was shot down and died three days later in a German hospital. Both my tanks were holed and I had to land.'

Von Richthofen was flying Albatros DIII Nr.2253/17.

Right: Lt W N Hamilton, sole survivor of trio who engaged Jasta 11.

Painting opposite: Victory No.62

Painting overleaf: Victory No.70

A
9299

DO NOT FLY WITH LESS THAN 160 LBS
IN THE GUNNERS COMPARTMENT

29 APRIL 1917

VICTORY NO.50

FE2D No.4898 (JAHORE No.14)
18 SQUADRON RFC
ENGINE No.866 WD 7476
GUNS: 17898; 20823

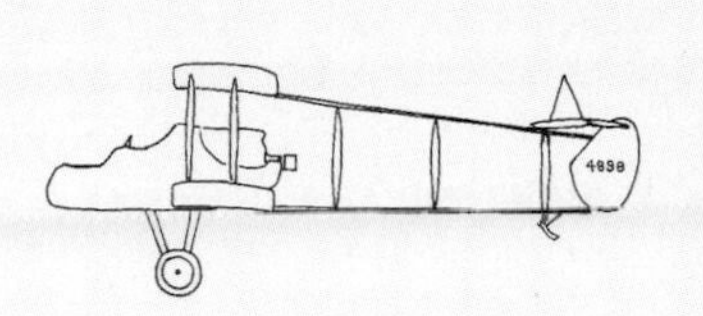

VON RICHTHOFEN'S Combat Report:
1655 hrs, south-west of Inchy, Hill 90, near Pariville, this side of the lines. Vickers 2. Occupants: Capt (sic) G Stead RFC. No details concerning the plane, went down burning in first line.

I attacked, together with five of my gentlemen, an enemy group of five Vickers. After a long curve fight, during which my adversary defended himself admirably, I managed to put myself behind the enemy. After 300 shots the enemy plane caught fire. The plane burnt to ashes, and the occupants fell out.

BARON VON RICHTHOFEN

Yet another Photo Op which Jasta 11 interrupted. How many RFC men died to bring back photographs of the front lines for the Generals and Army commanders?

Apart from giving Sergeant Stead the incorrect rank of Captain, and recording the location of the crash as Pariville instead of the assumed Pronville, this is Richthofen's victim. Like the previous action, this fight was again far south of the Arras-Vimy front, Jasta 11 operating in response to activity further south, on the Cambrai front.

The FEs had taken off at 1420, their task taking them to the 5th Army area, which ran from the east of Croissells, east of Noreuil, east of Boursies-Havrincourt; a line running in a south-easterly direction. They got as far as Marquion and had begun photographing an area around Marquion and Baralle, flying at 10,000 feet, but at around 1600, Second Lieutenant R C Doughty, observer to Second Lieutenant R W Reid (A5466) pointed out four red-coloured aircraft. However, they looked like Spads, so they thought they were British.

On the face of it, this seems incredible; why should a British crew think any Spads, British or French, would be red in colour, as opposed to the universal RFC colour of khaki-green, or the French grey/green? They paid for this folly.

Reid and Doughty had just taken their last photo as an enemy fighter came up on their tail, very quickly, and began firing. Doughty immediately jumped up to man the rear-facing gun as Reid stalled the FE in order to make the fighter overshoot prior to a rapid descent. Doughty got off just one round but then was hit and fell back into his front cockpit.

Reid went into a spiral dive to some clouds below, coming out over the Hindenburg Line at Inchy-en-Artois, but the fighter had followed them and attacked once more. Reid went into another spiral nose-dive and crossed the lines at 500 feet – British ground fire then driving off the fighter. Reid landed at Fremicourt, just east of Bapaume, to get aid to his wounded observer.

Meanwhile, Second Lieutenant George H S Dinsmore and his observer, Second Lieutenant G B Bate (L N Lancs & RFC), flying one of the escort FEs (A5483), were attacked by three fighters. Oddly enough, these two men had also wrongly identified four red aircraft as Spads, but larger. George Dinsmore saw his observer shoot down one fighter in flames and another out of control before he was hit and mortally wounded and the FE shot about. Dinsmore, like Reid, headed down and recrossed the lines at low level, ground fire driving off the pursuing fighter, flown by Kurt Wolff. Dinsmore got the FE down just behind the front lines, men of the Border Regiment helping the men from their aircraft. These same troops also confirmed seeing one enemy fighter wrecked on the ground in position D.5.6.55. As Jasta 11 suffered no recorded losses, one wonders if they had in fact seen the FE of Stead and Beebee crash. Bate in fact was found to be dead, and the FE was wrecked either in the forced landing or by the subsequent shelling. Reid landed sufficiently far away from the lines to be free of any shelling. Meantime, Richthofen's kill had come down south-west of Inchy which puts it near Pronville, the former home of his old Jasta 2, which was now right on the front line. Jasta 2 was now operating from Eswars.

Corporal Beebee had one victory to his name, having downed a hostile machine over Barelle during a bomb raid on 23 April, flying with Second Lieutenant H A Traylen (in 6987).

Von Richthofen was flying Albatros DIII Nr.2253/17.

Right: Rare picture of Manfred smiling broadly.

STEAD,
GEORGE
SERGEANT(No.2119) 18 SQUADRON

GEORGE STEAD, who lived before his marriage with his widowed mother at 18 Vere Street, Seedley, Salford, learnt to fly at his own expense, gaining the Royal Aero Club Aviators Certificate (No.4142) on 14 January 1917. He married and set up home at 27 Ossory Street, Moss Side, Manchester just before leaving for France on 21 April 1917. A brief eight days later his new wife, Ann, was a widow. His body was never recovered and he is commemorated on the Arras Memorial to the Missing, France. He was nineteen years old.

BEEBEE,
ALFRED
ACTING CORPORAL (No.14956) 18 SQUADRON
CROIX DE GUERRE (FRANCE)

BORN IN JULY 1898, Alfred was living with his parents, George and Alice Beebee, at 119 Broad Street in the heart of the city of Birmingham when war was declared. He was really too young to enlist but lied about his age, claiming that he was nineteen and so was allowed to join the Royal Flying Corps in October 1915. Within months, he had successfully completed his training and had qualified as an observer. Less than a week before his death, he had himself shot down an enemy machine over Barelle, a feat which earned him the award of the Croix de Guerre from the President of France (*London Gazette*, 14/7/1917, page 7095). The Commanding Officer of 18 Squadron, Major G R M Reid, described Beebee as 'by far the best gunner/observer we have'. His body was never found and he is commemorated on the Arras Memorial to the Missing, France. He was eighteen years old and shares, with Second Lieutenant K I MacKenzie (Number 39) and Donald Cameron (Number 68) the dubious distinction of being von Richthofen's youngest victim.

29 APRIL 1917

VICTORY NO.51

BE2E No.2738
12 Squadron RFC
Engine No.E674 WD 3023
Guns: 15775; 14469

VON RICHTHOFEN'S Combat Report:
1925 hrs, near Rouex, this side of the lines.
BE DD 2. No details, as plane is under fire.

Together with my brother, we each of us attacked an artillery flyer at low altitude. After a short fight my adversary's plane lost its wings. When hitting the ground near the trenches near Rouex, the plane caught fire.

Baron von Richthofen

Two crews took off from their airfield at Avesnes-le-Comte at 1645 to fly Art Obs sorties over the Front. The Arras battle still raged so there were a number of BEs working above the lines, and these two were unlucky onough to encounter the Richthofen brothers.

Davies and Rathbone did indeed crash near Rouex, which is right on the River Scarpe, below Fampaux, east of Arras. Lothar shot down the other BE (7092), crewed by Lieutenants Cyril John Pile (RFA & RFC, son of Sir Thomas Pile, Bart) and John Howard Westlake RFC (GL), between Monchy and Pelves, which is about three kilometres south-east of where brother Manfred's victims came down. Pile died shortly after being brought down, Westlake dying of his injuries on 7 May.

Obviously Jasta 11's patrol area for this evening sortie had moved further north, the locality being some 14 kilometres to the north-west of the earlier late afternoon combat area.

Von Richthofen was flying Albatros DIII Nr.2253/17.

Right: Formal portrait of Manfred von Richthofen.

DAVIES,
DAVID EVAN
LIEUTENANT 12 SQUADRON

BORN IN 1892, the son of Mr and Mrs Thomas Davies of 175 Crogan Hill, Cadoxton-Barry, Glamorgan, South Wales, 'Dan' Davies was educated at Barry County School and Cardiff University College. A brilliant scholar, he graduated Master of Science at Cardiff before securing a Government post which took him to the West Indies. Returning home when the war started, he enlisted as a private soldier in the Royal Welsh Fusiliers and served in France for a year before he was recommended for a commission. Following pilot training, Davies was sent to join 12 Squadron at Avesnes-le-Comte in France. Davies' body was never found and he is commemorated on the Arras Memorial to the Missing, France. He was twenty-five years of age.

RATHBONE,
GEORGE HENRY
LIEUTENANT 12 SQUADRON; ALBERTA REGIMENT

The son of lumber merchant George Rathbone and his wife, Elizabeth, of 15 Laxton Avenue, Toronto, Ontario, Canada, George junior was born on 30 June 1895. Educated locally, George joined his father's company as soon as he left school. He was a volunteer in the Militia, being a member of the 12th Regiment York Rangers. He enlisted in the 204 Btn Canadian Expeditionary Force on 14 February 1916, and sailed with his unit aboard the SS *Laconia* from Halifax, Nova Scotia on 27 September 1916, bound for Liverpool. He next successfully applied for transfer to the RFC which took effect on 15 February 1917. After training, he was awarded his 'Wing' and was sent to join 12 Squadron at Avesnes-le-Comte in France, arriving on 5 April 1917. His body, like that of his pilot's, was never found and he is commemorated on the Arras Memorial to the Missing, France. He was twenty-one.

29 APRIL 1917

VICTORY NO.52

SOPWITH TRIPLANE NO.N5463
8 SQUADRON RNAS

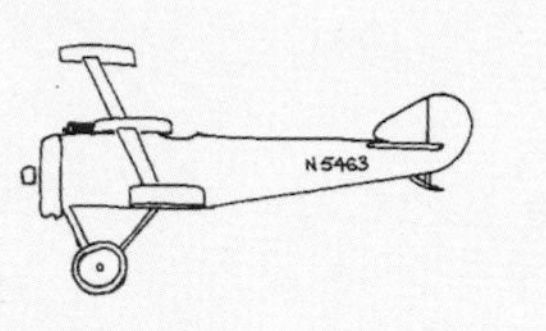

VON RICHTHOFEN'S Combat Report:
1940 hrs, between Billy-Montigny and Sallaumines, this side of lines. No details concerning enemy plane as it was burnt.

Soon after having shot down a BE near Rouex, we were attacked by a strong enemy one-seater force of Nieuports, Spads and Triplanes. The plane I had singled out caught fire after a short time, burned in the air and fell north of Henin Liétard.

BARON VON RICHTHOFEN

Above: Sopwith Triplane.

This fourth victory of the day was later to be erroneously identified as a Nieuport Scout and was among the most difficult of Richthofen's victories to identify as regards trying to match victim to losses.

Richthofen himself could have so easily ensured any such problem could not have arisen if only he had mentioned the type of aircraft he had shot down. That it was (a) a Triplane, (ie: it had three wings) and (b) it was the first (and as it turned out only) Triplane he ever shot down, one might have thought it a fact worth mentioning in his otherwise usually accurate reports.

It is understood the Nieuport theory came about because Floyd Gibbons, in the latter 1920's when researching his book *'The Red Knight of Germany'*, simply believed it was a Nieuport as there were no Spad losses and he assumed the loss must have been RFC rather than RNAS. This left a very obvious Nieuport Scout – A6745, flown by Captain Frederick Leycester Barwell of No.40 Squadron, who failed to return from an early evening sortie. To compound the error, Gibbons himself added 'Nieuport one-seater' to the combat report he recorded in his book, making it look as if Richthofen had himself stated his adversary had flown this nimble single-seater.

The strange thing in all this is that the Nachrichtenblatt clearly shows von Richthofen's claim to be a Sopwith Dreidekker (three wings), south-west of Billy-Montigny, as his 52nd victory.

Gibbons also built up the story from the fact that he had found an enemy infantry report stating that the fight, having been witnessed from the ground, had lasted almost half an hour. Unfortunately Gibbons does not quote a source for this, either by name or location, which could almost make it another figment to support his unfortunate theory. A brief look again at the combat report shows clearly that Richthofen had his adversary on fire '... after a short time.' Hardly a half-hour dogfight! That Barwell was a minor British ace was, supposedly, sufficent to assume he would have been a hard adversary for Richthofen to overcome.

The facts of the matter are that Barwell took off on patrol at 1820 (1920 pm German time), from Bruay, 16 kilometres west of Lens, where the Squadron had moved that very day, from Auchel (Lozinghem) where it had been for just four days. (Prior to this it had been at Treizennes, all three bases being north-west of Lens.) Gibbons, then, would have us believe Barwell flew to the lines while gaining combat height, headed over into enemy airspace, found Richthofen, fought him for almost 30 minutes and still be shot down at 1940 hrs German time, ie: twenty minutes after taking off!

The truth is less spectacular. Certainly there were patrols of Nieuports, Spads and Naval Triplanes in the area that evening. 19 Squadron would be the Spad outfit, but there are no combat reports by this unit, which supposes they did not claim anything.

There were, however, two Squadrons of Triplanes, 1 and 8 Naval. Four machines of 1 Naval had taken off from La Bellevue, on the Arras-Doullens road, at 1805, followed by a fifth at 1830 (1930 German time), to patrol west of Douai. Six of 8 Naval left Auchel earlier, at 1720 (1820 German time), to patrol Henin-Liétard-Vitry, led by Flight Commander A R Arnold. No.1 Naval in fact had their engagement, around Fresnoy and Gavrell at between 1900 and 1940, and despite them reporting a fight with 'red Nieuports' this was long after the Richthofen fight in which he downed Albert Cuzner, unless, as we shall see, someone recorded the time wrongly.

It was obviously 8 Naval that bore the brunt of Jasta 11's attack. The Squadron's six pilots were: Arnold (N5458), R A Little (N5493), A R Knight (N5477), P A Johnston (N5449), R McDonald (N5472) and Cuzner (N5472). Rex Arnold later reported engaging the enemy near Douai at 9,000 feet, timed at 1840 (1940 German time, spot on von Richthofen's report time). He spotted five Albatros Scouts 2,000 feet below, but as he attacked his engine began to pop and bang, threatening to cut out so he had to break off and head for the lines. Bob Little, meantime, reported going down on five red-painted Albatros Scouts and one green-coloured one. He spoke of seeing a red one attacking a BE near Monchy, which was probably Lothar, at 1815 (1915), but heavy AA fire caused him to lose sight of it. When he saw the Albatri again they were heading north and he attacked, also seeing another Triplane heading down, which in fact was R P Minifie of 1 Naval.

Strangely, while both pilots compliment each other in their reports, Minifie records the time as being 1915 – an hour later, but this has to be a mistake, a mistake compounded by a report by H V Rowley of 1 Naval who also records fighting a red Albatros at 1930.

By the time the fight started, Little and Minifie were almost over Douai aerodrome but then Little passed a Triplane going west with three red Albatri on its tail, and he thought he saw the number '16' on its fuselage. Both Little and Minifie fired at one Albatros whereupon it spun down and crashed on the aerodrome itself.

Richard Minifie was then desperately fighting off several hostile scouts, which were slowly driving him down. Little was also hotly engaged but both were experienced air fighters and managed to get themselves out of trouble. A last look at the aerodrome and Little saw several people running to the crashed German fighter.

Victor Rowley (N5425) attacked a red Albatros at 12,000 feet over Gavrelle firing 50 rounds from 50 yards. It went into a vertical dive, seemingly out of control, but he was then attacked by three hostiles and his engine cut out, probably hit, so he headed down and west for the lines, managed to scrape over and make a force-landing in a field south of Bapaume.

Minifie got back in his 'Manaos Britons No.1' marked Triplane (a presentation machine) having been fought down to 50 feet but he got back to land at Auchel with his left-hand longeron shot through, and nine other good sized holes in the Tripe. Cuzner failed to return. Canadian troops reported a Triplane down at Courrières, which seems a trifle north of Richthofen's location but it is in the general area. However, both 1 and 8 Naval reported one aircraft lost, 1 Naval losing N5441. Flight Sub Lieutenant H M D Wallace, after landing south of Bapaume having been wounded in the arm, believed he was inside German lines, so set fire to his machine, only to find he was on the right side of the trenches after all. Another 1 Naval pilot, FSL A P Heywood was also wounded but made a successful forced landing inside British lines.

Who did bring down Captain Barwell? In fact he got into a fight with Offizierstellvertreter Edmund Nathanael of Jasta 5, and was shot down over Beaumont, south of Henin Liétard, at 2000 (2100 German time), which is more than enough time to fly to the lines, get into a scrap, fight for half an hour (assuming that part of the story is correct) with an equally experienced air fighter, and be brought down.

Von Richthofen was flying Albatros DIII Nr.2253/17, but for the last time. On the 30th he finally went on leave, having achieved more than his 50 victories.

CUZNER,
ALBERT EDWARD
FLIGHT SUB-LIEUTENANT 8 SQUADRON RNAS

BORN ON 30 August 1890, 'Eddy' Cuzner was brought up and educated at the Model School and at the Collegiate Institute in the Canadian capital, Ottawa, before going on to the University of Toronto. A fine sportsman and a good scholar, Cuzner graduated Bachelor of Arts in 1915 and then took a course in forestry (1915-16). He volunteered for the Royal Naval Air Service in May 1916, taking private flying lessons at the Curtiss Aviation School, Toronto. He was awarded the Royal Aero Club Aviators Certificate (No.3627) on 3 September 1916 and sailed for England on the SS *Corinthian* on 16 September 1916. He received flying instruction at Redcar before being sent to Naval 8 on 8 March 1917. Eddy Cuzner had flown fifteen patrols with his Squadron before his final OP on 29 April 1917. His body was never recovered and he is commemorated on the Arras Memorial to the Missing, France. He was in his twenty-seventh year.

18 JUNE 1917

VICTORY NO.53

The Germans found the body of an airman named Ellis in the burnt out two-seater, but the other could not be identified, being too badly burned. This crew had taken off from their base at Proven, six kilometres north-west of Poperinghe, at 1100 to do a Photo Op. They reportedly fell at Sheet 28.C.8.c, the position given by the 38th Division Artillerymen who saw them fall.

Von Richthofen was flying Albatros DIII Nr.789/17. *(cont)*

RE8 No.A4290
9 SQUADRON RFC ENGINE
No.887 WD 4754
GUNS: 17045; A3903

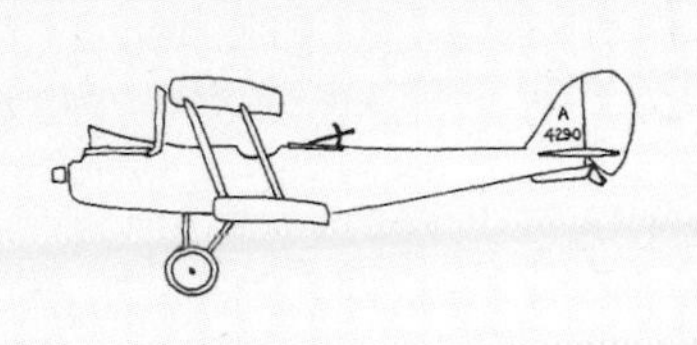

VON RICHTHOFEN'S Combat Report:
1315 hrs. Hof Struywe, Square V.42, this side of the line. RE2 (burnt).

Accompanied by my Staffel, I attacked at 2,500 metres north of Ypres, on this side of the line, an English artillery RE. I fired from shortest distance some 200 shots, whereafter I zoomed over the enemy plane.

In this moment I noticed that both pilot and observer were lying dead in their machine. The plane continued without falling, in uncontrolled curves to the ground. Driven by the wind, it fell into Struywe's farm * where it began to burn after hitting the ground.

BARON VON RICHTHOFEN

WEATHER: FINE IN THE MORNING, BUT HEAVY STORM IN THE AFTERNOON.

* Probably Stray Farm, map reference C 3c., ½ Km east of Pilckem, five Km north of Ypres.

Right: Next of Kin Memorial Plaque, British War Medal and Allied Victory Medal awarded, posthumously, to the family of Lt H C Barlow.

ELLIS,
RALPH WALTER ELLY
LIEUTENANT 9 SQUADRON; ROYAL GARRISON ARTILLERY

RALPH ELLIS lived at 'Crossdale', Berrylands Road, Surbiton, Surrey at the outbreak of war. He volunteered for service and was commissioned into the Royal Garrison Artillery. He learnt to fly at his own expense and was awarded the Royal Aero Club Aviators Certificate (No.4243) on 21 February 1917. Transfer into the RFC followed and, after pilot training, he was posted to 9 Squadron on the Western Front. His body was never recovered for burial and he is commemorated on the Arras Memorial to the Missing, France.

Below: Lt H C Barlow, surrounded by members of III Platoon, 'A' Company, 20th Battalion, Lancashire Fusiliers. A 'Bantam' Battalion, the 20/ Lancashire Fusiliers consisted of volunteers below the height of 5 foot, 3 inches.

BARLOW,
HAROLD CARVER
LIEUTENANT 9 SQUADRON; 20/LANCASHIRE FUSILIERS

THE SON OF Frank Barlow, JP, and his wife Mary of 'Woodville', Marple, Cheshire, Harold was born in 1891. He was educated at Leighton House School, Reading and Manchester University. A partner in the family firm of Thomas Barlow & Brothers, Eastern Merchants, he saw it as his duty to join one of the locally raised units and was gazetted into a 'Bantam' Battalion, the 20th (Fourth 'Salford Pals') Battalion, Lancashire Fusiliers, on 21 May 1915. He successfully applied for transfer to the Royal Flying Corps and after training he was awarded his 'Wing' and sent to join 9 Squadron in France. His body was never recovered and he is commemorated on the Arras Memorial to the Missing, France. He was twenty-seven years old.

23 JUNE 1917

VICTORY NO.54

SPAD VII No.B1530
23 SQUADRON RFC

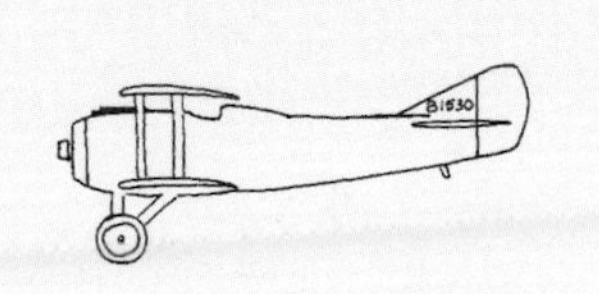

VON RICHTHOFEN'S Combat Report:
2130 hrs, north of Ypres. Spad one-seater.

I attacked, together with several of my gentlemen, an enemy one-seater squadron on the enemy's side. During the fight I fired at a Spad some 300 shots from shortest distance. My adversary did not start to curve and did nothing to evade my fire. At first the plane began to smoke, then fell, turning and turning to the ground, two kilometres north of Ypres, without having been caught.

BARON VON RICHTHOFEN

WEATHER: CLOUDY, WITH BRIGHT INTERVALS: VISIBILITY VERY GOOD AT TIMES.

Pilots of 32 Sqn. Left to right: H R Carson, C Wilderspoon, W Amory, A A Callender, J C Russell, E C Spicer, M A Tancock, R W Farquhar and Farson.

For years this victory has eluded historians' and researchers' efforts at identification. On the face of it, provided Richthofen's aircraft identification was correct, it had to be either a machine of 23 Squadron RFC (the other British Spad Squadron, No.19, was too far south at this time), a French or perhaps a Belgian aeroplane.

The problem with 23 Squadron, and its parent 22 Wing, is that virtually all its records have not survived. A study of the French units show that only GC12 – the Storks – were on the Ypres front at this period, and their only casualty this day was an NCO pilot of N.73 being seriously injured in a landing accident at 1840. Although it does not say if combat damage resulted in the crash, the time is still too early to agree with Richthofen's 2130 claim (2030 Allied time). We can also discount any Belgian involvement, as there were no Belgian-flown Spads at the Front at this time.

Continuing to dig, the 5th Brigade War Diary was perused, which embraced 23 Squadron and 22 Wing. Here was discovered a combat report by Second Lieutenant D P Collis which fitted exactly with all the known circumstances. Problem solved.

According to this report, three Spads were on an OP north of Ypres at 2015 – Collis (B1531), Farquhar (B1530) and Second Lieutenant D A A Shepperson (B1696). They were at 8,000 feet and sighted a formation of six Albatros Scouts, later increased to nine, north-east of the town. Collis led the attack and he saw Farquhar single out one Albatros, close right up to within 20 yards, firing, but then another German fighter slipped in behind him. Collis attacked this machine and drove it away, then attacked a second German, but was then engaged himself by three others. Shepperson came to his rescue, and then a general mêlée ensued, during which Collis observed an aeroplane go down on fire.

Collis then saw Farquhar hit and go down. The Spad had had its radiator and petrol tank shot through and he had to rapidly head down and away. It was

Above: Line up of 23 Squadron's Spads.

Right: 2/Lt D P Collis (in dress) while in PoW camp (with Capt G H Cock MC 45 Sqn). Collis had been in the fight with Jasta 11 on this evening and wrote the combat report which identified Farquhar as victory number 54.

undoubtedly the vaporising petrol and over-heating engine that produced the smoke and smoke-like plume Richthofen saw, as Farquhar headed down, fast, before his machine caught fire.

Collis himself, still fighting, headed back pursued by three hostile fighters, while Shepperson was hotly engaged by four others. This scrap continued for some minutes, the pilots now down to 1,500 feet, until the arrival of a patrol of Sopwith Pups, whereupon the Albatros pilots broke off and headed away eastwards.

Farquhar got back safely, although with a damaged machine, but not damaged sufficiently for a loss report to be completed; the damage was repairable at squadron level. On 7 July Farquhar who, because of Collis' report was credited with an Albatros in flames on the 23rd, was in combat again flying B1530 and gained his sixth and final 'victory' with 23 Squadron, an Albatros DV out of control over Zillebeke.

Richthofen, significantly, did not specifically mention that his victim had crashed, merely that it had gone down smoking to the ground without him seeing it pull out. Farquhar was obviously keen to get down as fast as possible, streaming petrol, and although we do not know if he force-landed behind the Front or managed to get back to his base at La Lovie – or even the forward airfield they used at Elverdinge – he most definitely survived and so did his Spad. The important thing, however, is that the time, locality and facts fit Richthofen's 54th victory claim.

Collis, Shepperson and Farquhar were all back in action the following morning, on a patrol led by Captain R L Keller (with other pilots). Significantly, Farquhar was not flying the shot–up B1530, but B3505. They were in combat at 1000, Collis being shot up this time and forced to land near Dickebusch (B1531) but he survived. Captain Douglas Percy Collis became a prisoner of war on 10 August 1917, brought down near Wervicq by three enemy fighters while suffering from engine trouble (Max Müller Jasta 28).

Von Richthofen was flying Albatros DV Nr.1177/17. This machine was reported as having a red fuselage and tailfin, red spinner, struts and wheel covers. Upper wing and elevator surfaces were mauve and green pattern camouflage, while undersurfaces were turquoise. The crosses were outlined in white. He was now flying the improved DV model, in place of the DIII.

FARQUHAR,
ROBERT WALLACE
SECOND LIEUTENANT 23 SQUADRON

BORN ON 4 February 1898, Robert was the son of a prominent local Food Preserve Merchant George Farquhar and his wife Florine C Farquhar of 528 Lordship Lane, Dulwich, London SE22. Robert was a student of music before joining the Royal Flying Corps in 1916. After qualifying as a pilot, he first flew in France with 18 Squadron with whom he claimed one 'victory'. He next was transferred to 23 Squadron and, becoming an adept Spad pilot, claimed five further 'victories' before July 1917, thus becoming an 'ace' in his own right. In the early summer of 1918, he was instructing in the No.1 School of Flying and Gunnery before finally joining 32 Squadron in the last great push to the victory he was destined never to see. On 24 September 1918, flying an SE5a, Farquhar added a Fokker DVII (OOC) to his list of 'victories'. Farquhar's luck finally ran out and he died of wounds on 30 October 1918, less than two weeks before the Armistice. At 0825 on the morning of the day he died, he took off in an SE5a (D6132) as part of an Offensive Patrol led by another 'Ace', an American from New Orleans Captain A A Callender (eight 'victories'). They were last seen fighting at the unusually low height of 1,000 to 1,200 feet over Ghislane, east of Douai. Incredibly, Farquhar, Callender (E6010) and Lt W Amory (D3440) all fell victims to von Richthofen's Jasta 2, although, happily, Amory survived. Their conquerors included the German 'aces', Leutnants Ernst Bormann (16 'victories') and Alfred Lindenberger (also 16 'victories', although 4 were achieved in the Second World War). Farquhar is buried in the Auberchicourt British Cemetery, France (Fr.1196). He was twenty years old.

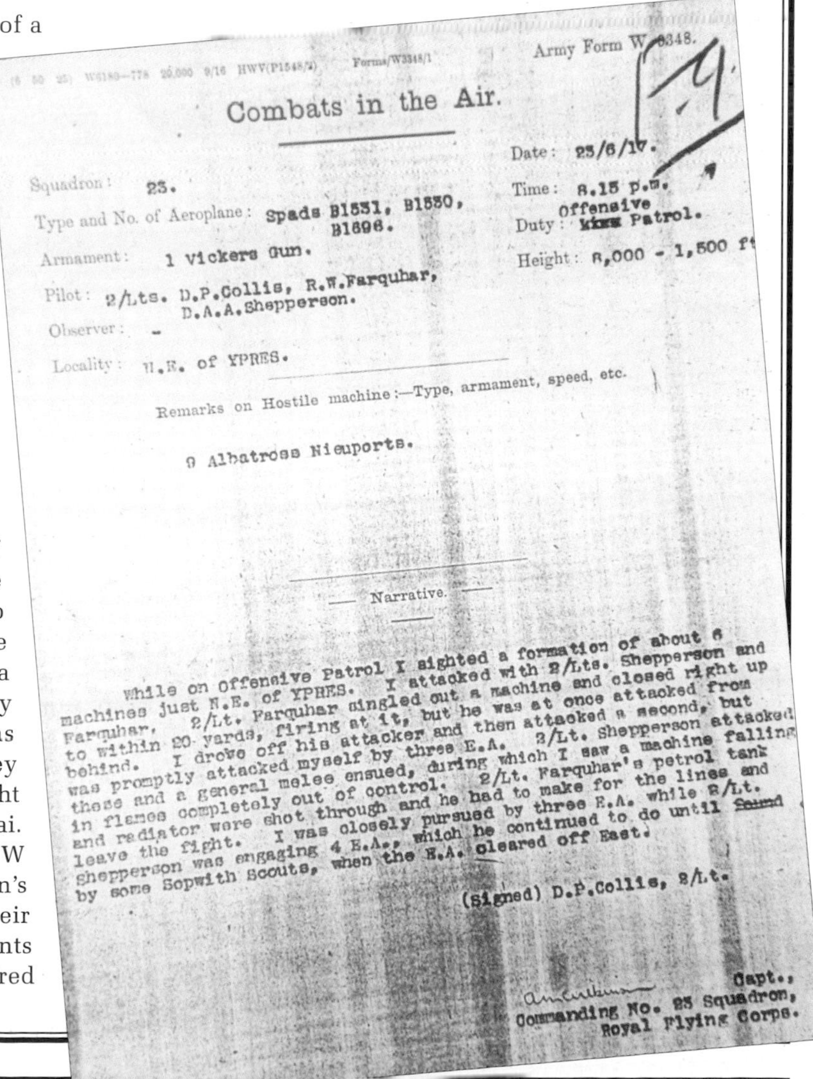

Army Form W. 3348.

Combats in the Air.

Squadron: 23.

Date: 23/6/17.

Type and No. of Aeroplane: Spads B1531, B1530, B1696.

Time: 8.15 p.m.

Armament: 1 Vickers Gun.

Duty: Offensive Patrol.

Height: 8,000 - 1,500 ft

Pilot: 2/Lts. D.P.Collis, R.W.Farquhar, D.A.A.Shepperson.

Observer: -

Locality: N.E. of YPRES.

Remarks on Hostile machine:—Type, armament, speed, etc.

9 Albatross Nieuports.

Narrative.

While on Offensive Patrol I sighted a formation of about 6 machines just N.E. of YPRES. I attacked with 2/Lts. Shepperson and Farquhar. 2/Lt. Farquhar singled out a machine and closed right up to within 20 yards, firing at it, but he was at once attacked from behind. I drove off his attacker and then attacked a second, but was promptly attacked myself by three E.A. 2/Lt. Shepperson attacked these and a general melee ensued, during which I saw a machine falling in flames completely out of control. 2/Lt. Farquhar's petrol tank and radiator were shot through and he had to make for the lines and leave the fight. I was closely pursued by three E.A. while 2/Lt. Shepperson was engaging 4 E.A., which he continued to do until ~~found~~ by some Sopwith Scouts, when the E.A. cleared off East.

(Signed) D.P.Collis, 2/Lt.

Capt.,
Commanding No. 23 Squadron,
Royal Flying Corps.

24 JUNE 1917

VICTORY NO.55

DH4 No.A7473
57 Squadron RFC
Engine No.2275173
WD 16052
Guns: 20473; A3353

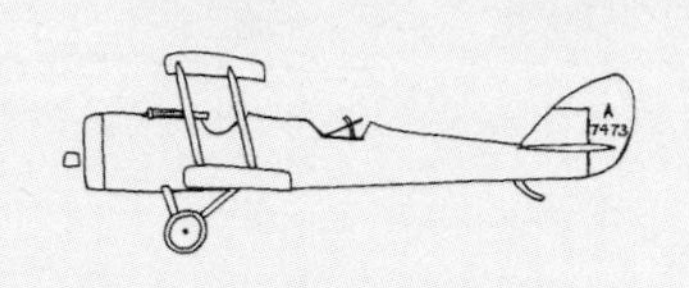

VON RICHTHOFEN'S Combat Report: 0910 hrs, between Keibergmelen and Lichtensteinlager, this side of the lines. De Havilland DD.

With six machines of my Staffel, I attacked enemy squad consisting of two reconnaissance planes and ten fighters. Unimpeded by the enemy fighters, I managed to break one of the reconnaissance planes with my fire. The fuselage fell with the inmates into a hangar between Keibergmelen (sic) and Lichtensteinlager, this side of our lines. The plane exploded when crashing on the ground and destroyed the hangar.

Baron von Richthofen

Weather: fine but cloudy, visibility good in early morning and again in the evening.

There were a number of problems for Floyd Gibbons in trying to identify this victory, despite it falling inside German territory. Firstly the report, or certainly the translation, showed the date as the 26th rather than the 24th. Secondly the time had been noted as 2110 (9.10 pm), instead of 0910. Thirdly, one place name was written as Keibergmelen, instead of Koelenbergmolen ('Cold Mountain Windmill'), and to confuse others, he again added something to the report, the words 'one-seater' after de Havilland DD (double dekker).

Once the correct date is discovered – the Nachrichtenblatt clearly shows it as the 24th, shot down near Becelaere – things become a little clearer. Koelenbergmolen is just south of Becelaere, and 57 Squadron were flying a Photo Recce sortie to Becelaere – two aircraft, only one of which returned.

However, these two machines – DH4s, ie de Havilland DDs – had taken off at 0740 and 0745 in the morning, not in the evening. A7473 was last seen in a spin at 9,000 feet over Becelaere, so one must assume that somewhere along the line, 'am' in Richthofen's report, became 'pm'. In any event it would seem, even for summer, to be a bit late in the day for a Photo Op, despite reported good visibility.

Obviously the Germans had an airfield south of Becelaere (Lichtensteinlager refers to a camp in a clearing or quarry), the luckless crew and their disintegrating 'Four' crashing into a hangar, where either its fuel tank exploded or perhaps other fuel or even some bombs in the hangar blew up, creating the explosion observed by Richthofen.

The two DH4s had an escort of eight Sopwith Triplanes of 10 Naval Squadron led by Flight Lieutenant Ray Collishaw (N5492), the pilots noting the 12 to 15 Albatros Scouts they engaged, as being bright red, mottled red or mottled green. They first spotted the hostile machines at 0805 high above the de Havillands and began to engage. Despite these Triplanes fighting off the Albatri and claiming at least one destroyed by Collishaw – he saw one set of wings rip away from the fuselage and the machine crash near Passchendaele – they were unable to prevent one 'Four' from being shot down. Flight Lieutenant J E Sharman (N6307) saw it happen but was too heavily engaged to help. He also saw an Albatros break up and thought it was one he had just shot at but it may have been Collishaw's victim. Two other Naval pilots suffered gun stoppages which did not help protect the DHs.

McNaughton and Mearns had been with 57 Squadron since the early spring, when the unit had been flying FE2b pushers. Their luck ran out this June morning.

Von Richthofen was flying Albatros DV Nr.1177/17.

MCNAUGHTON, NORMAN GEORGE

CAPTAIN 57 SQUADRON MC

THE SON OF barrister D Norman McNaughton and his wife, Christina, of 4 Grenville Place, Cornwall Gardens, South Kensington, London, Norman junior was born in May 1890. Like his three brothers, Norman was educated at Loretto School (1904-09). On leaving school, he secured a position on a cattle ranch in the Argentine but, on the outbreak of war, hurried home with the thousands of other British Latin American volunteers from all over the central and southern Americas. He secured a Special Reserve commission in the Royal Flying Corps on 21 July 1915, the very day that he graduated from flying school and gained the Royal Aero Club Aviators Certificate (No.1453). Pilot training with the RFC followed and he was awarded his 'Wings' on 1 December 1915. Posted to France, he joined 20 Squadron on 14 January 1916, and before long was flying operationally over the Front. On 21 April 1916, during a 2nd Army Reconnaissance, he was wounded in the leg. Despite his wound, he managed to land his machine without mishap at Abeele. After recovering from his injuries, McNaughton, by now an Acting Captain and Flight Commander, returned to the Front to join 57 Squadron. Captain McNaughton and his observers accounted for five hostile aircraft, including two 'out of control' between Gommecourt and Sailly on 4 March 1917 (with 2/Lt H G Downing in A1955) and, on 29 April 1917, again with Downing (A6365), one destroyed over Noyelles (pilot fell out). Saddened and angered by the news that his brother, Hamish Ian, a Second Lieutenant with 'E' Battery, Royal Field Artillery, had been killed in action in Macedonia on 24 April 1917, McNaughton redoubled his already considerable efforts. Now an 'ace', he was next awarded the Military Cross, the announcement being made in the *London Gazette* of 1/6/1917, page 5995:
'For conspicuous gallantry and devotion to duty when acting as a patrol leader in numerous combats. On one occasion he led his formation against an enemy patrol and himself drove down two hostile machines. He has set a fine example of courage and skilful leadership'.
His body was never recovered and he is commemorated on the Arras Memorial to the Missing, France. He was twenty-seven.

MEARNS, ANGUS HUGHES

LIEUTENANT 57 SQUADRON; 9/BLACK WATCH (ROYAL HIGHLANDERS)

BORN ON 13 December 1895, the son of Alexander Ashton Murray Mearns and his wife, Annie Webster Hughes Mearns, of 'Links', Montrose, Forfarshire. At the outbreak of war, Mearns, an exceptional scholar, was a student of medicine at St Andrews University, having already passed the first of his professional examinations. He had joined the University Officer Training Corps in 1913 and, as soon as his examinations allowed, he volunteered for active service, subsequently being commissioned into the 11th (Special Reserve) Battalion of the Black Watch. He was then posted to the 9th (Service) Battalion of his regiment on 14 March 1916, and remained on their strength until his successful application for transfer to the Royal Flying Corps was approved on 11 March 1917. Mearns often flew as observer to the Commanding Officer of 57 Squadron, Major L A Pattinson, before flying with McNaughton. His remains were never recovered for burial and he is commemorated on the Arras Memorial to the Missing, France. He was twenty-two years old.

25 JUNE 1917

VICTORY NO.56

RE8 No.A3847
53 Squadron RFC
Engine No. 569 WD 3685
Guns: A3544; 23595

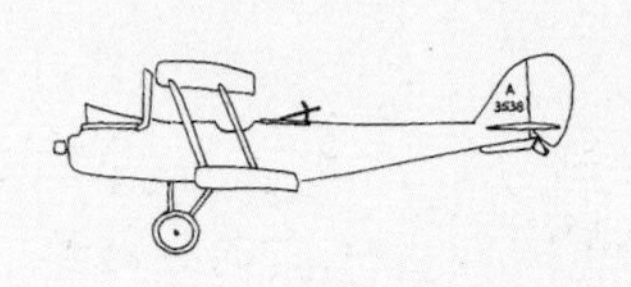

VON RICHTHOFEN'S Combat Report:
1840 hrs, above trenches near Le Bizet, other side of the line. RE plane.

I was flying together with Leutnant Allmenröder. We spotted an enemy artillery flyer whose wings broke off in my machine gun fire. The body crashed burning to the ground between the trenches.

Baron von Richthofen

Weather: fine, clouding over towards evening.

This crew set off from their base at Bailleul (town ground, just south of the town), just a couple of kilometres from the Belgian frontier, at 1635. They were tasked to carry out an artillery shoot.

A little over an hour later they were seen shot down by a hostile aeroplane, nose-diving into the front lines in position P.27.d.87.71; the position on the RFC loss report being given as Sheet 28, U.16.A.

The type of machine and location are correct, Le Bizet being just north of Armentières (over the border into Belgium). The hostile machine was also referred to as a red Albatros, and there were only three Allied planes claimed by the Germans this day: this RE8, a Triplane to Allmenröder later that evening, and a Spad by Off Stv. Walter Lang of Jasta 1. Von Richthofen was flying Albatros DV Nr. 1177/17.

Earlier, on 7 June, Bowman had been low flying over the British trenches, only to have his engine stop, but whether hit by a bullet from the ground was not determined. He crash-landed by a dressing station, and hit his mouth on the compass, but after three or four days at the 30th General Field Hospital (4 APO, BEF), he returned to the Squadron on the 10th, writing home that he and his observer were alright.

Right: Manfred's father visits Jasta 11. (L to R): Georg Simon, Karl Allmenröder, Kurt Wolff, Lothar von Richtofen, Manfred, Wolfgang Pluschow, Major von Richtofen, von Hartmann, Konstantin Krefft, Hans Hintsch.

BOWMAN,
LESLIE SPENCER
LIEUTENANT 53 SQUADRON; 4/KING'S OWN ROYAL LANCASTER REGIMENT

LESLIE BOWMAN was born on 21 June 1897, the only son of Dr Richard Oxley Bowman, MD, and his wife, Nora Louise, of 'Lightburn House', Ulverston, Lancashire. He was educated at Seascale Preparatory School and Clifton College (1911–14). As soon as he was old enough, he volunteered for service and was gazetted Second Lieutenant into the 4th (Territorial) Battalion of his county regiment on 23 December 1914. Sent to the Front in December 1915, he served in the trenches in the Picardy and Arras areas, being slightly wounded on 7 May 1916 when a bullet which had already passed through another man standing alongside him then hit him. He transferred to the Royal Flying Corps in July 1916 and was given his 'Wings' on 24 September 1916. He returned to France on 23 December 1916, but this time as a pilot with the RFC. Promoted to Lieutenant on 4 January 1917, he was again slightly wounded on 6 June 1917, but was fit enough to resume his duties by the 20th of that same month and to celebrate his birthday in the Squadron Mess the following day. Five days later he lay dead in no man's land. His remains were never recovered and he is commemorated on the Arras Memorial to the Missing, France. He was barely twenty years old.

POWER–CLUTTERBUCK,
JAMES EDWARD
SECOND LIEUTENANT 53 SQUADRON; ROYAL FIELD ARTILLERY

The only son of Surgeon Major E R Power-Clutterbuck, AMS and Mrs C A Power-Clutterbuck of 'Rockstowes House', Uley, Dursley, Gloucestershire, James was born in 1894. He 'joined up' as a private soldier in October 1914, before being gazetted Second Lieutenant into the Royal Field Artillery on 29 January 1915. He served and was wounded both in the Gallipoli campaign and on the Western Front before successfully applying for transfer to the Royal Flying Corps. He had only been with 53 Squadron for three weeks when he was shot down and killed. Unlike that of his pilot's, his body was recovered by British troops in the front line and he is buried in Strand Military Cemetery, Ploegsteert, Belgium (Bel.451). He was twenty-three years old. The family's only other child, a daughter, had died some years earlier.

2 JULY 1917

VICTORY NO.57

RE8 No.A3538
53 Squadron RFC
Engine No. 29460 WD 12293
Guns: A1695; 24051

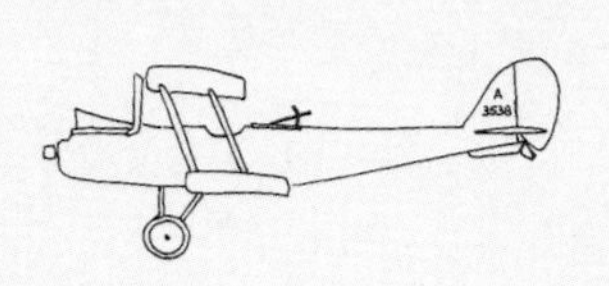

VON RICHTHOFEN'S Combat Report:
1020 hrs. Deulemont, between the lines. RE.
No details, as it fell burning.

I attacked the foremost plane of an enemy squadron. The observer collapsed with the first shots. Shortly thereafter, the pilot was mortally wounded. The RE reared up and I fired on the rearing aircraft from a distance of 50 metres with a few more shots until flames shot out of the machine and the opponent crashed burning.

Baron von Richthofen

Weather: cloudy but clear at times.

Once more it was 53 Squadron which suffered at Richthofen's hand. The REs were again providing their own escort aircraft to a camera-equipped machine for a Photo sortie to Tenbrielen, just north of Comines. Take off time is again not recorded, but the formation is reported as being attacked by nine hostile aircraft at 0840, behind Comines, and following a fight, A3538 went down.

Once more we have a time discrepancy of around 40 minutes; the German time would have been 0940, rather than 1020. The usual observer to Sergeant Whatley was Sergeant J I Moss, but on this sortie he flew with another pilot, whose machine carried the camera. As it happened, it was the first occasion Whatley and Moss had not flown together on a war flight.

A second escorting machine was also shot down, and the camera aircraft, according to Sergeant Moss, had to return to pick up another escort. Returning to the Front, Moss said that they were then attacked by the same bunch of enemy aircraft. Perhaps due to this time lapse, and if it was indeed Jasta 11 who engaged them a second time, this accounts for the time difference; that is to say, perhaps Richthofen incorrectly noted the time of the second indecisive fight when recording the earlier successful action.

Leutnant Gisbert-Wilhelm Groos claimed the second RE8, which fell near Messines, also in the British lines. It was his third of an eventual seven victories. His claim is noted as 1025 German time.

Messines and its famous and important (like Vimy) Kemmel Ridge, was right on the line, on the Ypres to Armentières road. Deulemont is located where the River Deule meets the River Lys, six kilometres north-east of Armentières. These were the only two RE8s shot down this day.

Von Richthofen was flying Albatros DV No.1177/17.

Note: There remains the question of which RE8 Richthofen actually did bring down. Another Squadron pilot, Sergeant Randall Kay, recorded in a letter to Whatley's mother that Whatley and Pascoe had fallen 1,000 yards north-east of Messines and were buried by the 3rd Division Australian Infantry.

Moss, also writing to Whatley's mother in August, recorded that they were seen falling, gliding into the front line trenches where he was buried. Moss does not mention the RE8 falling in flames, or crashing, but as he was writing to the mother he may not have done. The other crew were Captain Wilfred Palmer Horsley MC RFC (GL), who was killed, and Second Lieutenant A S Knight, severely wounded. They were flying A3249. However, Richthofen does say he attacked the foremost plane, so one might assume the camera aircraft – Whatley and Pascoe – would have been ahead of their escort. Also, as it was the first machine shot down, logic dictates that it would have fallen further east than the second loss (Horsley and Knight), and of course, Deulemont is further east than Messines.

Although Sergeant Kay noted a position more in keeping with Horsley and Knight – 1,000 yards north-east of Messines – he may be merely confusing the two aircraft, and he too was later wounded (on 12 July) and wrote from a hospital bed back in England, some time after the actual events.

Richthofen's confirmation witnesses on this occasion included Leutnant Wilhelm Bockelmann, Jasta 11, Hauptmann Kuhlman of AA Group 21, Leutnant Mann, Fluna Observer, and Leutnant Schröder, Air Defence Officer, Wijtschaete Gruppe.

WHATLEY,
HUBERT ARTHUR
SERGEANT (No.2056) 53 SQUADRON

HUBERT'S FATHER, AGRICULTURAL engineer Uriah Whatley, had had five sons with his former wife before marrying Eva, Hubert's mother. All in all, Hubert had five step brothers and two full brothers and so was well used to competing and handling himself in male company before he joined the Royal Flying Corps. The family lived at 7 High Street, Pewsey, Wiltshire, where Hubert had been born in 1898. Whatley was educated at his local council school where he demonstrated exceptional abilities. By the time Hubert joined the RFC in 1915, Uriah Whatley was dead and the family firm was in the charge of his two elder step brothers. Whatley's mature attitude and keen intelligence meant that he was quickly picked out for promotion. He learnt to fly at his own expense, gaining the Royal Aero Club Aviators Certificate (No.4515) on 16 April 1917. Within weeks, he had been awarded his 'Wings' and was flying with 53 Squadron in France. His usual observer, Sergeant J I Moss, had been allocated to another machine on the fateful day and so, for the first time, he was accompanied by an officer, Second Lieutenant F G B Pascoe. Although both bodies were recovered and buried by Australian troops, their graves were lost in the subsequent battles fought over the ground. Whatley is commemorated on the Arras Memorial to the Missing, France. He was nineteen years old.

PASCOE,
FRANK GUY BUCKINGHAM
SECOND LIEUTENANT 53 SQUADRON; 7/ROYAL IRISH FUSILIERS

THE SON OF the Reverend Frank Pascoe and his wife, Menella, of St George's Vicarage, Millom, Cumberland, Frank junior was born in 1897. He was educated privately and at St John's School, Leatherhead. He volunteered as soon as he was old enough to do so and was gazetted as a Second Lieutenant to the 7th (Service) Battalion, Royal Irish Fusiliers on 27 March 1915. Pascoe successfully applied for transfer to the Royal Flying Corps and, after training as an observer, was sent to join 53 Squadron in France. His first flight with Sergeant Whatley as his pilot was his last. His body was recovered from the crashed RE8 and buried by Australian troops who were in the vicinity. The grave was lost in the fighting that followed and so he is commemorated on the Arras Memorial to the Missing, France. He was twenty years old.

SHOT DOWN

It was unfortunate for the new Jagdesgeschwader that its commander was so soon knocked out of combat after his return from leave. But he was fortunate to survive the fate meted out to so many of his adversaries.

On this morning, the FE2s of No.20 Squadron flew a Central Offensive Patrol, taking off from their airfield at Ste-Marie-Cappel, located just south of Cassel, midway between St Omer and Bailleul. The patrol area would cover Comines-Warneton-Frelinghein, between Ypres and Armentières.

Six of the lumbering two-seat pushers lifted off at 0950 hrs led by Captain Donald Charles Cunnell, Hampshire Regt/RFC:

A6512 Capt D C Cunnell/2/Lt A E Woodbridge
A6376 Lt J Crafter/Lt A G Bill
A1963 2/Lt T W MacLean/Lt R McK Madell
A6547 2/Lt N V Harrison/2/Lt S F Thompson
A6498 2/Lt C R Richards/2/Lt A E Wear
A6419 2/Lt W Durrand/Lt S F Trotter

The RFC Communiqué for this day stated: 'An OP of 20 Squadron engaged about 30 Albatros Scouts in several formations. The German machines came much closer than usual and attacked keenly. Captain Cunnell and Second Lieutenant Woodbridge drove down four out of control. Second Lieutenant Richards and Lieutenant Wear also drove down one out of control. All our machines returned.'

The FEs usually took with them some 20 lb bombs to drop on targets of opportunity, and this day was no exception. Cunnell led his formation over a well known dump at Houthem and let go their bombs. Soon after turning back from the north, the large group of enemy fighters was seen approaching, having positioned themselves between the lines and the British machines. Soon the FE crews were involved in a fierce engagement over Comines-Warneton, at varying heights from 12,000 down to 3,000 feet, lasting from 1040 to 1120.

This is a long time for an air battle, but the FEs were involved in a deadly retreating, running fight, using their defensive circle tactics, much like the traditional scene of Red Indians attacking a wagon train, but moving.

The FE crews later reported that the hostile fighters showed considerably more spirit than usual of late and, of course, this was Richthofen's new formation and all were keen to do well and engage. It did, however, work both ways, for it enabled the FE gunners in particular the chance to engage the attackers at very close range.

None of the crews had any idea they were fighting Richthofen's new Circus, particularly Albert Edward Woodbridge, but he was later to acknowledge that several of the Albatros machines were red. Although none of the German machines appear to

Right; 2/Lt A E Woodbridge of 20 Squadron who was credited with wounding Richthofen on this day.

Left: FE2 crew, showing observer operating camera. Note pilot's fixed Lewis gun and observer's flexible Lewis guns.

Right: 2/Lt C R Richards, one of 20 Squadron's pilot's whose gunner 2/Lt Wear also claimed a Scout in this fight.

have been destroyed in this encounter, von Richthofen himself was hit in the head and went down to make a forced landing.

In November 1927, Woodbridge, by then a pilot in the RAF serving with No.58 Bomber Squadron at Worthy Down near Winchester, wrote to Floyd Gibbons. He had earlier met Gibbons concerning the encounter with von Richthofen and then, out of the blue received several letters from a complete stranger following the 'Liberty Magazine' articles which were the forerunner to Gibbons' book. Woodbridge says:

'Now all this is very nice but if I remember at the time of our interview, we didn't quite decide whether it was actually I who fired the shot which wounded the German ace. The fact that he was wounded in that particular scrap on that day in July 1917 is, I think, correct but what proof have you that it was my machine? As Cunnell was the leader with streamers, his machine might have been more conspicuous but then the deputy leader also had streamers arranged in a different manner. You see, there must have been more than one Hun shot down out of control in that fight and I fail to see why I should be given the credit unless you have some confirmation from the other side.'

To his credit, Woodbridge was quite right in wondering if he had indeed fired the bullet that hit von Richthofen a glancing blow to the head. However, what appeared in Gibbons' book, was either journalese or Woodbridge had been persuaded to revise his thoughts. In the book Woodbridge is supposed to have said as the Albatri attacked: '...I think the first one was Richthofen. I recall there wasn't a thing on that machine that wasn't red, and God how he could fly! I opened fire with the front Lewis, and so did Cunnell with the side gun. Cunnell held the FE to her course and so did the pilot of the all-red scout. Then something happened. We could hardly have been twenty yards apart when the Albatros pointed her nose down suddenly ... We saw the all-red plane slip into a spin. It turned over and over and round and round. It was no manoeuvre. He was completely out of control ..'

Von Richthofen, for a moment, was completely paralysed. His hands dropped to his side, his legs dangled off the rudder and, as something had obviously effected his optic nerve, he was blind. The red fighter went down but fortunately for Richthofen he regained some mobility, his vision returned and he was able to switch off the engine. Looking below he found an area in which to land, finally putting his machine down in a field of high grass, near Wervicq, just inside the Belgian border.

That Cunnell and Woodbridge were credited with four out of control victories and Richards and Wear one give the former a four to one chance of having scored the telling hit, but it might just have been the latter. Even Stuart Trotter, who died in No.53 CCS soon after landing, is supposed to have hit an Albatros. In any event, history seems to have given the kudos to Woodbridge.

As already mentioned, Woodbridge later became a pilot, and after the war spent some time in civil aviation before joining the RAF. Cunnell was killed by an exploding AA shell six days after the von Richthofen encounter, his observer, Lieutenant A G Bill (not Woodbridge on this occasion), managing to bring the FE down to a forced landing despite being wounded. Cecil Roy Richards MC, an Australian, was shot down, wounded and taken prisoner on 17 August.

Of the others in this fight, Crafter was reported missing on 8 July, Tom McLean killed 21 September, Thompson became a prisoner on 19 August, Albert Wear died of wounds 11 September, and even Woodbridge was wounded on 31 July, although he later returned, scoring more victories with Bill Durrand MC.

Of the other FEs on 6 July, A6376 had to make a landing at Abeele airfield, its oil tank shot through, A1963 landed at 42 Squadron's base at Bailleul, its magneto and tail boom damaged, while A6419 also landed at Abeele, its observer mortally wounded.

Richthofen had had a near encounter with death, but survived to return to his command in August, but he was never the same man again. He had made the mistake, if it was a mistake, of coming in too close to an adversary and giving the antagonist a shot too good to miss. He would only make one more mistake in his life, and that was to be his last – on 21 April 1918.

Left: Pilot and gunner positions in an FE2.

16 AUGUST 1917

VICTORY NO.58

NIEUPORT XXIII NO.A6611
29 SQUADRON RFC
ENGINE NO.T5480 J
GUN: 47117

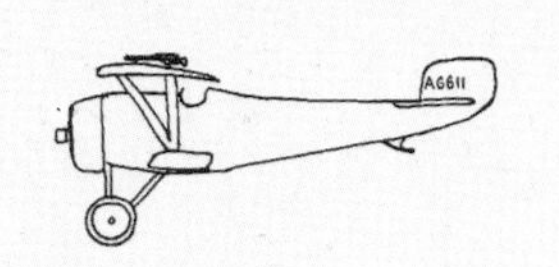

VON RICHTHOFEN'S Combat Report:
0755 hrs.

At about 0755, accompanied by four aircraft of Staffel 11, I pursued a small flight of Nieuports. After a long chase, I attacked an opponent and after a short fight I shot up his engine and fuel tank. The aeroplane went into a tail spin. I followed right after it until just above the ground, gave it one more shot, so that the aeroplane crashed south-west of Houthulst Forest and went right into the ground. As I was about 50 metres behind him, I passed through a cloud of gas from the explosion that made it hard to see for a brief moment.

BARON VON RICHTHOFEN

WEATHER: FINE.

As far as is known, this was the first patrol Richthofen flew following his wounding. The British had opened their attack at Langemarck (Ypres) due to the improved weather, so activity around the area began early, Jasta 11 having to rise early too.

For a long time the identity of the British pilot was not known. Despite a feeling of nausea and dizziness, von Richthofen spotted a Nieuport, stalked it, gained a firing position and sent it down to crash in the Polygon Wood area.

No.29 Squadron were flying a ground patrol which began at 0625, to the 11 Corps front. There were four Nieuports, going out in pairs: Second Lieutenants J Collier and C W Cudemore, J D Payne and W H T Williams. Payne later reported that he and Williams were attacked by eight Albatros Scouts, the leader of which dived on Williams. Payne turned and fired at the enemy leader but after about five rounds his gun jammed. He last saw Williams at about 600 feet, going down but appearing to be under control, with some of the enemy machines on his tail.

According to the RFC War Diary, 29 Squadron had been engaged on ground strafing around Zonnebeke and Polygon Wood. Williams had fired an estimated three drums of Lewis ammunition into the Wood, and Collier reported firing three more into the Iron Cross Redoubt and the Wood. It was then that the Albatros Scouts struck.

It had not been a good week for Williams. Two days earlier he had crashed in A6784 as he was landing back at 1805, following an OP and the machine was wrecked.

Von Richthofen was flying Albatros DV Nr.2059/17, and due to his feeling unwell, he quickly returned to base after this combat.

WILLIAMS,
WILLIAM HAROLD TRANT
SECOND LIEUTENANT 29 SQUADRON

BORN IN 1898, the son of Dr William Griffiths Williams and his wife of 5 Dingle Hill, Liverpool, Will Williams was educated at Liverpool College and Liverpool University. From school, he decided to follow his father's profession and passed the Northern Universities Matriculation Examination to join an MB degree course at Liverpool University. He had passed the first year's examinations and embarked upon the second year when he suddenly decided he had to volunteer to fight for King and Country. Having been a member of the University OTC, he was immediately sent for cadet training to the Inns of Court OTC on 23 October 1916. Next, he was directed to the RFC Cadet School and, on 19 April 1917, he was gazetted Second Lieutenant. Pilot training followed and he was awarded his 'Wings' in the early summer of 1917. His first posting was to 28 Squadron in England, where he built up his flying hours prior to being sent to No.2 AD in France on 1 August. Now with 46 flying hours in his logbook, he was sent to join 29 Squadron at the Front. Returning from an OP on 14 August, he executed a poor landing and, in the process, crashed and completely wrecked A6784. His good fortune in walking away from the crash unhurt ended abruptly barely two days later when he fell under the guns of von Richthofen. Picked out of the wreckage by German troops, he was carried to a nearby Military Hospital. His wounds, however, were extremely severe and despite excellent medical attention he died six days later on 22 August 1917. He is buried in the Harlebeke New British Cemetery, Belgium (Bel.140). He was nineteen.

Right: Four German ground personnel salvage items from a downed Nieuport 17, believed to be one brought down by Manfred von Richthofen.

26 AUGUST 1917

VICTORY NO.59

Spad VII No.B3492
19 Squadron RFC
Engine No.15293
Gun: L1639

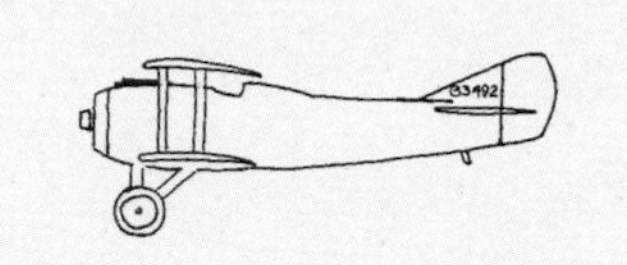

VON RICHTHOFEN'S Combat Report:
0730 hrs, between Poelcapelle and Langemarck, this side of our lines. Spad one-seater. English.

During a fighter patrol with four gentlemen of Staffel 11, I saw beneath me a single Spad flying at an altitude of 3,000 metres above a solid cover of cloud. The adversary was probably trying to find flying German artillery planes.

I attacked him, coming out of the sun. He tried to escape by diving, but in this moment I shot at him and he disappeared through the clouds. Upon pursuit, I saw him beneath the cloud, first plunge straight down, then at about 500 metres altitude explode in the air.

Due to the new, very poor incendiary ammunition my pressure line, intake manifold, exhaust, etc, were again so damaged that I would not have been able to pursue a merely wounded opponent. Consequently, he would have escaped and I had to see that I glided as far from the Front as possible.

Baron von Richthofen

Weather: fine.

Captain John Leacroft (B3559) led the patrol of Spads out from Poperinghe at 0540 – a sortie recorded as a Special Mission – to attack airfields at Bisseghem and Marche. With him were Lieutenants H C Ainger (B3616), A A N D Pentland (B3620), A R Boeree (B3520), R L Graham (B3618), and J G S Candy (B3552). C P Williams and Lieutenant F E Barker (B3570) had taken off about 20 minutes earlier and were in roughly the same area.

On the way out the larger patrol met two DFW C-type two-seaters. One flew right across the front of the formation, turning towards the Spads and was fired on by Candy and Graham.

Ainger then fired and two more Spads went after it. The two-seater turned on its side and went down in a fairly steep spiral in front of Jerry Pentland who also fired. Ainger followed it down and saw it crash into a field near Moorsele, without coming out of its spiral. The observer seemed to have been hit (in fact he had been killed) as his gun was pointing straight up, doing nothing. The DFW had streamers attached to its elevators and mainplane struts, and was an aircraft of Flieger Abteilung Nr.5, the observer being Leutnant Max Haase. Little seems to have been recorded about the eventual attack on the airfields, but on the way home ground targets were attacked, then more enemy aircraft were engaged.

A number of Albatros Scouts came up from the general direction of Bisseghem and Heule, on the north-east outskirts of Courtrai, Leacroft shooting one down out of control, seen by Ainger to crash near the aerodrome. While all this was going on, it seems that Williams and Barker became embroiled with German fighters on the edge of this action. Barker was hit, wounded, and forced to land with a damaged aircraft inside British lines (20T.22.B.9-5). Now on his own, Williams was picked off by Richthofen, crashing near Poelcapelle, eight kilometres north-east of Ypres.

Von Richthofen was flying Albatros DV Nr.2059/17.

WILLIAMS,
CONINGSBY PHILIP
SECOND LIEUTENANT 19 SQUADRON

'CON' WILLIAMS was living with his parents at 'Avondale', Holmfield Road, Leicester when the war started. His father, Coningsby Ford Williams, ran a cycle shop in London Road, Leicester, where his son had picked up his keen interest in engineering. Con was educated at Wyggleston School and was an active member of the local St Philip's Church. His

body was never recovered and he is commemorated on the Arras Memorial to the Missing, France.

Right: Informal pose, and on another mode of transport.

1 SEPTEMBER 1917

VICTORY NO.60

RE8 No.B782
6 Squadron RFC
Engine No.278 WD 3558
Guns: 45722; A5170

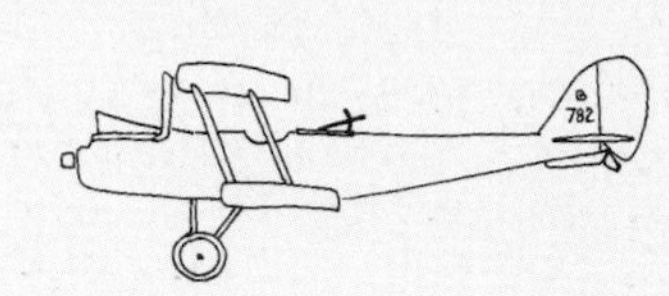

VON RICHTHOFEN'S Combat Report:
0750 hrs, near Zonnebeke, this side of the lines.
RE 2, English.

Flying my Triplane for the first time, I attacked, together with four of my gentlemen, a very boldly flown artillery-reconnaissance aircraft. I approached and fired twenty shots from a distance of 50 metres, whereupon the adversary fell out of control and crashed this side, near Zonnebeke. Apparently the opponent had taken me for an English Triplane, because the observer in the machine stood upright without making a move for his machine gun.

Baron von Richthofen

Weather: low clouds and rain with bright intervals.

For many years the date of this combat has been recorded as 2 September, mainly due to the casualty report being so dated, but the War Diary does confirm this crew as being lost on the first, which coincides with Richthofen's report.

The RE8 crew had taken off from their base at Abeele, south-west of Poperinghe, at 0550 to fly the inevitable Art Obs sortie to Polygon Wood, east of Ypres. If what Richthofen supposed, that the two British airmen thought they were seeing a Naval Sopwith Triplane approaching, is true, we can only imagine those last fateful moments as, perhaps, a sense of relief at knowing some friendly fighters were nearby, turned initially to a trace of anxiety as the approaching aircraft seemed to be coming a little too close for comfort, and then to incredulity and shock as it opened fire. Did they even then wonder why this Allied aircraft was firing at them, had its pilot mistook them for a German two-seater, was it a German flying a captured Sopwith…

Observers on the ground saw the RE8 attacked and begin the long spin into the ground. Zonnebeke is just six kilometres east of Ypres, its high ground much sought after, and nearby Polygon Wood a well known landmark. A crew of No.4 Squadron also reported seeing an RE8 attacked by an enemy aircraft at this time, and watched it go down in a spin over Polygon Wood before losing it in ground mist. When Madge returned from Germany in late 1918, he confirmed that he had been wounded in the back by Richthofen's fire and he lost consciousness, waking up several days later in a German hospital.

Von Richthofen was flying Fokker F1 Nr.102/17. It was not red, but displayed the standard Fokker dope-streaked finish, natural aluminium cowling, the black crosses on a white background and white rudder. Under-surfaces were turquoise. Its Werke Nr.1729, it was first tested on 16 August and delivered to JG1 on the 21st. Kurt Wolff was to be killed in it during a fight with 10 Naval Squadron on 15 September.

MADGE,
JOHN BRISTO CULLEY
LIEUTENANT 6 SQUADRON; ROYAL FIELD ARTILLERY

BORN IN CALCUTTA, India in 1892, John Madge was educated at George Watson's College (1909-12) and at Edinburgh University (1912-14) where, when war broke out, he was studying medicine and living at 116 Gilmore Place in the Scottish capital. Volunteering immediately, he was gazetted as Second Lieutenant to the Royal Field Artillery on 19 September 1914. Promotion to Lieutenant followed on 19 March 1915 and, in 1916, he transferred to the Royal Flying Corps. He first joined 18 Squadron on 5 August 1916 as an observer on probation, before qualifying as a pilot and going on to join 6 Squadron at Abeele on 1 September 1917. Madge was badly wounded in his fight with von Richthofen and spent much of his captivity in German hospitals until he was finally repatriated on 17 December 1918. On his return, Madge's hospitalisation continued for some months before he finally returned to his studies at Edinburgh University. John Madge qualified as a Doctor of Medicine (MB ChB Univ Edin) in July 1924, twelve long years and a World War having intervened since the commencement of his degree course in 1912. Doctor Madge's medical career took him around the country. In the Twenties, he lived in East Ealing, London. The Thirties and Forties saw him residing and working in Shipton-Thorpe, York before, in the early Fifties, he moved on to Warsop Vale, Shirebrook, Nottinghamshire. John Madge died at his retirement home in the tiny village of Newton by Toft, Lincolnshire on 2 February 1957 leaving a widow, Gladys Marie.

KEMBER,
WALTER
SECOND LIEUTENANT 6 SQUADRON; 7/LANCASHIRE FUSILIERS

BORN ON 2 February 1891, Kember was the son of dentist Walter Kember and Mrs Kember of 'Sarina', 5 Dover Road, Birkdale, near Southport, Lancashire. He was educated at Bickerton House School, Birkdale and at Liverpool University, where he was studying for a Licentiate in Dental Surgery when the war came. Volunteering immediately, he left his studies to join his local Territorial Battalion, the 7th King's Liverpool Regiment, as a private soldier. Kember accompanied his battalion to France on 8 March 1915, and went 'over the top' on 15 May 1915, the first day of the Battle of Festuburt. He was wounded in the action, suffering flesh wounds in the legs. After recovering in a London hospital, he was selected for officer cadet training and was eventually gazetted as Second Lieutenant in the 7th Battalion, Lancashire Fusiliers. Transferred to the Royal Flying Corps in July, 1917 he had been with 6 Squadron only a matter of days when he was killed. He is buried in Harlebeke New British Cemetery, Belgium (Bel.140). He was twenty-six years old.

3 SEPTEMBER 1917

VICTORY NO.61

SOPWITH PUP NO.B1795
46 SQUADRON RFC
ENGINE NO.35123 WD 10972
GUN: A4723

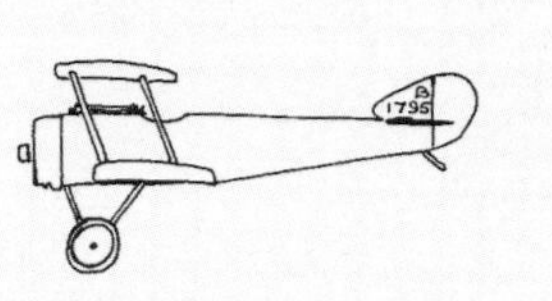

VON RICHTHOFEN'S Combat Report: 0735 hrs, south of Bousbecque, this side of the lines. Sopwith 1, B1795; Motor No: 35123 (80 hp Le Rhône Type 'R') Occupant: Lieutenant A F Bird, made prisoner, unwounded.

Along with five planes of Staffel 11, while engaged in a fight with a Sopwith single–seater, I attacked, at a height of 3,500 metres, one of the enemy machines. After a fairly long dogfight, I forced him to land near Bousbecque. I was absolutely convinced I had a very skilful pilot in front of me, who even at an altitude of 50 metres did not give up, but fired again, and opened fire on a column of troops while flattening out, then deliberately ran his machine into a tree.

The Fokker Triplane FI No.102/17 was absolutely superior to the British Sopwith.

BARON VON RICHTHOFEN

WEATHER: FINE.

The Pup formation took off from their airfield at Ste-Marie-Cappel, which is just south of Cassel, at 0545, to carry out a Southern Offensive Patrol. They were engaged by Jasta 11, and obviously Bird fought gallantly until his machine was knocked out, and even then made the most of his last moments by firing his gun at some ground troops, and then deliberately smashed up his aircraft by running it into a tree. Richthofen's location is confirmed, as British observers reported the Pup falling over Wervicq, which is just below Bousbecque on the Menin to Armentières road. When he returned from Germany in November 1918, Bird reported that his engine had been hit and that he in fact, had suffered a slight flesh wound.

Bird's Squadron suffered severely this day. Apart from him, three other pilots were lost: Lieutenant K W McDonald (RE & RFC), an acting Flight Commander, Lieutenant S W Williams (4th Sussex Regt & RFC) and Lieutenant F B Barager RFC (SR), a Canadian, wounded. They were not all lost in this first patrol, but all went down during the morning's efforts.

Von Richthofen was indeed flying Fokker F1 No.102/17.

From Richthofen's testimonial of Bird's skill, it seems he had improved from an unsteady beginning. Earlier, on 30 August 1917, Bird was ferrying Pups to the Squadron. He crashed B1701 at St Omer at 1215, having flown the machine over from England. Taking A648 from No.1 AD, he crashed this on landing at St-Marie-Cappel having collided with another Pup on the ground.

BIRD,
ALGERNON FREDERICK
LIEUTENANT 46 SQUADRON; 2/5 NORFOLK REGIMENT

THE SON OF Mr and Mrs F A Bird of 'The Retreat', Hunstanton, Norfolk, Algy Bird was born in 1896. He was educated at Hunstanton, Lowestoft and Felsted School (1910-13). After the turn of the century, the family moved to 'St. Augustine's Priory', Chapel Street, Lynn, Norfolk. From Felsted School, Bird went on to the City and Guilds College, London, where he interrupted a course in engineering to volunteer for the Army. On 2 June 1915, he was commissioned as a Second Lieutenant into the 2/5th Battalion, Norfolk Regiment. Transfer to the Royal Flying Corps followed and by September 1917 he was flying as a scout pilot with 46 Squadron. After his shooting down, and following an exchange of pleasantries with von Richthofen, Bird was marched away to a prison camp where he was confined until 14 December 1918 when he was, at last, repatriated and could return to Norfolk and to running the family firm of F A Bird, Downham Mills Ltd, Flour Millers and Merchants. Algy Bird married soon after the war and he and his wife, Winifred, lived at 'The Beeches', London Road, Downham Market, Norfolk until his death on 24 August 1957.

Below left: Von Richthofen and Anthony Fokker lounging on the fuselage of the former's 61st 'victory' (Lt A F Bird). Fokker is wearing the vanquished pilot's helmet and flying coat!

Below right: Bird's wrecked Pup B1795 'Z'.

Bottom: Lt A F Bird, Norfolk Regiment and RFC. Von Richthofen (on left) greets his latest 'victory' in person.

23 NOVEMBER 1917

VICTORY NO.62

DH5 No.A9299
64 Squadron RFC
Engine No.101287 WD 15883
Gun: A6038

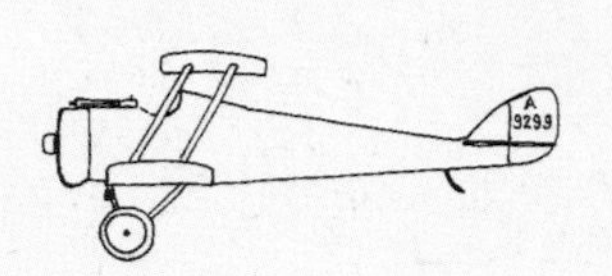

VON RICHTHOFEN'S Combat Report:
1400 hrs, south-east corner of Bourlon Wood.
DH5. Englishman.

At 1400 hrs, shortly after I had forced an Englishman to land at the west side of Bourlon Wood, I attacked a DH5 north of Fontaine (Notre Dame) at about 100 metres height. After the first shots, the Englishman started to glide downwards, but then fell into the south–east corner of Bourlon Wood. I could not observe the plane hitting the ground.

Baron von Richthofen

Weather: low clouds

No.64 Squadron were based at Le Hameau, west of Arras, but were operating from an advanced landing ground on this afternoon. They had been flying in support of the Battle of Cambrai for several days; in his own account after the war, Boddy stated that on the 20th his machine had been hit by rifle fire and had to return drenched in petrol.

On the 23rd they were detailed to support an infantry attack against Bourlon Wood. They took off at 1240 and during the ground strafing Boddy had noticed '.. some of the red machines of Richthofen's "Circus" a few thousand feet above, but there were some SE5s up there too, so I left it at that.'

Obviously he had no idea about Richthofen's attack. A bullet fractured his skull and he crashed between two trees into the Wood, breaking both thighs, one being completely crushed by the engine as it was pushed back into the cockpit area.

From his report it does seem as if Richthofen had accounted for two aircraft in this fight, but had only submitted a claim for one. Boddy himself reported that one of the Squadron pilots, who had had a forced landing near the front lines – the first of Richthofen's victims? – brought a rescue party out to Boddy's wrecked machine, under heavy fire, and got him back to a dressing station on board a tank. His smashed leg was later amputated.

This other pilot was Captain Henry Thornbury Fox Russell (1/6 Royal Welsh Fusiliers TF & RFC), who'd been downed by a 'shell' (A9490). He reported his DH5 had had its tail blown off at low level by a shell but he had survived and scrambled into the front lines. He had then seen Boddy come down and as the pilot did not get out of the wreck he decided to help. Reaching the crash-site he got the badly injured Boddy out and, with the help of a passing tank and its crew, got him back safely. For his rescue of Boddy, Fox Russell received the Military Cross. Fox Russell, from Anglesey, had a brother, a doctor serving with the Royal Army Medical Corps who won the Victoria Cross for exceptional gallantry in bringing in

Left: The crudely altered Balkenkreuze taken from the right side of von Richthofen's Fokker Triplane 425/17 which was auctioned in London in 1994. It had been cut from the machine by L/Cpl A E Putman, 32 Battalion, AIF, who later gave it to a doctor who saved his life. Until its sale it had hung on the doctor's wall.

Below: The Balkenkreuze taken from the left side of the same Fokker Triplane which currently resides in the Royal Canadian Military Institute in Toronto, given to them by Captain Roy Brown. The bare fabric in the centre shows the signature of 209 Squadron pilots in April 1918.

Overleaf:The central monument of the combined Memorial to the Missing of the Royal Flying Corps, the Royal Naval Air Service and the Royal Air Force.

BODDY, JAMES ALEXANDER VAZEILL

LIEUTENANT 64 SQUADRON OBE (1953)
18/DURHAM LIGHT INFANTRY

BORN ON 17 July 1895, James Boddy was the only son of the Rev A A Boddy FRGS and Mrs G G Boddy of Pittington, County Durham. His father was Vicar of All Saints, Monkwearmouth, Sunderland. Boddy's mother, a relation of John Wesley, was of Huguenot descent, hence all of her children bore the name 'Vazeill'. He was educated at Monkton School ('the best goalkeeper we have ever had') and Emmanuel College, Cambridge. He interrupted his university education to join up, being commissioned Second Lieutenant into the 18th (Service) Battalion of his county regiment on 18 September 1914. Promoted Lieutenant on 16 March 1915, he and his Battalion left Liverpool on the SS *Empress of Britain* in December of the same year, bound for Egypt. The voyage was eventful, their ship colliding with an empty French troopship and one of their escorting cruisers, HMS *Dublin*, being torpedoed. Dreary duties on the Suez Canal came to an end when the Battalion was ordered to France, arriving in Marseille on 11 March 1916. Boddy successfully applied for transfer into the RFC in November 1916, serving first as an observer with 11 Squadron. James's introduction into the air war was unfortunate in that on his very first sortie, with 2/Lt F Crisp as pilot, he was shot down. Their FE2b was brought down at Hebuterne on 22 November 1916, a year and a day earlier than his eventual exit from the war under the guns of the Red Baron. They were shot down into the front line trenches by Halberstadt Scouts, a spent bullet hitting Boddy between the eyes, smashing his goggles and knocking him out. Just at the moment he regained consciousness, they crunched into the ground. In another of his actions, on 25 March 1917 he and his pilot, 2/Lt G Mackrell, encountered seven aircraft over the Scarpe Valley. Together with another crew, they drove down one of the enemy which was believed to have crashed, while another went down in a vertical nose-dive. Pilot training followed his period of service as an observer and, after graduating, he accompanied 64 Squadron to France on 15 October 1917. Boddy was badly wounded in the fight with von Richthofen and, although his life was undoubtedly saved by Captain Fox Russell (who received the MC for his bravery) the doctors had to amputate his leg. Boddy married Marjorie D'arcy in 1920 and lived for the rest of his life at 'Orchard House', Swithland Lane, Rothley, Leicestershire. He became a member of the Executive Council of the Royal British Legion, a Justice of the Peace and a Deputy Lieutenant of his county. Despite his disability, he served in the Home Guard throughout the Second World War. Boddy was awarded the OBE in the new Sovereign's Coronation Honours List in 1953 (*London Gazette* 1/6/1953 page 2957). He died the following year at the age of fifty-nine.

Right: Capt. H T Fox Russell.

wounded men. Their father was also a doctor.

Yet another pilot of 64 Squadron came down around the Bourlon Wood area, this being Lieutenant A A Duffus (A9295), escaping uninjured following a forced landing in some barbed wire. He'd been hit in the engine and fuel tank. Duffus had fired briefly at four enemy fighters, at some distance, before being hit, following a strafing attack. He just managed to clear the trees, flying west, and flopped down on the right side of the advance. Yet another candidate for the possible 'unclaimed' Richthofen victory on this day.

Either could have been the aircraft hit initially by von Richthofen, with perhaps a slight emphasis on Duffus, as Fox Russell, we must assume, knew what hit him. As von Richthofen later had in his collection the serial number of Boddy's DH5, it would seem to clinch the matter. However, with three DH5s coming down in or near the Wood, it is possible that somehow someone cut the serial number of Boddy's machine and sent it on to the Baron. One would not expect Richthofen to have been so near the Front himself to get the number, as it was a very active front line, and one could easily forgive someone sent up to the fighting zone to get it, for cutting one from the first crashed aircraft he found. There has to be, therefore, a slight question: ie: did whoever cut the number, do so from the easiest wrecked aircraft rather than 'the' actual one Richthofen shot down? One could say too, that perhaps Richthofen was claiming the first aircraft, which he said landed, and not the second which he said he did not see hit the ground.

The three locations given for the three DH5s were: Boddy F.20.a; Fox Russell F.14.d; and Duffus F.19.c. During the afternoon, 64 Squadron were to lose two more aircraft in this area to ground fire, in positions F.20.b and E.29.d. Both pilots survived.

Floyd Gibbons selected Lieutenant A Griggs of 68 (Australian) Squadron as Richthofen's victim on this occasion. Griggs, despite his unit, hailed from Meridan, Mississippi, USA. However, Griggs was seen still in the air at 1545, one hour and 45 minutes after Richthofen made his claim, although the position was stated as that same south-east corner of Bourlon Wood. He came down nearby but reportedly to ground fire, dying of his wounds.

The Fokker Triplane had been found to be defective, just as the early Albatros Scouts had been, when Richthofen swapped to the Halberstadt. Now, with the Triplanes withdrawn for modifications, Richthofen and his pilots reverted to the Albatros DV. On this occasion he flew a DV Nr.4693/17, with red engine cover, fuselage and tail, a machine later displayed in the Berlin Museum.

30 NOVEMBER 1917

VICTORY NO.63

SE5A No.B644
41 SQUADRON RFC
ENGINE No.1083 WD 8658
GUNS: 47634; A6597

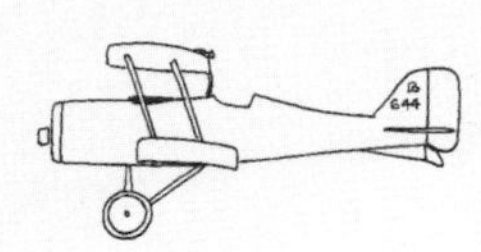

VON RICHTHOFEN'S Combat Report:
1430 hrs, near Moevres. Englishman; burnt.

Together with Leutnant von Richthofen and Leutnant Gussmann, we attacked an enemy one-seater squadron of ten Englishmen right above the trenches at 1430. After I had fired at several Englishmen, I fired from close range behind a single-seater, which after 100 rounds crashed in flames in the vicinity of Steinbruch Forest.

BARON VON RICHTHOFEN

WEATHER: CLOUDY

Above: SE5a.

Floyd Gibbons once again made a snap selection of a Captain P T Townsend of 56 Squadron as Richthofen's likely victim, just as he'd done with victory No.62. Townsend went down near Le Tronquoy, just to the north of St Quentin, whereas Moeuvres is 34 kilometres away to the north-west. Townsend went down at 1445 (1545 German time), so he loses out on two counts. In fact, OffStv Josef Mai of Jasta 5 got him.

The SEs of 41 Squadron were airborne from Lealvillers at 1300; they had only recently swapped their DH5s for SE5s. Captain Loudoun James MacLean (B38) and MacGregor were over Inchy-en-Artois at 1330, patrolling west of Bourlon Wood. Two enemy scouts were seen at 2,000 feet. Both SE pilots attacked, MacLean getting to within 50 yards of one German, fired 30 rounds and saw the EA turn over and go down in a spin and crash into the ground.

Turning to engage the other German, MacLean saw MacGregor fighting with it and went to help. Both British pilots came at it from opposite directions, MacLean from the front, MacGregor from the rear. MacLean then had to climb to avoid a collision and as he again turned, he saw MacGregor above the hostile but immediately afterwards saw him going down in flames, the enemy machine then making off north-eastwards.

Captain Meredith Thomas led the other Flight, including Lieutenant Russell Winnicott. They engaged three red Albatros Scouts north of Bourlon and to the west, Winnicott claiming one shot down and crashed, near Fontaine, which was seen by Thomas. Thomas himself claimed one shot down and crashed, just east of Rumilly at 1345. They followed this up at 1400 by Thomas, MacLean, Winnicott and Lieutenant Frank Howard Taylor downing a two-seater out of control over Rumilly.

Second Lieutenant Ernest Francis Hartley Davis, also in this patrol, was forced to return after a head-on attack by a German fighter. All pilots mentioned (other than MacGregor) were to become British aces. Jasta 10 lost Leutnant Friedrich Demandt on this day, shot down and killed near Flesquières, five kilometres south-east of Moeuvres.

Von Richthofen makes mention of his victim going down in flames, and says it was burnt. Everything else fits too: the time, place, quite a dogfight, etc. MacGregor had claimed an Albatros Scout out of control the previous day flying this same SE5a over Douai at 1050.

Von Richthofen was flying Albatros DV Nr.4693/17.

MACGREGOR, DONALD ARGYLE DOUGLAS IAN

LIEUTENANT 41 SQUADRON; ARMY SERVICE CORPS

THE ELDER SON of Councillor John and Mrs Elizabeth Stewart MacGregor of Leith, Midlothian, Donald MacGregor was born in 1895. He was educated at George Watson's Boys College, Edinburgh (1904–12) where he excelled both in his studies and on the playing fields. Leaving Watson's, he went on to a technical college in London to study motor engineering. Moderately 'well off' in his own right, he was settled into his house, 'Balnagowan', Finchley Road, Golders Green, when war broke out. He immediately offered his services and was commissioned into the Army Service Corps on 28 October 1914, being sent to France with the Indian Motor Ambulance shortly afterwards. Transfer to the Royal Flying Corps followed and he served first as an observer before qualifying as a pilot. After service with a squadron on the Front, he was brought home and, for a time, acted as a test pilot at Vickers. MacGregor turned down an offer of a post as a flying instructor which would have taken him to comparative safety in Canada, asking instead to be returned to France. His wish granted, he was ordered to join 41 Squadron at the Front. His body was never recovered and he is commemorated on the Arras Memorial to the Missing, France.

Right: [Late 1917] Fokker FI 102/17 flown by von Richthofen and later by Kurt Wolff.

12 MARCH 1918

VICTORY NO.64

BRISTOL F2B NO.B1251
62 SQUADRON RFC
ENGINE NO.275 WD 18637
GUNS: 55335; C9601

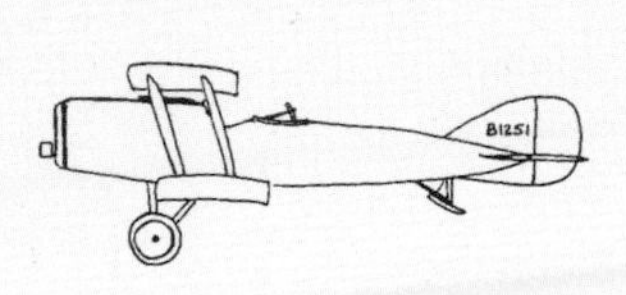

VON RICHTHOFEN'S Combat Report:
1110–1115 hrs, north of Nauroy, square 2858. Bristol Fighter No.1251. Motor: Rolls-Royce 200 hp 12 cylinder V-shaped No.275. Englishman.

Together with Leutnant Lothar von Richthofen and Leutnant Steinhauser, both of Jasta 11, we attacked an enemy squadron between Caudry and Le Cateau at an altitude of 5,500 metres, far behind our lines. The plane I attacked immediately dived down to 1,000 metres and tried to escape.

The observer had only fired high up in the air, had then disappeared in his seat and had only recommenced shooting shortly before the machine landed. During the fight we had been driven off to Le Catelet. There I forced my adversary to land and after doing this both occupants left their plane.

BARON VON RICHTHOFEN

WEATHER: FINE WITH FAIR VISIBILITY.

NB – the one hour time difference between Allied and German forces had ended on 10 March 1918, and would remain the same until 16 April, at which time the Germans were once more one hour ahead.

Although this is the first Bristol Fighter he had brought down since the famous fight with 48 Squadron back in April 1917, he appears to have made short work of this machine on this day. His fire had indeed wounded the observer, making it easier for him to finish them off and force them to land.

Nine Bristols had taken off at 0930 to fly an Offensive Patrol over the line Cambrai-Caudry-Le Catelet, in support of the British 5th Army front, going more than 20 miles over the lines. The British pilots saw the three hostile aircraft, but also saw a two-seater diving at the latter. Engaged then by the three Fokkers, B1251 was seen by the rest of the patrol to go down east of Cambrai, at about 1110; exactly the time of Richthofen's claim. Nauroy is ten kilometres north of Cambrai.

Captain Douglas Stewart Kennedy MC had been leading the patrol and they had been over the lines for nearly two hours and were due to break off within a few minutes but were then engaged by enemy aircraft. When the air fight finally began, Clutterbuck (aircraft letter 'T') endeavoured to secure a good position for his observer to fire, but then von Richthofen came at them, a burst of fire hitting Sparks in the left shoulder and arm, and he collapsed. Seeing this, Clutterbuck tried to dogfight the Triplane, but then his front gun jammed and he knew he was in trouble. His predicament was not helped by having an ejected cartridge from the rear Lewis gun flying into his front cockpit during the early stage of the action as Sparks tested his gun. This is what Richthofen had seen, recording that the observer '... had only fired high up in the air'. It had lodged between the tank and control column, which curtailed movements to climb and he had to descend. As he finally cleared the stick, they were then attacked. Sparks regained consciousness and tried to man his gun again, but the effort was too great and he crumpled once more. The Brisfit was severely shot about, with cut wires streaming back, then the fuel tank was holed. Switching to the emergency tank, he

Above: The brothers, Lothar and Manfred von Richthofen in front of a Fokker Triplane.

headed for the lines, but then this second tank was hit, and losing pressure the engine packed up. When he finally came down, Clutterbuck was just two miles short of the trenches, and both men were captured immediately. In fact they had come down in the German reserve line and were immediately taken by a German officer. Sparks had his wounds dressed in a dug out before they were both taken to Le Cateau where they were separated by their captors.

Sparks was taken to a hospital and on the second day was visited by a German air force officer sent, his visitor told him, by Baron von Richthofen himself. Following a very short interview he bade him farewell, offering Sparks half a dozen cigars, which he gratefully accepted. It was the start of four months in hospital for Sparks, then prison camp.

When he returned home, Clutterbuck said he'd been attacked by four Triplanes (the number also confirmed by Sparks), and one had followed him down, shooting both fuel tanks through. Once he'd landed, he was unable to set fire to the machine as German soldiers had arrived while he was still trying to get Sparks, wounded in both arms (sic), out of his cockpit.

No.62 Squadron were to lose four aircraft. Lothar brought down two at Maretz and at Clary, while Steinhauser brought his down north of Caudry. One of them was Captain Kennedy and his rear man, Lieutenant H G Gill (10th West Yorks & RFC), both leaping from their burning Bristol (B1247). The other two lost were B1520, Second Lieutenant C B Fenton RFC (GL)/Lieutenant H B P Boyce (15th Canadian Reserve & RFC), C4824, Lieutenant J A A Ferguson RFC (GL)/Sergeant L S Long.

Von Richthofen was flying Fokker Dr1 Nr.152/17 (Werke Nr.1864), the Triplane once more in favour and certainly a favourite of the Baron. It had red upper wings, cowling, wheel covers and tailplane. Also red were the rear aft fuselage (from edge of the cross) and the wing struts. The rest of the machine was in standard Fokker factory finish. The rudder was white and the crosses edged white also.

This Triplane had been tested on 2 November 1917 and delivered on 13 December. It was returned to the Fokker works at Schwerin on 18 March 1918 for wing modifications.

CLUTTERBUCK,
LEONARD CYRIL FREDERICK
SECOND LIEUTENANT 62 SQUADRON

CLUTTERBUCK LIVED AT 175 James Avenue, Brighton, at the time of the Great War. He served as a Sergeant (No.1973) with the Royal Fusiliers before transferring with the same rank (No.773) to the Motorised Machine Gun Section, Royal Artillery, going to France with that unit on 9 April 1915. He was commissioned Second Lieutenant on to the General List/Royal Flying Corps on 16 December 1916. After a period as an observer, he qualified as a pilot then received further extensive training on Bristol Fighters before he flew over to France with 62 Squadron in January 1918. Following his forced landing, Clutterbuck did not have the time to set fire to his Bristol Fighter. German troops swarmed up out of the shell holes surrounding them and took pilot and observer prisoner almost before their machine came to a halt. Clutterbuck remained in captivity until he was repatriated on 17 December 1918.

SPARKS,
HENRY JAMES
SECOND LIEUTENANT 62 SQUADRON MC; KING'S ROYAL RIFLE CORPS

A 'LONDONER', SPARKS was born on 28 March 1890, receiving his education at the local board school in Trafalgar Square, Stepney. In January 1908, he enlisted as a musician into the Royal Marines Band. Five years later, in January 1913, he purchased his discharge and entered civilian life. When the war came, Sparks, like so many others, thought that 'it would be over before Christmas'. By October 1915, it had become obvious that the war would last for years and so he joined the Royal Highlanders (Black Watch) as a private soldier (No.11803). Sent to France on 22 January 1916, he fought with his regiment in the trenches until selected for officer training in England. Commissioned as a Second Lieutenant into the 21st Battalion, King's Royal Rifle Corps in April 1917, it was not long before he returned to Flanders to join his new regiment as the Battalion Lewis Gun officer. On 31 July 1917, the opening day of the Third Battle of Ypres (the battle later to be better known by the single emotive word 'Passchendaele') the 21/KRRC were in support of the 123rd Infantry Brigade in the area of Zillebeke. After a day of extremely heavy fighting in torrential rain which churned up the ground and turned trenches into veritable quagmires, the enemy counter-attacked on the right flank of the 123rd Brigade at 1000. Two companies of the 21/KRRC were sent forward to stem the advance, and, in causing the enemy to retreat with heavy losses, Henry Sparks won the Military Cross *London Gazette* 29/9/1917, page 9979; Citation 9/1/1918, page 644:

"For conspicuous gallantry and devotion to duty, when all the officers of his company had become casualties, he took command and by his coolness and contempt for danger inspired confidence in the men left in his charge, holding the front line for forty-eight hours at a most critical time under terribly severe weather conditions. His capable handling and personal gallantry set a wonderful example to the men of his company".

In August 1917, a successful application for transfer to the RFC was followed by observer training and a posting to Home Service for a period from September 1917 to December 1917. In December 1917, Sparks was posted to 62 Squadron in France and was able to claim three 'victories' before being shot down himself. Wounded in the arm and shoulder by von Richthofen, Sparks was carried to a German dressing station, his wounds cleansed and bandaged, before being put on the back of a horse to be led away to the rear and into captivity. Two days later, laying in his hospital bed, he received a present of half-a-dozen cigars, sent with the compliments of Baron Manfred von Richthofen! Sparks remained a prisoner of the Germans until 13 December 1918, when he was repatriated. After the war, Sparks secured a position with the Inland Revenue as an Inspector of Taxes, living at 88 Murston Road, Sittingbourne, Kent.

13 MARCH 1918

VICTORY NO.65

Sopwith Camel No.B2523
73 Squadron RFC
Engine No.1527 WD 14656
Guns: C5739; A6499

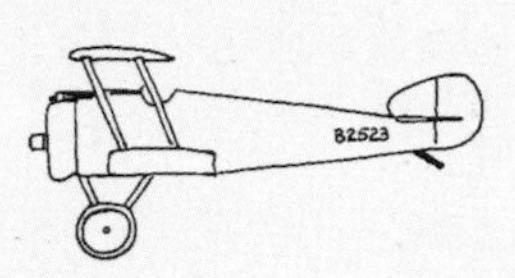

VON RICHTHOFEN'S Combat Report:
1035 hrs, between Gonnelieu and Banteux, in square 1853. Sopwith Camel. Englishman, wounded.

I started with Jasta 11 and fought later on with two Staffels of my group against 20 to 30 Englishmen (DH4s, SE5s and Sopwith Camels). I forced down a DH4 from 4,000 to 2,000 metres. My opponent glided down in the direction of Caudry with only very slowly working engine. The fight took place quite a distance behind our lines. The Englishman landed south of Le Terrière in square 2256. Harassed by Albatroses of another Staffel, I let my doomed adversary off, climbed to 3,200 metres, where I fought with several Sopwith Camels.

In this moment I saw an Englishman attacking one of my Staffel's planes. I followed him, approached to within 20 metres, and put holes through his benzine tank. Apparently I had hit the pilot, as the machine dived and plunged to the ground. The Englishman tried to land in the fighting area near Gonnelieu but smashed his machine just behind our lines.

Baron von Richthofen

Weather: fine; visibility fair.

The interesting thing about the beginning of this report concerns the DH4 he starts to shoot down. It appears disabled, with, seemingly, its propeller slowing down, indicating to Richthofen that its engine was working only very slowly. Rather than finish it off for another confirmed victory, he leaves it to two others. In fact it was not a DH4 but a Bristol F2b. (German pilots often confused the DH4, the BF2b and the AWFK8 machines, von Richthofen not being an exception.)

This machine was from 62 Squadron who lost two aircraft: one was B1207 flown by Second Lieutenant C Allen RFC (GL)/Lieutenant NT Watson (20th Middlesex Regt & RFC); the other, B1268, by Second Lieutenant NB Wells RFC (GL)/Lieutenant G R Crammond (Lancs Fusiliers & RFC). They were part of a ten-machine OP east of Cambrai, having taken off at 0900 and were last seen engaged by many enemy aircraft.

Pilots of Jasta 56 got the Bristols, Leutnant Franz Schleiff, the Staffelführer, finishing off Richthofen's target, which came down at Le Terrière, Leutnant Rudolph Heins bringing the other BF2b down at Marcoing. It is interesting that von Richthofen, presumably, did not contest this victory claim, for with his fame and standing he would more than likely have had it awarded as his 65th. It was Schleiff's eighth kill, gaining four more before he was wounded on 27 March, losing his left hand.

The Camels Richthofen now engaged were a patrol of 73 Squadron that had taken off from their airfield at Champien, east of Roye, way down on the southern sectors, to fly an OP south-east of Cambrai. At 1025 they became embroiled in an air battle losing two Camels, one flown by Heath, the other by Second Lieutenant James Noble Layton Millett, another Canadian, flying B5590.

One Camel was seen to go down in flames, which if correct must have been Millett as he was killed. Richthofen says his victim crashed, so is more likely to have survived, and Heath had been wounded as Richthofen thought. The other Camel came down north of Vaucelles, shot down by Leutnant Edgar Scholtz of Jasta 11, timed at 1040, his second of an eventual six victories. (He was killed in a crash on 2 May 1918.) Gonnelieu and Banteux are situated just to the west of the St Quentin Canal, 12 km south of Cambrai. Vaucelles is just a couple of kilometres north-east of this position.

Returning from prison camp on Christmas Day 1918, Heath wrote a long report on his final flight, saying their ten-man OP had met the Richthofen Circus totalling 22 fighters in all, in two groups, one above and one below. To quote:

'We immediately attacked the group below not noticing the group above. I engaged two EA and believe I brought both down but on my last dive was attacked by three EA from above, who shot my engine and both petrol tanks; two bullets hit me in the buttock. At the same time both my guns jammed. I broke off the fight as I was unable to do anything and tried to get back to our lines, followed by three EA which kept firing at me until about 1,500 feet from the ground, they stopped. I kept gliding to the lines and at about 200 feet loosened my belt as I expected to land in no-man's-land. In trying to land in trenches and shell holes, the machine turned upside-down and I was therefore unable to destroy it. It was impossible for me to get out, but several Germans gathered around, lifted the machine up so I could get out, surrounded me and captured me at the point of a bayonet.'

After some interrogation at the local battalion HQ, where his wounds were dressed, he went to Walincourt, was questioned again, then moved to Le Cateau where he was interrogated yet again, by a Corps Intelligence Officer. Each time Heath refused to divulge the number of his Squadron. He was finally sent off to the hospital at Walincourt after his flying kit had been taken away.

From 73 Squadron's viewpoint, Captain A H Orlebar (B7282) reported engaging some 35 Triplanes and Albatros Scouts south-east of Cambrai at 1015. He sent one Albatros down upside down, then dived on a Fokker which nose-dived and lost its top wing. He then saw a Camel under attack by four enemy fighters – probably flown by Second Lieutenant Hyatt, who landed at 23 Squadron's base badly shot up, but his guns jammed as he tried to intervene.

Captain Maurice LeBlanc Smith (B5572) also saw a Triplane diving on the tail of a Camel, which burst into flames. He saw the Triplane make a half-circle and he got in a good burst broadside on. The Fokker dived vertically then went into a wide right-hand spiral, but he had to leave it. Later a machine was reported lying on its side, smoking, in the German front line trenches.

Orlebar was credited with a Triplane destroyed, having seen the top wing break away. In fact the Dr1 was flown by Lothar von Richthofen, Nr.454/17, Staffelführer of Jasta 11. Rather than losing the whole of his top wing, only the top centre section came off, leaving the ailerons 'in situ', so Lothar was able to glide down, but stalled in trying to avoid some high-tension cables and crashed, near Awoingt. He was badly injured and away from the Front for four months.

There is another claimant for Lothar, Captain Geoffrey Forrest Hughes (an Australian) and his observer, Captain H Claye, in C4630. Soon after the end of the war, Hughes gave a graphic account of this whole action.

'... our big scrap on March 13 ... was by far the most amazing fight I ever had. We started off with 11 Bristols in two formations to patrol the Cambrai-Le Cateau road to keep the air clear for some DH4 bomb raids. I was leading my Flight with C Flight on top. A single Albatros came under my nose and went gently east in front of me. It was rather too obvious a decoy and a careful search revealed about 30 Huns in three formations down below, waiting for us.

'I decided to try and bait the Huns and manoeuvred to try and draw one formation away so that we could mop it up. This game of cat and mouse went on for an hour ... [but] I could not see an opening to attack. Meantime, another formation of Triplanes was coming in from the east at our height. 'By this time we had completed our 90 minute patrol ... so decided we'd done our job. To my horror, as I turned, two of my Flight began to dive on the 30 Huns below us. There was nothing for it but to go after them. The fight that followed is beyond description. I dived on a Triplane that was on the tail of one of my Bristols, firing till I had to pull away for fear of a collision. I have never seen anything like the tracers that streaked the air from the Triplanes that were round our tail in a semi-circle.

'Claye shot one down – its top wing fell off – but then his gun jammed and I was hard put to keep the Huns off our tail and I dived steeply. Then a single bright red Triplane came at us from above and when I saw he was gaining on us I decided to turn and fight him with the front gun. I did a sudden climbing turn and first got my sights on him, when he simply half-rolled over me and came down vertically, firing both guns. He was the only Hun I ever met who really was a wonderful shot, and the splinters fairly flew from my old Bristol. I did a half-roll, dived and managed to get clear, though he followed us to the lines. Staton got back, his machine shot about too, and later all but two got home.'

Hughes and Claye received the MC soon afterwards; Hughes died in 1951. Staton was Captain W E Staton MC DFC, another successful Bristol Fighter pilot. He and his observer claimed a Triplane and an Albatros out of control in this fight (C4619), his first two of an eventual 26 victories. Hughes claimed 11 victories in WW1.

Von Richthofen was flying Fokker Dr1 Nr.152/17.

HEATH, ELMER ERNEST

LIEUTENANT 73 SQUADRON; CANADIAN EXPEDITIONARY FORCE

BORN AND EDUCATED locally in Wallaceburg, Ontario, Canada, Heath was deeply interested in the military from an early age. A keen volunteer, he received his commission in the 24th Kent Regiment (Militia) in November 1915. He left Canada for England as part of an Artillery draft on 24 April 1917, and was soon sent across to France in charge of a party of replacements for the 3rd Division Ammunition Column. Shortly afterwards, a successful application to join the Royal Flying Corps saw him seconded to Reading on 3 July 1917. Following training, he was sent to join 73 Squadron who, equipped with Camel F1s, were set to depart for France on 9 January 1918. As part of 'A' Flight, he had flown only ten patrols with his Squadron before his encounter with von Richthofen, gaining the dubious distinction of becoming the Red Baron's first Camel 'victory'. Badly wounded in the fight, he was taken to a German Military Hospital where the doctors were able to remove some, but not all, of von Richthofen's bullets; three remained in various parts of his anatomy for the rest of his life. He was eventually repatriated on Christmas Day 1918, and was glad to return home to Canada early in the new year. He died in his home town of Wallaceburg in April 1965, following a long illness.

18 MARCH 1918

VICTORY NO.66

SOPWITH CAMEL NO.B5243
54 SQUADRON RFC
ENGINE NO.35751 WD 9400
GUNS: A2768; C6720

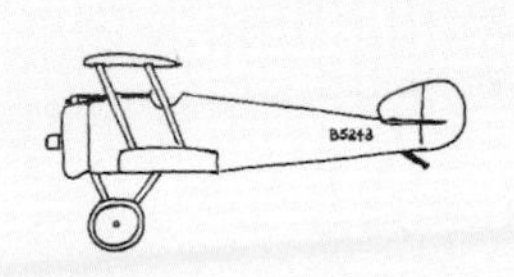

VON RICHTHOFEN'S Combat Report:
1115 hrs. Above the Molain-Vaux-Andigny road.
Sopwith Camel B5243. Engine: Clerget 35751.
1 Canadian, made prisoner.

I started with 30 planes of my Geschwader and flew to the Front, commanding all three Staffeln at 5,300 metres. Just as we were approaching the Front, I saw several English squadrons crossing our lines and flying in the direction of Le Cateau. The first squadron we came across was approximately at 5,500 metres altitude, and together with Leutnant Gussmann, Jasta 11, I shot down the last opponent, a Bristol Fighter. He lost his wings, and Leutnant Gussmann brought him down.

Thereupon, I took my 30 planes in hand, climbed to 5,300 metres and pursued two enemy squadrons which had made their way right through to Le Cateau. I attacked just when the enemy tried to fly aside and retreat. The enemy machine flying nearest to me, apparently a Bréguet or a Bristol Fighter, was fired upon by me and Leutnant Löwenhardt of Jasta 10. The tank was shot to pieces and I observed how the aircraft crashed straight down. Leutnant Löwenhardt brought it down.

Then I attacked from the centre of two English one-seater squadrons a plane flying pennants, and forced it to land near Molain.

BARON VON RICHTHOFEN

WEATHER: FINE

This is one of the few occasions Richthofen records being at the head of his Geschwader, and noting (confirming) other pilots' victories but in which he had a hand. It was obviously a morning of much activity, with so many British squadrons in evidence. The two-seaters were neither Bristols nor Bréguets, but DH4s.

No.54 Squadron had taken off from their base at Flez, 18 km due west of St Quentin, at 1000 to fly an OP to Busigny, 24 kilometres north-east of St Quentin, which was a long way over, and Le Cateau is a further eight km further north-west from there. In fact they were part of an escort to the DH4 bombers of 5 Naval Squadron attacking Bohain aerodrome, along with ten SE5a fighters.

Leutnant Siegfried Gussmann's Bristol (sic) went down south of Jancourt at 1050. Löwenhardt's adversary went down south of Le Cateau at 1110. It is recorded as a French Bréguet but once again it was a DH4. It was Erich Löwenhardt's 13th victory of an eventual 54, and Gussmann's third of an eventual five. One DH4 failed to return while another got back riddled with bullets, the pilot having been wounded in three places but still managing a good forced landing not far from his home base at Mons-en-Chaussée, west of St Quentin.

The Camels were hard hit. No fewer than five fell in this battle: Captain F L Luxmore (C6720), Lieutenant N Clark (B5421), Second Lieutenants G Russell (C1566), W G Ivamy (B5243) and E B Lee (C1576). Two SEs also failed to get back. One of the Naval DH4 pilots involved, Captain C P O Bartlett DSC, described the fight as one of the greatest aerial battles of the war. Captain F M Kitto of 54 Squadron also reported it as the biggest scrap he'd ever been in.

Of the Camels, one fell to Vizefeldwebel Edgar Scholtz, Jasta 11, east of Bohain at 1115. Leutnant Fritz Friedrichs of Jasta 10 got another over Awoingt at 1125. Leutnant Hans Kirschstein, Jasta 6, shot one down south-west of Vaux-Andigny. A non-Circus pilot, Vizefeldwebel Benedikt Jehle of Jasta 16, shot down one over the airfield at Busigny at 1115, his first and only victory. Hans Joachim Wolff of Jasta 11 got one of the SEs.

Ivamy was last seen in a fight with a large number of enemy aircraft two miles east of Busigny, which is in the fight area. The combat had developed around 1100 hrs five miles east of Busigny aerodrome, 54 Squadron's ten Camels up against an estimated 40 to 50 hostile fighters. This would be about right if Bavarian Jasta 16 had reinforced JG1's 30. Second Lieutenant Eric A Richardson (C6703) was one of only two claimants in this fight, reporting a Triplane in flames, Second Lieutenant N M Drysdale claiming an Albatros DV out of control (B5241). Jasta 16 lost Leutnant Franz Riedle, killed near Molain in this combat.

When Ivamy came home from Germany in mid-December 1918 he said they had been engaged with 50 German fighters and he'd been hit in the petrol tank. The engine would not pull up [start] on the gravity tank, so he had to go down.

Some time after the war, Ivamy recalled that this day they were escorting DH4s to bomb the German aerodrome at Molain, along with ten SE5s. They crossed the lines south of St Quentin, flying at 12,000 feet, 3,000 feet above the 'Fours'. Just after the bombers dropped their bombs, the German fighters attacked. Flying this day as deputy flight leader and at the rear of the formation, he carried wing streamers, just as Richthofen described in his report.

He was at the back and in the highest position, which was why he was hit first. He immediately collected bullets in the main and emergency fuel tanks, being saturated with petrol, blinded, and with a now dead engine. He put his nose down and dived vertically, landing up the side of a hill amongst German troops. He understood that in addition to his Squadron's losses there were two SE5s and one DH4 lost.

Von Richthofen flew Fokker Dr1 Nr.152/17.

IVAMY, WILLIAM GEORGE

SECOND LIEUTENANT 54 SQUADRON; ROYAL ENGINEERS

BORN ON 14 February 1890, W G Ivamy was educated in the south coast resort town of Bournemouth, Hampshire, where he lived with his parents at their home in Torbet Hill Road, Winton. On leaving school, he was apprenticed to a firm in nearby Christchurch with whom he eventually qualified as an electrical engineer before, in 1911, at the age of 21, he left for Canada, en route for his intended destination, Australia. When he arrived in Vancouver, he was offered a position with the British Columbia Electric Power Company and decided to stay in Canada. Following the outbreak of war, he returned to England and, in March 1915, joined the cable unit of the Royal Engineers. He was sent to France in November 1915, as a sergeant in charge of a Cable Section. In July 1916, bored and fed up with the mud and the mules, he successfully applied for transfer to the Royal Flying Corps, training first as an observer. Ivamy joined No.1 Squadron as an artillery observer on probation in October 1916, and, after only one month, was given a commission and transferred to No. 7 Squadron, then stationed on the Somme. Ivamy served with No. 7 throughout the period of the German retreat to the Hindenburg Line, afterwards moving north in support of the British 'push' on the Messines Ridge. Next, Ivamy was sent home for a month's leave and for pilot training. Following the usual training at Gosport and Reading, he was sent back to France in November 1917 as a pilot with 54 Squadron, and by January 1918 he was flying patrols over the St Quentin front. After being shot down, apart from temporary partial blindness caused by the gasoline spraying from his damaged tanks, Ivamy was unhurt and was taken prisoner. He spent most of his captivity at Holzminden before being repatriated on 14 December 1918. He decided to return to Canada after the war, taking up his old job and setting up home in Burnaby, British Columbia. By the end of his working life, he had risen to be the Chief Engineer of Sub-stations. He died in his adopted home town in March 1958, at the age of sixty-eight.

24 MARCH 1918

VICTORY NO.67

SE5A No.C1054
41 SQUADRON RFC
ENGINE No.115259 WD 34086
GUNS: 27914; B358

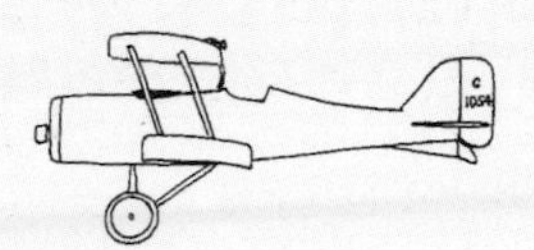

VON RICHTHOFEN'S Combat Report:
1445 hrs, above Combles. SE5. Brought down behind the enemy's lines.

During a protracted single-seater fight between ten SE5s and 25 machines of my own Group, I attacked an Englishman at an altitude of 2,500 metres. Under my machine gun fire, both wings broke away from the aeroplane in the air. The pieces were scattered in the vicinity of Combles.

BARON VON RICHTHOFEN

WEATHER: FINE.

Floyd Gibbons in his early research identified Richthofen's victim as Second Lieutenant Wilson Porter Jr (an American) of 56 Squadron (C5389). However, he was shot down at 1315 near Peronne, a victim of Bavarian Jasta 34b which claimed two SE5a machines downed. This was an hour and a half before von Richthofen's fight, although Combles, ten kilometres south of Bapaume, is only ten kilometres north-west of Peronne.

Captain R W Chappell (B624) had led 41 Squadron's patrol, and he reported meeting 30 Triplanes and Albatros Scouts between Sailly and Havrincourt, shooting down one Triplane out of control. He then found a red Triplane on his tail but managed to get on the Tripe's tail, firing 200 rounds with both guns (Lewis and Vickers) and saw it turn over on to its back. At 2,000 feet above the ground it was still going down in a spin.

Second Lieutenant H D Arkell (B663) flying above Havrincourt saw a hostile machine over Le Transloy and he too claimed a Triplane out of control, until he lost sight of it in some ground smoke at 200 feet. He also saw another going down in flames east of the Bapaume-Peronne road. This was the Dr1 attacked by Second Lieutenant A S Hemming (B8267) south-west of Havrincourt. The red Triplane was hit by 150 rounds from 25 yards and fell smoking from the cockpit area. Second Lieutenant H E Watson (B8235) sent another Triplane down in a vertical dive but did not make a claim. Jasta 10 may have lost a pilot on this date.

McCone failed to get home, as did Second Lieutenant D C Tucker (C6399). The latter was wounded, and came down inside German lines and was captured. As von Richthofen's adversary could not possibly have survived his machine disintegrating, having also lost its wings, it follows that his victim must have been McCone, who was killed.

'Shorty' McCone had claimed two out of control victories while with the Squadron, an Albatros Scout on the 22 January, flying B68, and an unidentified enemy aircraft which he last saw diving into Beugny village on 23 March, flying C1054.

Von Richthofen was flying Fokker Dr1 Nr.477/17 (Werke Nr.2103), described as having a red cowling, red upper decking, wheel covers, and tail unit.

McCONE, JOHN PERCY

LIEUTENANT 41 SQUADRON; CANADIAN ENGINEERS

BORN IN QUEBEC, Canada on 11 March 1891, J P McCone was the son of J E and Mrs McCone who, in later years, lived at 2452 West Iowa Street, Chicago, Illinois, USA. A Surveyor by profession, McCone had spent a year with the Mexican Army during the unrest and insurrection in that country. On the 24 April 1915, he attested into the Canadian Cyclists. Service in the Canadian Engineers followed until, in February, 1917 he applied for transfer and was sent for flying training to Reading. His appointment as Flying Officer, RFC on 7 November 1917 was followed by a posting to France on 5 December 1917, and service with 41 Squadron. At 5 foot 4 inches, McCone attracted the inevitable sobriquet of 'Shorty', but he also attracted admiration for his bravery and flying abilities and his death was met with unusually deep regret by his comrades in the Squadron. His body was never recovered and he is commemorated on the Arras Memorial to the Missing, France. He was just over twenty-seven years of age.

Above: Lt J P McCone, Canadian Engineers and RFC flanked by W J Gillespie (41 Squadron) and K P Campbell (60 Squadron).
Credit: W J Gillespie via S K Taylor

Right: Fokker Drl with Balkenkreuze insignia

25 MARCH 1918

VICTORY NO.68

SOPWITH CAMEL NO.C1562
3 SQUADRON RFC
ENGINE NO.35759 WD 9408
GUNS: C8563; A8745

VON RICHTHOFEN'S Combat Report:
1555 hrs, above Bapaume-Albert road, near Contalmaison. Sopwith 1; burnt. Englishman (Beginner).

With five planes of Jasta 11, I attacked several low-flying English one-seaters north-east of Albert. I approached to within 50 metres behind one of the Englishmen and shot him down in flames with a few shots.

The burning machine crashed between Contalmaison and Albert, and continued to burn on the ground. The bombs it apparently carried, exploded a few minutes later.

BARON VON RICHTHOFEN

WEATHER: STARTED FINE, BECOMING CLOUDY; WINDY LATER.

Cameron was indeed a beginner, having joined the Squadron just a month previously on 19 February. And he was carrying bombs, for the mission on this March afternoon was low bombing of German troops, transport and strong points along the British 3rd Army front. He had taken off at 1530, from Vert Galant, having moved there from Warloy that very day, and had not lasted half an hour.

Contalmaison is situated six kilometres north-east of Albert, and just to the south of the Albert to Bapaume road, which also runs north-east, a continuation of that straight, long road which begins at Amiens.

Von Richthofen was flying Fokker Dr1 Nr.477/17. *(cont.)*

Right: One of the famous Sanke portraits of Manfred.

CAMERON,
DONALD
SECOND LIEUTENANT 3 SQUADRON

THE ELDER SON of civil engineer James Cameron and his wife, Mary S Cameron, of 'Wellbrae Park House', Strathaven, Lanarkshire, Donald was born on 3 May 1899. James Cameron, a civil engineer of some distinction, had been involved in the construction of the Glasgow underground railway and in the reconstruction of Belfast Harbour. Donald was educated at the Collegiate School, Glasgow, Strathaven Academy and Glasgow High School, where he was a member of the OTC. He entered directly into the Royal Flying Corps on 22 May 1917, and, after training at Farnborough, Denham and at the Cadet School at Oxford, he was gazetted Second Lieutenant on 31 August 1917. His flying training completed, he was awarded his 'Wings' on 31 December 1917. At last, he was sent to France on 9 February 1918, being posted to 3 Squadron as a scout pilot. Cameron's 'war flying' training was barely completed when the great German offensive began on 21 March 1918, and he was killed within days. After the war, a relative living in South Africa claimed to be 'in touch', spiritualistically, with the late Donald Cameron and relayed 'messages' from him to his mother, messages from which, apparently, Mary Cameron took comfort. Her son's body was never recovered and he is commemorated on the Arras Memorial to the Missing, France. He was eighteen years old.

26 MARCH 1918

VICTORY NO.69

SE5a No.B511
1 Squadron RAF
Engine No. 1925 WD 21825
Guns: 33985; A7572

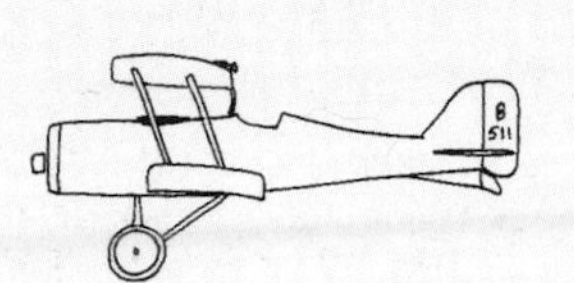

VON RICHTHOFEN'S Combat Report:
1645 hrs. Wood south of Contalmaison. Sopwith 1; burnt in the air. Englishman.

Flying with five gentlemen of Jasta 11, at low level, I encountered a Sopwith single-seater at the Front, with Leutnant Udet. At first the adversary attempted to escape me by skilful flying. From a distance not more than the length of a plane, I shot him down in flames. During the fall it disintegrated. The fuselage crashed into the small wood of Contalmaison.

Baron von Richthofen

Weather: fine with strong winds, overcast at times.

Floyd Gibbons chose Second Lieutenant William Knox of 54 Squadron as Richthofen's victim (C1553), but unfortunately, Knox was shot down on the 24th, two days earlier.

Later historians then chose Second Lieutenant A T W Lindsay, of the same Squadron (C1568), but he took off at 1245 and was last seen near Roye. (Lindsay had already been out and shot about by ground fire on an early OP (B9135) but had got home again.) Apart from the time element – Lindsay would have had to have been flying for four hours to have been shot down by Richthofen – Roye is also more than 30 kilometres to the south of Contalmaison. He was also taken prisoner, which von Richthofen's adversary could not have been.

There were a number of single-seaters in action during the afternoon of this day, and several shot down or shot up. Eliminating the fighter types, No.1 Squadron had a bad day, three of its SE5s being lost in the afternoon. One pilot was killed and two captured. The man who died was Second Lieutenant Allan McNab Denovan, but 1 Squadron would normally be operating further north, although, with the fierce ground battle raging, squadrons were operating over the southern sectors giving ground support. 1 Squadron were, in fact, operating from 40 Squadron's base at Bruay, where they had flown that morning, (attached to 10th Wing for the day) still 50 kilometres to the north of the battle front, but they were nevertheless flying further south. Jasta 26 claimed two SE5s, at 1700 and 1720 pm at Beaucourt (on the Ancre River), and north-west of Tamechou Wood, which is only about six kilometres north of Contalmaison. Jasta 26 were operating from Erchin.

Two Camels were lost; possible credits go to von Richthofen, and to Leutnant Gussmann of Jasta 11, timed at 1700, north of Albert. This, of course, is in the same general area as Richthofen's action, but the Camel candidates do not help. A 3 Squadron machine returned shot up, so that is out; a 70 Squadron Camel also landed back shot up at 1720, so that too must be discounted. 54 Squadron lost Lindsay as already stated, but the time is out, while another Camel was shot down by MG fire, but survived to be sent for repair to 2 AD. Two more SE5s, of 40 Squadron, were shot up in the afternoon, but both got safely down, although away from their base, so they cannot be involved. 41 Squadron also lost a machine but again the time is out, having taken off at 1210, going down near Bapaume.

This leaves 19 Squadron's Sopwith Dolphins. A comparatively new Sopwith type to reach France, it began to arrive in late February. Certainly von Richthofen, as far as we know, had not yet met them in the air, and it is perhaps significant that in his report, he does not specifically mention the name Camel, so did he in fact realise he was fighting Sopwith Dolphins?

No.19 Squadron lost two Dolphins. Because they were new types to the Front, neither were claimed specifically by German pilots, and in any event, they would mostly be flying ground attack sorties, but on this day we do know they were engaged by German fighters. It is significant that three German pilots claimed Martinsydes this afternoon. Martinsydes, of course, had been away from the battle zones for four months, but one can easily imagine a German pilot thinking a Dolphin looked like a Martinsyde from certain angles.

The problem with the 19 Squadron losses is the arithmetic: while they lost two aircraft, three were claimed, five if you add Richthofen and Gussmann. In the Nachrichtenblatt, Gussmann is credited with a Camel but Richthofen is credited with just a Sopwith Einzister – Sopwith one-seater!

The Dolphins were based at Ste-Marie-Cappel, which being south of Cassel is on the northern part of the Front, but, like 1 Squadron, they were obviously operating further south due to the battle front. There was a combat in which an Albatros DV was claimed by 19 Squadron at Grevillers, which is just west of Bapaume. The Dolphins had taken off at 1640 on a low flying patrol but unfortunately Richthofen does not make any reference to the height of his adversary.

The two Dolphins lost came down, according to the German pilot's 'Martinsyde' claims, at:

Leutnant H Lange, Jasta 26 – SW Grandcourt at 1700 hrs
Leutnant R Plange, Jasta 2 – Grevillers Wood at 1715 hrs
OffStv O Esswein, Jasta 26 – at 1745 hrs

Add Richthofen and Gussmann:

Rittm M v Richthofen JG1 – S of Contalmaison 1645 hrs
Leutnant S Gussmann Jasta 11 – N Albert at 1700 hrs

All the noted locations are in an area south-west of Bapaume, between Bapaume and Albert, Grevillers being nearer to Bapaume, Grandcourt mid-way while Contal-maison and 'N of Albert' are closer to Albert.

If the two missing Dolphin pilots took off at 1640, there is little time for either of them to get to the Front and be shot down by Richthofen at 1645 (the times being the same for both sides) and in any event were reported downed at approximately 1725, more in keeping with Plange and Esswein's claim times (although is it significant that the latter's claim has no locality?).

So what or who went into the wood south of Contalmaison, under the guns of the Red Baron has yet to be determined. It is understood that 1 Squadron took off at around 1620, and the two SEs that were brought down by Jasta 26 still leaves one SE unaccounted for, within the time scale of Richthofen's combat. If the Jasta 26 pilot's victories resulted in British prisoners, then the one killed might well have been the pilot who fell from the aircraft shot down by von Richthofen – Second Lieutenant A McN Denovan. Did Richthofen mis-identify an SE5 for a Camel?

However, Lieutenant A Hollis (B643), flying on this same patrol, was seen to be shot down by an enemy fighter near Bapaume, his SE5 losing a wing just before he crashed. As Hollis is one of the two SE5 pilots captured, he obviously got down safely. The other was Second Lieutenant W M R Gray (B641) seen to force-land in enemy territory and turn over. Denovan looks favourite.

Von Richthofen was flying Fokker Dr1 477/17.

DENOVAN, ALLAN McNAB

SECOND LIEUTENANT 1 SQUADRON

BORN ON 8 January 1895, Allan was the son of barrister A McN Denovan and his wife, Elizabeth, of 64 Highlands Avenue, Toronto, Ontario, Canada. His father gave him the best local education money could buy at University Schools and at Upper Canada College, Toronto. He was a member of the Militia and in January 1916 he joined the 180th Battalion, Canadian Expeditionary Force. Shortly afterwards, the city of Toronto was visited by Captain Lord A R Innes-Ker, DSO, Royal Horse Guards and a Flight Commander in the Royal Flying Corps. Innes-Ker had been sent by the War Office to comb Canada for suitable candidates for the RFC. Denovan asked for an interview and was eventually transferred to the RFC in November 1916. A month later he was aboard the SS *Missanabie* bound for Liverpool. Denovan was commissioned Second Lieutenant into the RFC and his training began on the first day of the new year. He qualified as a pilot with 50 hours flying at the end of April and was posted to 3 Squadron in France on 8 May 1917. On 15 June 1917, Denovan's Morane was engaged by a German scout. His observer fought off the attack but not before Denovan was wounded in the left hand. Using his right hand, Denovan flew the Morane back to their base at Lavieville. His wound took some time to heal and it was seven months before an impatient Denovan was allowed to return to France, this time joining 1 Squadron on 1 February 1918. Denovan soon earned himself a reputation as an aggressive, even reckless pilot, always in the thick of the fights. His body was never found and he is commemorated on the Arras Memorial to the Missing, France. He was twenty-three years old.

26 MARCH 1918

VICTORY NO.70

RE8 No.B742
15 Squadron RFC
Engine No.29556 WD 12387
Guns: 18184; A6344

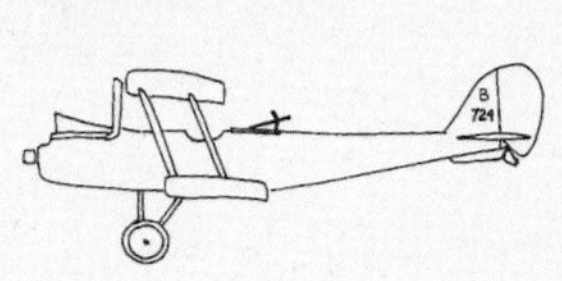

VON RICHTHOFEN'S Combat Report:
1700 hrs, two kilometres north-east of Albert. RE old type, burnt; Englishman.

A quarter of an hour after my first victory on this day, I detected in exactly the same spot, at an altitude of 700 metres, an RE two-seater. I went into a dive behind it, and from close range I fired about 100 rounds, and set him on fire. At first the Englishman defended himself with his observer's machine gun. The plane burned in the air until impact. Half an hour later, the machine continued to burn on the ground.

Baron von Richthofen

This machine had taken off from Fienvillers, south-east of Doullens, at 1640. The Squadron had only moved there on this day, from Lahoussaye, north-east of Amiens, where it had been one day, evacuating from Lavieville on the 22nd.

It had just about reached the Front, in order to carry out the assigned task of contact patrol and bombing over the Corps area when von Richthofen swooped down on it. So short had been their sortie that the crew had not even had a chance to send, by Morse code, any report or message.

Von Richthofen was flying Fokker Dr1 No.477/17.

READING,
VERNON JACK
SECOND LIEUTENANT 15 SQUADRON

Born on 13 September 1895, Jack Reading was the only son of caterer Arthur Vernon Reading and Mrs Reading of 'Knodeshall Lodge', Saxmunden, Suffolk. He was educated at the Grammar School (1907-12) in nearby Woodbridge, Suffolk where he was a founder member of the Officer Training Corps. After training, Reading joined 15 Squadron in France on 8 February 1918. Initially reported as 'Missing', his demise was confirmed a month later on 26 April 1918. In a letter to Jack's father after his death at the hands of von Richthofen, his commanding officer wrote:
"during the great offensive *(the German offensive which commenced on 21 March 1918)* he did good work, brought back reports of the highest value, bombed and machine gunned enemy troops in a way that one could not feel but the greatest admiration for his initiative and courage."
Reading's body was lost in the subsequent fighting over his burial place and he is commemorated on the Arras Memorial to the Missing, France. He was twenty-two years old.

LEGGAT,
MATTHEW
SECOND LIEUTENANT 15 SQUADRON; 5/LANCASHIRE FUSILIERS

Born in 1897, Matt Leggat was the son of Peter and Agnes Leggat of 16 Fotheringham Road, Ayr. He joined the Royal Engineers as a sapper in October 1915 and, after training, was sent to France in February 1916. A little more than a year later, in April 1917, he was picked out as potential officer material, brought home and sent to the Officer Training Corps at Chatham. After successfully completing the course in October of the same year, he was gazetted Second Lieutenant to the 5th Battalion, Lancashire Fusiliers. He married his fiancée, Celia Ellen, on 30 September 1917, and they set up home at 10 Argyle Street, Ayr. Two months later he succeeded with a request for transfer to the Royal Flying Corps. Following training at Reading and Winchester, he passed out as an observer and was awarded his 'Wing'. Leggat was sent to France on 28 January 1918, joining 15 Squadron three days later. He flew operationally virtually every day until he was killed. His body was never recovered and he is commemorated on the Arras Memorial to the Missing, France. He was twenty-two years old.

27 MARCH 1918

VICTORY NO.71

SOPWITH CAMEL NO.C6733
73 SQUADRON RFC
ENGINE NO.54595 WD 46148
GUNS: 11002; 10895

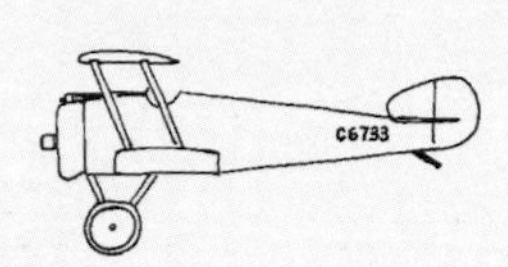

VON RICHTHOFEN'S combat report:
0900 hrs. Ancre, one kilometre north of Aveluy, north of Albert. Sopwith – 1, burned; Englishman.

With five machines of Jasta 11, I attacked at low height an English one-seater plane and brought him down from a very close range, with 150 bullets. The plane fell into the flooded part of the Ancre.

BARON VON RICHTHOFEN

WEATHER: FINE, SOME LOW CLOUDS.

Originally identified as being Lieutenant H W Ransom of 70 Squadron, flying Camel B8234. However, Ransom had only left his base at Marieux, south-east of Doullens (they were about to evacuate to Fienvillers) at 0900, the same moment as Richthofen was finishing off his 71st victim 20 kilometres away to the south-east.

Floyd Gibbons also said that Richthofen's report shows the Camel went down in flames, which the above translation does not. As Ransom was killed, the 'in flames' statement was probably added to make it seem more authentic. The reference to 'burned' – as it is not mentioned in the air fight – most likely referred to what happened to the Camel once it hit the ground.

The Camels of 73 Squadron, based at Remaisnil, north-west of Doullens (where it had moved on the 24th, evacuating from Cachy), had left at 0700, to fly a low-bombing and strafing sortie against the advancing Germans, near Albert. Sharpe was last seen by Second Lieutenant R N Chandler in combat with enemy aircraft, low down east of Albert, but then Chandler himself became engaged with enemy fighters and lost sight of his Flight Commander.

Aveluy, where Richthofen said his victim fell, is just to the east of Albert, the time scale fits and, as the flooded Ancre river area hereabouts was now in German hands, any pilot surviving a crash would indeed be taken prisoner, as Sharpe was.

Only three other Camels were claimed in air combat this day, one to Unteroffizier Karl Pech of Jasta 29, one to Leutnant Heinrich Bongartz, Jasta 36, and one to Leutnant Hans Kirschstein, of Jasta 6. Pech's victim (2/Lt W C Dennett in B9167) came down in the front lines near Albert, but was timed at 0715, Bongartz got his south-west of Albert at 0800, while Kirschstein's fell north-east of Albert, but at 1520. The other Camel losses were two from 70 Squadron, Ransom and 2/Lt C J Wilsdon (C8219), both having taken off at around 0900, and a 46 Squadron machine, Lt G D Jenkins (B7311), last seen at 1815, in combat.

When Sharpe returned from Germany, arriving in England on 25 December, he recorded in his report that he had been shot down and wounded by machine gun fire from the ground and that both fuel tanks had been hit. Whether he had indeed been hit by ground fire as well, or had not seen Richthofen attack, or simply did not like to admit being brought down by a German pilot (he wouldn't be the first), we shall never know. Certainly he was in combat, as witnessed by Robert Chandler.

Von Richthofen was flying Fokker Dr1 No.127/17 (Werke Nr.1838), described as having red upper decking and hood, tail and wheel covers. Tail cross with white border, wing crosses on white fields. It had been tested on 15 October 1917, and delivered on the 29th.

SHARPE,
THOMAS SYDNEY
CAPTAIN 73 SQUADRON DFC; 3/GLOUCESTERSHIRE REGIMENT

Sharpe was born in Gloucester on 24 February 1889. He was commissioned into the 3rd (Reserve) Battalion, Gloucester Regiment on 17 April 1915. Formal transfer to the Royal Flying Corps followed the award of the Royal Aero Club Aviators Certificate (No.2471) on 19 February 1916. He was first posted to 24 Squadron, with whom he flew from May 1916 to July 1916. A skilled and gallant pilot, he achieved rapid promotion to captain's rank and was eventually appointed a flight commander with 73 Squadron. In March 1918, he claimed six 'victories', and so became an 'ace' in his own right. Sharpe was one of the earliest winners of the newly introduced gallantry decoration, the Distinguished Flying Cross, the award of which was announced almost six months after his battle with von Richthofen, *London Gazette*, 21/9/1918, page 11254:

'A gallant officer who has always led his patrol with marked skill and judgement. On one occasion he chased down an Albatros scout and caused it to crash. He afterwards attacked five enemy machines destroying two. On the following day, encountering four Albatros scouts, he engaged one, which crashed. Proceeding on his patrol, he met a formation of enemy scouts; he chased one and destroyed it'.

Wounded and taken prisoner after his encounter with the Red Baron, Sharpe's incarceration lasted until December 1918 when, at last, he was repatriated and able to return to civilian life. After the war, he lived at Courthorpe, Tuffley, Gloucester and ran a building company for many years.

27 MARCH 1918

VICTORY NO.72

AWFK8 No.B288
2 SQUADRON RFC
ENGINE No.1094 WD 7704
GUNS: 27861 E; A3918

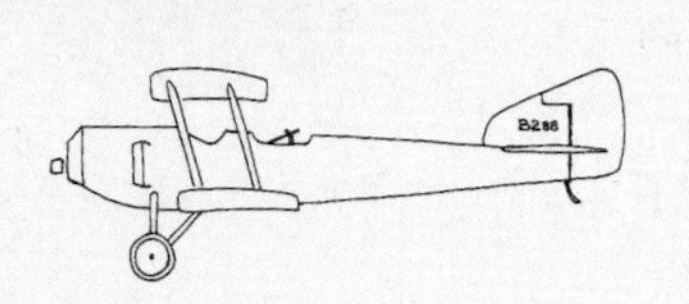

VON RICHTHOFEN'S Combat Report:
1630 hrs, two kilometres west of Foucaucourt. Bristol Fighter – 2, burned: Englishman.

With six machines of Jasta 11, I attacked enemy infantry flyers molesting our movements. I managed to approach unnoticed a Bristol Fighter within some 50 metres and then I succeeded in shooting him down after some 100 shots. The machine fell burning and hit the ground not far from some German columns.

BARON VON RICHTHOFEN

Once again we have the problem of what Richthofen thought he had attacked, and what he'd actually attacked. Having recorded his victim as a Bristol Fighter, this naturally led historians to look for this type in the casualty returns. For some reason, Floyd Gibbons chose B1156 of 20 Squadron, crewed by Captains K R Kirkham MC and J H Hedley CdeG. The problem was that no times were given on the loss report for their hour of departure from 20's base at Ste-Marie-Cappel, south of Cassel, and the Squadron Record Book (which would show flying times) was missing.

Despite the northerly area of their base, they too had headed south to the Amiens battle area to carry out a low-flying and bombing sortie north of Albert. Fortunately, in Wing records three or four copy pages of these last March days were located, which clearly show that this crew took off on their final mission at 1005. Therefore they could not have been shot down by Richthofen at 1640.

The Nachrichtenblatt notes five other pilots claiming BF2bs on this day: Leutnant Heinrich Bongartz and Unteroffizier Alfred Hubner of Jasta 26, Leutnant Karl Gallwitz of Jasta 2, Vizefeldwebel Franz Hemer of Jasta 6, and Vizefeldwebel Edgar Scholtz of Jasta 11. Bongartz and Hubner in fact shot down DH4s (25 Squadron), Hemer's claim turns out to be a Dolphin of 79 Squadron, while Scholtz' claim for a Bristol is timed at 1205. Karl Gallwitz of Jasta Boelcke in fact downed Kirkham and Hedley, at 1100, his eighth of an eventual ten victories.

There were, of course, certain similarities which fooled Gibbons, such as the type of sortie they were flying, but then almost everyone was trying to stem the German advance by low strafing and bombing. Gibbons also interviewed Hedley after the war, and although he makes no mention of knowing or otherwise that he had been brought down by Richthofen at the time, he does confirm being shot down by a fighter. However, he did say they came down 12 miles behind the German lines, which north of Albert was at this time,

SMART,
EDWARD TRELOAR
LIEUTENANT 2 SQUADRON; ROYAL GARRISON ARTILLERY

THE ONLY CHILD of the Reverend John Racstar Smart and Mrs Smart of 'Springfield', North Road, Hythe, Kent, Edward Smart (right) was born in 1898. He was educated at Castle School, Tonbridge and at Tonbridge School (1911–14) where his father was a Master. Fascinated by railways, and keen to make them his profession, he secured a post in the Traffic Department of the South Eastern Railway at London Bridge in 1914. When the war came, he volunteered as soon as he was old enough, receiving a commission in the Special Reserve of the Royal Garrison Artillery on 13 October 1915. In 1916 he was given command of a section of the 149th Anti-Aircraft Battery, RGA, serving variously at Edinburgh, Echlin and on Inchcolm Island in the Firth of Forth. A successful application to transfer to the Royal Flying Corps was confirmed on 27 March 1917. After training, he was appointed Flying Officer on 14 July 1917, and was sent to join 'B' Flight of 2 Squadron in France on 25 August. In a letter to his parents, the Second in Command of his Squadron wrote:

'It was not his turn for the last trip that he made, but he was so eager to take his share in the big battle that he prevailed on another pilot to let him take his place'.

Edward's body was never found and he is commemorated on the Arras Memorial to the Missing, France. He was twenty years of age.

BARFORD,
KENNETH PURNELL
LIEUTENANT 2 SQUADRON

BORN IN 1899, Kenneth Barford (inset) was the son of Coventry town councillor Henry Widdowson Barford and his wife, Mary, of 'The Bungalow', Kenilworth Road, Coventry. In 1917, as soon as he reached the age of acceptance, he interrupted his university studies and successfully applied for a commission in the Royal Flying Corps via the General List. His body was never found and he is commemorated on the Arras Memorial, France. He was nineteen years old.

whereas Foucaucourt, some ten kilometres to the south-east, was further still.

Once again we see the problem of identification by the Germans, with Bristol Fighters being confused with DH4s and Dolphins. Von Richthofen now confuses a BF2b with a 'Big Ack' – AWFK8 – an Armstrong Whitworth FK8, two-seat Corps aircraft. It could be, and was, used as a reconnaissance aircraft as well as for artillery spotting, contact patrol work and day as well as night bombing. It was not new to the Front, having been around for a year, but there are few if any reports that Richthofen had faced one before.

No.2 Squadron was based at Hesdigneul, having more than the range and endurance to come south to operate in the battle area. They had been flying down throughout the day, but formations had become split due to the poor low-level visibility, so most aircraft were operating independently over the battle front. That morning had already seen one AWFK8 of the Squadron badly shot about and brought down on fire into no-man's-land, its pilot being recommended for the Victoria Cross. This was Second Lieutenant Alan Arnett McLeod (B5773) from Winnipeg, Manitoba, and his observer Lieutenant A W Hammond MC. They'd been shot down by Hans Kirschstein of Jasta 6, his second of an eventual 27 victories. Wounded and burned, McLeod dragged his wounded observer to safety before their bombs exploded, and got him to the British lines.

Lieutenant E T Smart and Second Lieutenant K P Barford, had taken off at 1520 for another low-sortie to the Albert area. Termed as a 'Special Mission' it was however, a sortie to bomb, strafe and harrass German troops, which is exactly the task identified by Richthofen in his report, ie: '.. infantry flyers molesting our movements'. By which he meant the movements of German soldiers. The German line now reached from the Ancre through Albert, past Morlancourt, Chipilly, Proyart, Raincourt, Vauvillers, Bouchoir, Guerbigny and then to Beauvraignes, where the French line began.

Another reason they were undoubtedly overlooked earlier, is that for some strange reason their loss was not recorded in the RFC War Diary, but they are listed in No.1 RFC Wing records.

Fifteen minutes after Richthofen claimed his victory, Second Lieutenant Horace Ison Pole RFC, with Lieutenant L C Spence MC of 2 Squadron (in AWFK8 C3575), engaged on a similar 'Special Mission', were 2,000 feet over the same locality – Foucaucourt, situated on that long straight Amiens to St Quentin road, unbending for some 56 kilometres. They were attacked by seven enemy fighters, one Albatros Scout and six Fokker Triplanes. They dived on the Big Ack in succession, and Spence managed to drive off the first two. The third, a Triplane, was then hit and it turned sharply, dived vertically and burst into flames, later seen burning on the ground west of Estrées.

Von Richthofen was flying Fokker Dr1 No.477/17.

NB – in the book *'Above the Lines'* by Franks, Bailey and Guest, Grub Sreet, 1993, the authors (one of whom is involved in this book) stated that Richthofen's 72nd victory was a DH4 of 5 Naval Squadron. This has now been amended, having since discovered that although the time and the location match, the attacking aircraft were not Triplanes but Pfalz DIII Scouts.

27 MARCH 1918

VICTORY NO.73

SOPWITH DOLPHIN No.C4016
79 SQUADRON RFC
ENGINE No.116137 WD 44644
GUNS: 5256A; 10066C; 62757

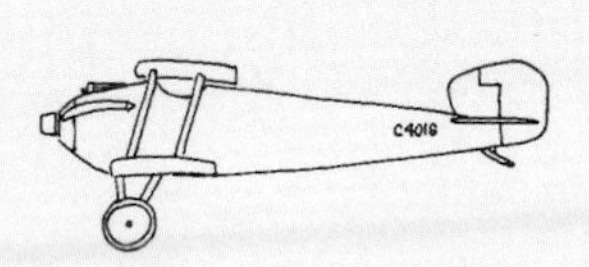

VON RICHTHOFEN'S Combat Report:
1635 hrs, one kilometre north of Chuignolles, south of Bray-sur-Somme. Bristol Fighter – 2, burned; Englishman. Seat of observer was closed, only one occupant.

Soon after I had shot down my 72nd opponent in flames, I attacked once more with the same gentlemen of the Jasta. Just then I observed that one of my gentlemen was attacked by a Bristol Fighter. I put myself behind this machine and shot him down in flames from a distance of 50 metres.

I noticed that there was only one occupant. The observer's seat was blocked and I surmise it was filled with bombs. I first killed the pilot; the machine was caught on the propeller. I fired a few more shots and the plane then burned and broke up in the air; the fuselage fell into a small wood and continued to burn.

BARON VON RICHTHOFEN

WEATHER: FINE, SOME LOW CLOUDS.

This was the Baron's third kill of this extraordinary day. Extraordinary in that it was his third kill and the third wrong identified type and/or crew.

Once again we see the reason, the misidentification of aircraft type. Not that von Richthofen was alone in this, but historians have, it is clear, not fully appreciated the complexities of air combat, and assume that an aircraft type noted and written down by a fighter pilot has to be correct. This sort of oversight is compounded when someone believes something quite out of the ordinary, such as a Bristol Fighter having its observer's cockpit closed so it can be filled with bombs.

Not since early 1917 had the RFC foolishly sent out two seaters without an observer (usually BE2s) in lieu of extra bomb weight. And as all WW1 aircraft carried external bombs, why would anyone suddenly believe this particular 'Bristol' had its observer's cockpit full of bombs, and how was the pilot going to drop or dispose of them? And, if we suppose he still carried the bombs, why was he attacking a fast, nimble Fokker Triplane?

In this particular instance, von Richthofen was again up against a type not only new to the Front but new to him (especially if we believe he did not have a fight with 19 Squadron Dolphins on 26 March). What confused German pilots was the unusual double bank of wing interplane struts, making it look, at first glance, like the BF, the DH4 or even the AWKF8.

George Harding had taken off to fly an Offensive Patrol at 1530 from the unit's base at Beauvois, east of Hesdin. An hour later he made a valiant attempt at attacking one of JG1's aircraft, and was promptly shot down by the Rittmeister in short order.

As to the supposed pilot of the 'Bristol Fighter', this was said to have been Captain H R Child of 11 Squadron (B1332). Just why he was chosen by historians could only stem from the fact that his was a convenient BF2b loss, seeing that Richthofen had claimed one. That Child was indeed carrying a backseat observer – Lieutenant A Reeve – seems to have been overlooked or ignored. Not only that, but the fact that this crew took off on their sortie at 1115, five and a quarter hours before Richthofen claimed his victory, was also ignored.

Von Richthofen was flying Fokker Dr1 No.477/17.

HARDING, GEORGE HALLIWELL

SECOND LIEUTENANT 79 SQUADRON

BORN IN SEPTEMBER 1893, George Harding was the son of Grain Commissioner George P Harding and his wife, Mary, of 1815 Colfax Avenue South, Minneapolis, Minnesota, United States of America. George Junior was educated locally at West High School, Minneapolis. After leaving school, George joined E S Woodworth & Co, where his father was vice - president. As soon as the United States entered the war in April 1917, George volunteered for the US Army Air Service but was disappointed to discover that because there were so many other aspirants, he would have to wait for many months for his chance. Not content to wait, he travelled up to Canada and there joined the Royal Flying Corps. A naturally gifted pilot, he not only gained his 'Wings' in a very short time but, within weeks of his 'graduation', was himself helping to train novice pilots. In the autumn of 1917, after enjoying a week's embarkation leave in his home in Minneapolis, he sailed for England. After further training, he was selected for a scout squadron and, early in March 1918, was sent to join 79 Squadron stationed at Beauvais, France. More than a year after his death, George's actress sister, Ruth, happened to be in France with a drama company entertaining the troops. Showing a determination and courage equal to her brother's, she set out to find his grave. After several attempts, she eventually found a small graveyard containing the bodies of a number of unidentified aviators. Remarkably, she managed to prevail upon the officials of the Imperial War Graves Commission to disinter the remains, and after identification, saw to it that her brother's body was moved to an appropriately marked grave at Dive Copse British Cemetery, France (Fr.141). He was twenty-four years old.

28 MARCH 1918

VICTORY NO.74

AWFK8 No.C8444
82 SQUADRON RFC
ENGINE No.1559 WD 20593
GUNS: A8131; E48724

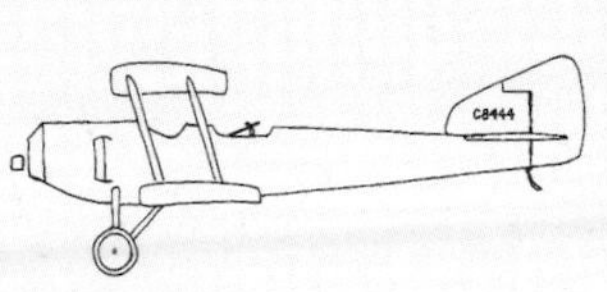

VON RICHTHOFEN'S Combat Report:
1220 hrs. Forest near Mericourt.
Armstrong – 2, burned; Englishman.

Flying at a very low height, I saw shell-explosions near the scene of a victory. Coming nearer I recognised an Englishman at 500 metres altitude, flying home. I cut him off and approached him. After 100 shots the enemy plane was burning. Then it crashed down, hit the ground near the small wood of Mericourt and continued to burn.

BARON VON RICHTHOFEN

WEATHER: HIGH WINDS ALL DAY; SOME RAIN IN THE AFTERNOON.

This time von Richthofen recognised the Armstrong Whitworth, one of a number operating over the battle zone. Unfortunately, while the Squadron Record Book survives, the entry for this day is incomplete as there is no reference to this crew flying or being lost. However, they are reported as lost on 28 March in the RFC War Diary, one of two that failed to return, the other being Second Lieutenants Thomas Watson RFC and T Taylor (C8456), but this one fell on the German side.

Betley was the usual observer to Second Lieutenant J G W March but he was wounded on 25 March. Taylor appears to be a new pilot as his name does not feature in the previous Record Book pages. One wonders if this was his first sortie, and Betley, being pilotless at this moment, was told to show the new boy the ropes.

Their Big Ack was brand new, having just one hour and 45 minutes flying time noted on its flying record; just time for an air test or two.

Von Richthofen was flying Fokker Dr1 Nr.127/17. *(cont.)*

Right: An AWFK8 'Big-Ack'.

TAYLOR,
JOSEPH BERTRAM
SECOND LIEUTENANT 82 SQUADRON

BORN ON 25 August 1898, Joseph Taylor was the son of Mr and Mrs Albert H Taylor of 17 Crosby Road, Forest Gate, London E7. He received his education at St Lawrence, Ramsgate. After leaving school, he was sent to Ceylon to study teaplanting. In May 1917, he left his home and job in Kotiyagalla, Bogawantalawa, yet another of the many volunteers who came over from the plantations and commercial centres of the then British colony of Ceylon to fight for the King Emperor. He was sent first to the RFC Officer Cadet School at Oxford from where he was commissioned a temporary Second Lieutenant in the Royal Flying Corps. He learnt to fly at Spittlegate aerodrome, Grantham, Lincolnshire, where he gained his 'Wings' in March 1918. As soon as he qualified, he was immediately ordered overseas to 82 Squadron,stationed in France. The undue haste was caused by the commencement of the great German offensive on 21 March 1918, and the urgent need of reinforcements for the beleaguered squadrons in the path of the advance. Taylor was killed on what was almost certainly his first patrol. His body was never recovered for burial and he is commemorated on the Ceylon Roll of Honour and on the Arras Memorial to the Missing, France. He was nineteen years old.

BETLEY,
ERIC
SECOND LIEUTENANT 82 SQUADRON; ROYAL GARRISON ARTILLERY

THE SON OF James E and Elizabeth Betley of 39 Victoria Avenue, Didsbury, Manchester, Eric was born in 1897. He was educated at South Manchester School (1907–09) from where he gained a scholarship to Manchester Grammar School. A brilliant student, he became the captain of MGS and also captained the lacrosse team. He gained a classical scholarship at Hertford College, Oxford, but decided his studies could wait until after the war was won and, instead, applied for a commission. Commissioned into the Royal Garrison Artillery in January 1916, he soon became bored with routine duties and successfully applied for transfer to the Royal Flying Corps. After the usual training, he was sent to 82 Squadron in France. Betley generally flew with Second Lieutenant J G W March as his pilot but, as March had been wounded on 25 March, he went up for what was to be his last flight with J B Taylor. Betley's body was never found and he is commemorated on the Arras Memorial to the Missing, France. He was twenty-one years old.

2 APRIL 1918

VICTORY NO.75

RE8 No.A3868
52 Squadron RAF
Engine No.1207 WD 4576
Guns: 50190; C2613

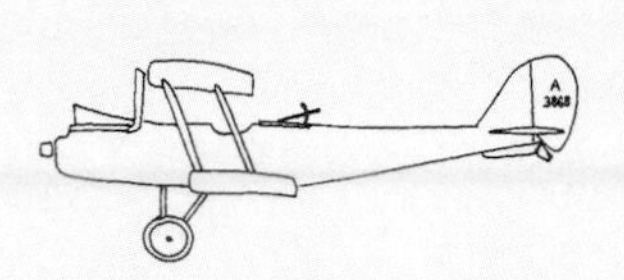

VON RICHTHOFEN'S Combat Report:
1230 hrs. Hill 104, north-east of Moreuil.
RE 2; Englishman.

Around 1230 I attacked, above the wood of Moreuil, an English RE at an altitude of 800 metres, directly under the clouds. As the adversary only saw me very late, I managed to approach him to within 50 metres. From ten metres range I shot him until he began to burn.

When the flames shot out, I was only five metres away from him. I could see how the observer and pilot were leaning out of their plane to escape the fire. The machine did not explode in the air but gradually burnt down. It fell uncontrolled to the ground where it exploded and burnt to ashes.

Baron von Richthofen

Weather: fine, good visibility, but cloudy over lines at 2,000 feet.

This RE8 (Richthofen's reference to a RE 2 merely means it was a two-seater RE) had taken off from the base at Abbeville at 1200 hrs to fly a patrol and bombing sortie to the front lines. The occupants could only just have started having a look round for any suitable targets by the time Richthofen surprised them, the crew once more being caught looking at the ground rather than watching the clouds above.

Moreuil is 20 kilometres south-east of Amiens, on the River Avre.

Von Richthofen was flying Fokker Dr1 Nr.477/17. *(cont.)*

Right: A relaxed Manfred von Richthofen.

JONES,
ERNEST DAVID
LIEUTENANT 52 SQUADRON

BORN ON 6 March 1899, Ernest Jones was the son of Benjamin and Matilda Jones of 38 Orchard Street, Llanfaes, Brecon. Ernest enlisted in the Army Reserve on 24 January 1916, but was, at that time, too young for active service and had to wait until May 1917 when he was sent to the Officer Cadet Wing, Farnborough with further subsequent postings to Grantham and Jesus College, Oxford. On 12 September 1917, he was appointed to a temporary commission as a Second Lieutenant on the General List for duties with the RFC. The next five months were taken up with flying training, first at the 49th Training Squadron, then with the 20th TS, before finally graduating at the Central Flying School, Upavon on 24 January 1918. A month later, on 27 February 1918, he was sent to join 52 Squadron in France. As the Royal Flying Corps and the Royal Naval Air Service had combined to become the Royal Air Force on 1 April 1918, Jones and his observer, Bob Newton, became not only von Richthofen's seventy-fifth 'Victory' but also the Baron's first against the new Service. His body was never recovered and he is commemorated on the Arras Memorial to the Missing, France. He was nineteen years old.

NEWTON,
ROBERT FRANCIS
SECOND LIEUTENANT 52 SQUADRON

ROBERT NEWTON WAS the son of bank clerk John Bertram Newton and Mrs Newton of 48 Cotham Road, Cotham, Bristol. Von Richthofen is reported to have been particularly struck by Newton's courage:
'a tough fellow, a first class fighting man. I flew within five metres of him. Even to the very last moment, he kept shooting at me'.
Newton's remains were never found and he is commemorated on the Arras Memorial to the Missing, France.

Painting opposite:
Victory No.73

Painting overleaf:
Victory No.76

Fok.DR I 477/17

6 APRIL 1918

VICTORY NO.76

SOPWITH CAMEL NO.D6491
46 SQUADRON RAF
ENGINE NO.54644 WD 48144
GUNS: C3919; A846

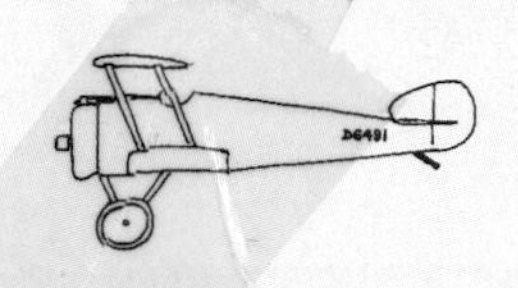

VON RICHTHOFEN'S Combat Report:
1545 hrs, north-east of Villers-Bretonneux, near east edge of Bois de Hamel.
Sopwith Camel, burned; Englishman.

With five of my planes of Jasta 11, we attacked several enemy one-seaters at low altitude, flying north-east of Villers-Bretonneux. The English plane which I attacked started to burn after only a few shots from my guns. Then it crashed burning near the little wood north-east of Villers-Bretonneux, where it continued burning on the ground.

BARON VON RICHTHOFEN

WEATHER: LOW CLOUDS AND RAIN.

With the RAF continuing to fly low-bombing and strafing sorties into the battle area, there was no shortage of targets for the German fighter pilots. 46 Squadron had sent out aircraft at 1445 from Filscamp Farm, next to Le Hameau, to operate over the British 3rd Army front.

Smith, in an almost brand new Camel – it had only eight and a half hours of flying time on its record – was last seen over Lamotte at 1530, by Lieutenant McConnell. Smith's patrol had consisted of himself as leader, and Lieutenants J R Cole, V M Yeates, and R K McConnell. They found and attacked troops and transport vehicles in La Motte, dropping 16 x 25 lb bombs and firing 450 rounds of ammunition, but Smith failed to return.

Smith is identified as 'Beal' in Victor Yeates' classic *Winged Victory* novel. He was a very press-on type, according to Yeates, and the suggestion is that on this last sortie, he was too intent on attacking ground targets to see hostile aircraft swooping down. He was warned at the last minute by another member of his patrol but had only just commenced a turn when he was shot down. Over the previous days he had been much in evidence during the ground offensive. Twice he had returned with Camels sufficiently shot up by ground fire to warrant major repairs – D6407 on 27 March and D6489 on the 30th.

He had previously been wounded on 1 May 1917 – by a red machine; However, von Richthofen was on leave from the Front at the time.

Von Richthofen was flying Fokker Dr1 Nr.127/17.

(cont.)

SMITH, SYDNEY PHILIP

CAPTAIN 46 SQUADRON; ARMY SERVICE CORPS

BORN ON 10 May 1896, S P Smith was the son of Mr and Mrs Arthur H Smith of 'Morningside', Cargate, Aldershot, Hampshire. He was educated at King's College School, Wimbledon where he was a member of the OTC for more than four years. A crack shot, he captained his school rifle team at the annual Public Schools 'Shooting Blue Ribbon' at Bisley. Smith preferred his second forename, invariably signing himself as 'S. Philip Smith'. Immediately upon the outbreak of war, Smith enlisted as a private soldier in the Public Schools Battalion. Before long, he was selected for a commission and gazetted as a temporary Second Lieutenant into the Army Service Corps on 21 October 1914. Smith accompanied the Wessex Division (ASC) to France in March 1915, and, after many attempts, was at last allowed to transfer to the Royal Flying Corps in the spring of 1916. He gained his Royal Aero Club Aviators Certificate (No.3056) on 24 May 1916, and was accepted into the Royal Flying Corps the following month. Smith was sent to join 6 Squadron on 22 June 1916. His skilful piloting of the Squadron's BE2s earned him an appointment as a Flight Commander on 22 December 1916. Smith's heavy flying schedule continued unabated and, on 26 January 1916, he and his observer, Lieutenant Handsworth, barely escaped with their lives from the persistent attacks of one lone enemy scout. Handsworth received severe wounds in his right arm which later caused it to be amputated. Less than two months later, on 17 March 1917, he and another observer, 2AM Backhouse, claimed an Albatros Scout, one of five who had attacked their Flight, some small consolation for the loss of their comrades, 2/Lt Aaron Appleton and Corporal Cooper, who had been shot down in flames moments earlier. At 1400 on 1 May 1917, Smith took off for the fourth time that day, this time piloting RE8 (4196) with Lt Hayman as his passenger. Returning two hours later from an Artillery Observation patrol, he was attacked by five Albatros Scouts. Smith's own laconic observations on the action read:

'the leader (ALL RED) shot machine to Hell. 2 bullets thro' right foot. Forced landing, O.K., at 15 Heavy Battery near Reninghelst. Observer thinks he got a Hun'.

Having recovered from his wounds, he next joined 46 Squadron as a Flight Commander on 6 March 1918. Between that date and the day of his death, he claimed four further 'victories', so becoming an 'ace' in his own right. His Commanding Officer, Major R H S Mealing, described Philip Smith as 'wonderfully brave, perhaps too brave' and he was recommended on at least four occasions for a decoration of some sort. His body was never recovered and he is commemorated on the Arras Memorial to the Missing, France. He was twenty-two years old. After the war, Smith's father, determined to trace his son's remains, crossed to France with former Camel pilot, Donald Gold. Gold, having just been shot down by Jasta 11 himself, had stood and watched helplessly as von Richthofen relentlessly pressed home his attacks until Smith's Sopwith Camel exploded into flames and fell to earth. Although Mr Smith was successful in locating and mapping the positions of the various pieces of the Camel's wreckage, he was never able to discover his son's body.

GvRI

Dieu et mon Droit

HE whom this scroll commemorates was numbered among those who, at the call of King and Country, left all that was dear to them, endured hardness, faced danger, and finally passed out of the sight of men by the path of duty and self-sacrifice, giving up their own lives that others might live in freedom.

Let those who come after see to it that his name be not forgotten.

Capt. Sydney Philip Smith
Royal Army Service Corps (T.F.) & 46th Sqdn Royal Air Force

War Office (A.G.10.)
27, Pilgrim Street
London, E.C.4
12th May 1921.

Sir,

I am directed to transmit to you the accompanying "1914-15 Star" which would have been conferred upon Captain S.P. Smith, The Army Service Corps & Royal Air Force had he lived, in memory of his services with the British Forces during the Great War.

In forwarding the Decoration, I am commanded by the King to assure you of His Majesty's high appreciation of the services rendered.

I am to request that you will be so good as to acknowledge the receipt of the Decoration on the attached form.

I am, Sir,
Your obedient Servant,

A. H. Smith Esq.

P. M. W. Macdonogh
Adjutant General.

Temporary.

George R.I.

George by the Grace of God, of the United Kingdom of Great Britain and Ireland, and of the British Dominions beyond the Seas, King, Defender of the Faith, Emperor of India, &c.

To Our Trusty and well beloved Sydney P. Smith Greeting.

We reposing especial Trust and Confidence in your Loyalty, Courage, and good Conduct, do by these Presents Constitute and Appoint you to be an Officer in Our Land Forces from the Eighth day of December 1914. You are therefore carefully and diligently to discharge your Duty as such in the Rank of 2nd Lieutenant or in such higher Rank as We may from time to time hereafter be pleased to promote or appoint you to, of which a notification will be made in the London Gazette, and you are at all times to exercise and well discipline in Arms both the inferior Officers and Men serving under you and use your best endeavours to keep them in good Order and Discipline. And We do hereby Command them to Obey you as their superior Officer and you to observe and follow such Orders and Directions as from time to time you shall receive from Us, or any your superior Officer, according to the Rules and Discipline of War, in pursuance of the Trust hereby reposed in you.

Given at Our Court, at Saint James's, the Fifth day of December 1914 in the Fifth Year of Our Reign.

By His Majesty's Command.

Sydney P. Smith
2nd Lieutenant
Land Forces.

PRIVY PURSE OFFICE,
BUCKINGHAM PALACE, S.W.

25th January, 1921.

Dear Sir,

The King and Queen have during the War invariably sent messages of sympathy to the nearest relative of those who have lost their lives in the service of their Country.

In cases of doubt, however, Their Majesties have refrained from sending any message, always hoping that the report might not be true.

The King and Queen have now heard with deep regret that the death of your son, Captain S.P. Smith, is presumed to have taken place in 1918, and I am commanded to convey to you the expression of Their Majesties' sympathy with you in your sorrow, and to assure you that during the long months of uncertainty Their Majesties' thoughts have been constantly with you and those who have been called upon to endure this exceptional burden of anxiety.

Yours very truly,

Keeper of the Privy Purse.

A.W. Smith, Esq.

Top left: One of more than a million illuminated Scrolls sent to the families of British and Empire casualties of the Great War.

Top right: Letter from the War Office forwarding, posthumously, the 1914/15 Star conferred upon Captain S P Smith for his service in France and Flanders with the British Expeditionary Force.

Above: The King's 'Commission'.

Right: Letter from the Keeper of the Privy Purse sent, on behalf of the King and Queen, to all relatives of men previously posted as 'Missing' but subsequently known to have died.

7 APRIL 1918

VICTORY NO.77

SOPWITH CAMEL NO.D6550
73 SQUADRON RAF
ENGINE NO.1609 WD 50208
GUNS: C7827; C3602

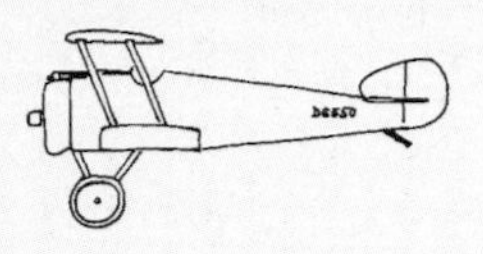

VON RICHTHOFEN'S Combat Report:
1130 hrs, near Hangard. SE5; broke up in the air. Englishman.

With four machines of Jasta 11, I attacked several 'SE5's' near Hangard. I shot at an enemy plane some 200 metres away. After I had fired 100 shots, the enemy plane broke apart. The remnants came down near Hangard.

BARON VON RICHTHOFEN

WEATHER: GOOD VISIBILITY BUT CLOUD COVER AT HEIGHT.

Again, the identity of his victim is not clear. While Richthofen does seem to identify the machine as an SE5, it is not clear as to why he noted the type in inverted commas in the text, unless he meant to show he was not certain of the type himself. (And there is the question of victory No.78; see page 194.)

Evidence of the problems facing historians is shown by Floyd Gibbons' choice of victim. Taking the SE5 statement at face value, he came down in favour of Captain Guy Borthwick Moore MC, of No.1 Squadron, who was killed this day. However, Moore's machine (C1083) was seen to be blown apart by a shell over Hollebeke, having taken off at 1252. Hollebeke is 112 kilometres north-east of Hangard, therefore he cannot by any stretch of the imagination be a candidate.

Eyes then fell on Lieutenant Philip John Nolan DFC of 24 Squadron (SE5a B63). The problem here, however, is that Nolan is shown in the loss report as taking off at 1500, over three hours after Richthofen claimed. Nolan is reported to have hit a tree, which, it has been suggested, might have been seen by Richthofen as breaking up. However, Richthofen's report makes no mention of being low down, and he clearly states that the SE5 broke to parts (pieces) and the remnants came down near Hangard. This surely indicates that they were higher than tree height. Finally, Nolan has to be discounted, provided Richthofen's timing is correct, for a 5 Brigade combat report clearly shows that Nolan was in a fight at 1550 and was shot down by an Albatros DV, witnessed by Lieutenant R T Mark, crashing into Moreuil Wood, six kilometres south-west of Hangard, in a position given as 66E/C.22. Nolan went down under the guns of Leutnant Fritz Pütter of Jasta 68 over Moreuil at 1545 hrs, his 19th of an eventual 25 victories.

Others have also said that Captain G E H McElroy MC and Bar, of 40 Squadron, came to the rescue of some SE5s fighting some Albatri and Triplanes in the area of Moreuil and claimed three; two DVs and one Triplane, timed at between 1040 and 1115, which is a little before Richthofen's combat.

If the 'SE5' (in quotes) gave question to the actual type, then perhaps this fight was in fact the combat between Camels of 73 Squadron and Triplanes in this same area. Captain Maurice LeBlanc Smith (D1839), who was involved with Richthofen back on 24 March, led an OP to the Bray-Caix area, taking off at 1010. The patrol encountered about 20 Triplanes, the fight going on above Lamotte-Warfusée.

Two Camels were brought down, one flown by Gallie, the other by Lieutenant R G H Adams (D6554). Gallie came down 1,500 yards west of Villers-Bretonneux, perhaps four kilometres north of Hangard, but survived. Adams fell too and is supposed to have been the victim of Jasta 6's Hans Kirschstein. Kirschstein reported his kill down north-east of Harbonnières, which is nine kilometres east of Hangard. Adams later reported that a German staff officer told him he was von Richthofen's 77th victory, which is of interest considering the overall problem. Adams' machine certainly smashed to pieces and he was left for dead under a tarpaulin alongside a railway track. It was only when he moaned, and was heard, that the German troops nearby realised he was alive.

Jasta 11 only made one claim, Hans-Joachim Wolff sending down an SE5a north of Domart-s-la-Luce, just west of Hangard, at 1150, but this victory was not confirmed. One wonders if this was a disputed claim with Richthofen and Richthofen won, especially if the type was wrong. Other Camels were shot down during this mid-morning period, but they were not in this area.

Jasta 11 had Siegfried Gussmann wounded on this day, and apart from McElroy's actions, Second Lieutenant R R Rowe and Captain G A H Pidcock of 73 Squadron each claimed a Triplane out of control, east of Villers-Bretonneux and north of Lamotte, between 1130 and 1200.

Von Richthofen was flying Fokker DrI Nr.477/17.

GALLIE,
ALBERT VERNON
SECOND LIEUTENANT 73 SQUADRON

Gallie, commissioned on 17 October 1917, was perhaps the luckiest of von Richthofen's victims in that he was able to walk away from his wrecked aeroplane, comparatively unscathed. Just six days earlier, on 1 April, the very day that the Royal Flying Corps and the Royal Naval Air Service combined to become the Royal Air Force, Gallie had run out of fuel returning from patrol and had crashed another Camel, No.C1578. Gallie was unhurt but the machine, a total wreck, had to be written off. Having had two miraculous escapes in seven days, Gallie went on to learn well his trade as a fighter pilot, gaining four 'victories' in the remaining months of the war. All were Fokker DVIIs: one crashed east of Montdidier on 6 June although Gallie's Camel (No. D6504) was also badly shot about; another crashed north-west of Conchy on 11 June; then came two 'out of control' 'victories' in Camel D8202 on 16 July over Château Thierry and another east of Launoy on 25 July.

Below: Camels of 73 Squadron.

7 APRIL 1918

VICTORY NO.78

SOPWITH CAMEL NO. D6554
73 SQUADRON RAF ENGINE
NO: 1613 WD 30212
GUNS: C3632; A9958

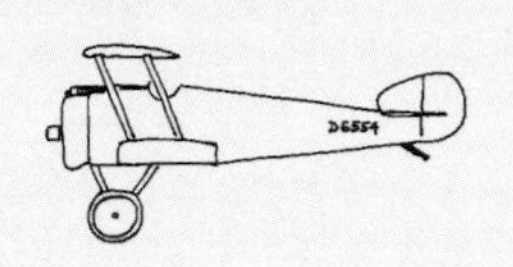

VON RICHTHOFEN'S Combat Report:
1205 hrs, 500 metres east of Hill 104, north of Villers-Bretonneux. Spad, fell down: Englishman.

I was observing, and noted that a Kette [three] of German planes pursuing an English plane was being attacked from the rear. I dashed to their aid and attacked an English plane. After putting myself behind him several times, the adversary fell. The plane crashed into the ground and I saw that it smashed to pieces. This happened 500 metres east of Hill 104.

BARON VON RICHTHOFEN

This second kill of the patrol does little to help with the previous question concerning victory No.77. Firstly there were no longer any British Spads at the Front, although French ones were in the area as evidenced by the fact that two days earlier French Spads had downed an Albatros DV which today stands in the Smithsonian Institute in America. However, he does say specifically it was an English machine, so one imagines he could clearly make out the RFC roundels on the wings, rather than those of the French Air Force. In any event, there are no French Spad losses recorded this day. So once more we are faced with a possible problem of identification by von Richthofen.

At this time, Hill 104, just south of the Somme River, was held by Australian troops, with Villers-Bretonneux 1,000 metres due south and Hangard south again.

Once more we can examine the known casualties. It could still be the fight with 73 Squadron and probably is. Perhaps this was Gallie's Camel, which came down less than a mile from Villers-Bretonneux. 73 Squadron had two other machines badly shot up – Captain M LeBlanc Smith (D1839) and Lieutenant A N Baker (D1823) – but both got back to their base.

A Camel of 208 Squadron was lost this day, shortly after noon, but it fell way up north of Douai. 4 AFC Squadron lost one too, at 1115, near Illies, but that was to AA fire and was again up on the northern sectors. All the other casualties in the RAF War Diary were the results of ground fire.

Having claimed a Spad, of course, would preclude him from being considered for a second Camel claim by the Germans, so if in fact Richthofen attacked and damaged either LeBlanc Smith or Baker, and perhaps then saw Adams crash and thought this was his victim hitting the ground, then this would have no basis for a credit. It would, however, go some way towards explaining why Adams was later later told by his captors that he had been brought down by the Baron, despite the confusion and that Richthofen later was only credited with one

Camel – Gallie's. Significantly, of course, Richthofen did record going down to aid three other aircraft attacking the 'Spad' – more than likely this was Kirschstein going down after Adams. Obviously, too, that as Richthofen claimed a Spad, and no wrecked Spads were located in the general area, he would not be in line for any dispute over Kirschstein's victory. The bulk of the evidence, however, is that Richthofen was in combat with Adams and was involved in his being brought down, but it was credited to Kirschstein. Adams was last seen over Lamotte, just as the fight started, which is only four kilometres east of Villers-Bretonneux.

Von Richthofen was flying Fokker Dr1 No.477/17.

ADAMS, RONALD GEORGE HININGS

LIEUTENANT 73 SQUADRON; 15/MIDDLESEX REGIMENT

Born in Bromyard, Worcestershire on the last day of 1896, Adams was educated at University College, London. He was still not eighteen years old when he was commissioned temporary Second Lieutenant into the 15th (Reserve) Battalion of the Middlesex Regiment on 2 December 1914. Transfer to the Royal Flying Corps followed and Adams qualified as an observer before going on to pilot training. He served with 18 Squadron and flew Camels with 44 Squadron on Home Defence before joining 73 Squadron in France. Wounded and taken prisoner after his fight with von Richthofen, Adams spent the next eight months in hospitals and prison camps until finally being repatriated on 17 December 1918. After the war, Adams qualified as a chartered accountant but, finding that a less than exciting existence, tried his luck at theatre management, taking on the Embassy Theatre, London, and then gravitated to the acting profession itself, and, in the process, altered his name slightly to 'Ronald Adam'. He also wrote books and several of his plays were staged. As he matured, he found film parts came his way. His urbane manner, his tall figure and distinguished demeanour guaranteed him many 'character' roles in a film career which started in 1936. His dozens of films, American and British, included, *'Q' Planes, The Lion Has Wings, Song of Freedom, Escape to Danger, Angels One-Five, The Lavender Hill Mob, Captain Horatio Hornblower R.N., The Million Pound Note, The Man Who Never Was, Reach For The Sky, Cleopatra, etc.* During the Second World War, Adams rejoined the Royal Air Force and was, among other appointments, Fighter Controller at Hornchurch during the Battle of Britain. By the war's end, Adams had reached the rank of Wing Commander. His first marriage to Tanzi Cutana Barozzi was dissolved and he married for a second time to Allyne Dorothy Franks, living in Surbiton in Surrey. He died on 28 March 1979, in his eighty-third year.

20 APRIL 1918

VICTORY NO.79

SOPWITH CAMEL D6439
3 SQUADRON RAF
ENGINE NO: 9204 WD 31691
GUNS: C10397; C10005

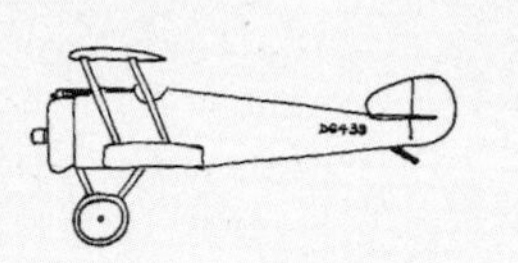

VON RICHTHOFEN'S Combat Report:
1840 hrs, south-west of Bois de Hamel.
Sopwith Camel, burned; Englishman.

With six planes of Jasta 11, I attacked large enemy squadron. During the fight I observed that a Triplane was attacked and shot at from below by a Camel. I put myself behind the adversary and brought him down, burning, with only a few shots. The enemy plane crashed down near the forest of Hamel where it burned further on the ground.

BARON VON RICHTHOFEN

WEATHER: FINE AT FIRST; CLOUDY AND OVERCAST LATER.

Fortunately, after the difficulties of identifying the last two victories, his 79th and 80th are both clear-cut. Captain D J Bell MC (C6730) led the patrol of 3 Squadron, Major Raymond-Barker being amongst the pack.

At 1800, east of Villers-Bretonneux, they spotted five or six Fokker Triplanes in solid colours – one red, one blue, etc. In the fight that followed, Bell saw a Camel burst into flames and go down out of control, and then saw another Camel go down, catch fire, but then it seemed to go out. He also saw a Triplane crash west of Hamel Wood. Captain C M Lemon MC (5446) engaged a Triplane which had sent a Camel down in flames (Richthofen), fired 100 rounds, but saw no results. Lieutenant L A Hamilton (D6519) engaged in the fight, being at the back of the formation, and almost at once saw a Camel burst into flames. He attacked and fired into a blue Triplane, the pilot putting his machine into a spin. Second Lieutenant C M Kinney (C1629) also saw a Camel go down on fire and he dived on a red Triplane, firing about 150 rounds at it. He then saw a green and white Triplane on his tail and broke off the combat against the red machine.

It seems as though the Triplanes initially fired at the Camels at long range, and at least one pilot thought that Raymond-Barker had been killed instantly after he'd been hit.

Von Richthofen was flying Fokker Dr1 No.425/17.

RAYMOND – BARKER, RICHARD

MAJOR 3 SQUADRON MC; NORTHUMBERLAND FUSILIERS

DICK RAYMOND-BARKER was born on 6 May 1894, the son of Edward and Rose Raymond-Barker of 'Paulmead', Bisley, Gloucestershire. He was educated at Wimbledon College and Mount St Mary's College. Dick assisted in the laying of submarine cable from Sydney to Auckland aboard the telegraph steamer, *Silverton*, and later, other cable work on the west and south-east African coasts. Just before the start of the Great War, he had gone to Canada to farm but returned immediately and enlisted as a private soldier in the Middlesex Regiment. Within three months he had been promoted to Sergeant and was then commissioned into the 5th Battalion, Northumberland Fusiliers on 30 November 1914. Next he learnt to fly at his own expense, gaining the Royal Aero Club Aviators Certificate (No.1460) on 18 July 1915. Transferring to the Royal Flying Corps on 6 August 1915, he gained his 'Wings' on 19 October, before being posted to France on the 22 November following. He flew with both 6 and 16 Squadrons over the next 13 months. Promotion and posting to 48 Squadron, which was equipped with Bristol Fighters, followed on 12 May 1917. Shortly afterwards, on 2 July, he was sent to 11 Squadron, another of the Bristol Fighter units. During these periods, he and his observer claimed six 'victories' and he was awarded the Military Cross, *London Gazette* 17/9/1917, page 9581:

'For conspicuous gallantry and devotion to duty when leading a fighting patrol. He attacked a large hostile formation, destroying two of them. He has also done excellent work in leading distant photographic reconnaissances, notably upon two occasions when his skilful leadership enabled photographs to be taken of all the required hostile area in spite of repeated attacks from enemy aircraft. He has helped to destroy seven hostile machines and has at all times displayed conspicuous skill and gallantry'.

In the same month that his MC was announced in the *London Gazette*, Raymond-Barker, now an 'ace' in his own right, was promoted to Major and given command of 3 Squadron. Yet another brilliantly promising career was cut short with his death at the hands of von Richthofen on 20 April 1918. Dick's younger brother, Lt Aubrey Basil Raymond-Barker, was a pilot with 12 Squadron and had been taken prisoner of war on 21 October 1916. On that day, the youngest Raymond-Barker was piloting a BE2c on a bombing raid; he was last seen flying just below 2/Lt J G Cameron (von Richthofen's eighth 'victory') when he was attacked by a fast biplane of Jasta 2, the British machine going down in a steep spiral and crashing north of Bullecourt. The eldest brother, Lt Henry Edward Raymond-Barker, formerly Ceylon Planters Rifle Corps and later 3/Brahmans, Indian Army, saw service in Egypt, Mesopotamia and Arabia. The Raymond-Barker boys' parents were descendants of John Raymond, who had inherited his aunt-in-law's Fairford estates and fortune and, at her request, had added her name, Barker, to his own. Dick's body was never recovered and he is commemorated on the Arras Memorial to the Missing, France. He was just over twenty-four years of age.

20 APRIL 1918

VICTORY NO.80

SOPWITH CAMEL NO.B7393
3 SQUADRON RAF
ENGINE NO.101026 WD10398
GUNS: A6576 & B168

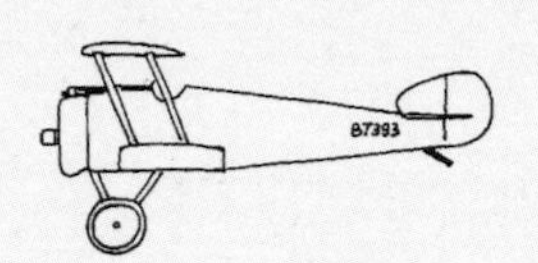

VON RICHTHOFEN'S Combat Report:
1843 hrs, north-east of Villers-Bretonneux.
Sopwith Camel, burned: Englishman.

Three minutes after I had brought down the first machine, I attacked a second Camel of the same enemy squadron. The adversary dived, caught his machine and repeated this manoeuvre several times. I approached him as near as possible when fighting and fired 50 bullets until the machine began to burn. The body of the machine was burned in the air, the remnants dashed to the ground, north-east of Villers-Bretonneux.

BARON VON RICHTHOFEN

During the same fight, Lewis was also hit and went down. He'd seen the red Triplane come round behind his tail and Richthofen's bullets set his seven-gallon gravity tank afire. Lewis, however, was more fortunate than his CO had been, and somehow survived the impact with the ground. He came down only some 50 yards from Raymond-Barker's machine the wreckage of which was burning furiously.

As he stood between the two burning machines, Lewis saw a Triplane fly by at low level, the pilot waving. Presumably this was Richthofen and he must have assumed the man to be a German soldier, for it seems certain he believed his two victories had resulted in two men dead. He undoubtedly wanted someone on the ground to recognise his red machine in order to gain confirmation of his two kills.

Leutnant Hans Weiss of Jasta 11 was credited with a Camel shot down, south-west of the Bois de Hamel at 1840, but this appears to be a 201 Squadron machine. Another 3 Squadron pilot, Second Lieutenant G R Riley RFC (GL) in D6475, returned wounded having been hit on the left shoulder by a machine gun bullet, his Camel damaged. There are no apparent personnel losses amongst JG1's pilots.

Von Richthofen gained his 80th victory and his second of the day, flying Fokker Dr1 No.425/17. This machine is understood to have had red sides and top deck of fuselage, red upper surfaces of all wings, struts, wheel covers and tail, but white rudder. The former Patee crosses had been overpainted with the new broad style Balken crosses. Wing and fuselage undersurfaces were turquoise.

Its engine was a 110 hp Oberursel type, serial Nr.2478. This Dr1's Werke Nr. was 2009, built in Frankfurt and first tested on 8 January 1918. It was in this same Dr1 that von Richthofen flew out to do battle with 209 Squadron the next day – and failed to return.

LEWIS,
DAVID GRESWOLDE
SECOND LIEUTENANT 3 SQUADRON

DAVID LEWIS CAME to England from his home in Bulawayo, Rhodesia as soon as he was old enough to offer his services in the Royal Flying Corps. Born on 15 October 1898, he had spent most of his life in Africa but now took up residence at 'Melvin Hall', Golders Green, London whilst awaiting his acceptance into the Inns of Court OTC which finally arrived on 16 February 1917. Two months later, on 16 April, he was posted to the RFC Cadet School before finally being commissioned on 16 June 1917. Following training with 198 TD (June to September) he was sent to 78 Home Defence Squadron (September to 27 March, 1918). Lewis was friendly with Captain Douglas Bell, MC, and, finding that Bell was about to be sent as a Flight Commander to 3 Squadron in France, managed, on 29 March 1918, to 'wangle' a 'joint' posting with his friend. Lewis flew in Bell's Flight during one of the most fraught periods for the BEF of the whole of the war. Three weeks of intensive patrolling followed his arrival in France until, on 20 April, he met the Red Baron. Thankfully, he lived to 'tell the tale' and enjoy, in later life, some small fame as von Richthofen's last 'victory'. His subsequent incarceration at Graudenz lasted until 1 December 1918 when, at last, he was repatriated. After the war, Lewis returned to live on the family 'ranch' at Gwanda, southern Rhodesia. In the mid-thirties, Lewis was Assistant Native Commissioner of the Native Affairs Department at Balanago, Southern Rhodesia. In 1938, he was invited to Germany to attend the dedication of the new Richthofen Geschwader. By the time he retired in 1958, at the age of sixty, he had become an Under-Secretary (Administration) in the Government of Rhodesia. Lewis was to enjoy yet another miraculous escape in his lifetime. During the Rhodesian War of Independence, his car was ambushed by terrorists, the vehicle being raked from end to end by machine gun fire. Lewis walked away from the wreck, unhurt. He died in Salisbury on 10 August 1978, more than sixty years after his encounter with the Red Baron.

FINALE

Any self-respecting historian or enthusiast of WW1 aviation will know that Manfred von Richthofen was brought down and killed on Sunday 21 April 1918, just as any schoolboy should know the date of the Battle of Hastings.

Much has been written and many have argued about who brought him down, but at this distance in time nobody will ever be able to prove with any certainty whether it was from ground fire or a bullet from a Sopwith Camel. We do not wish to extend that particular debate, merely to record the brief factual details of the last morning of Manfred von Richthofen's life.

Both the German and British air forces were still engaged in the bitter air fighting above the ground battles that had begun with Germany's March Offensive. Exactly one month after the commencement of the offensive, on 21 April, the Germans knew that while they had achieved much it, like all the other offensives mounted by German, British or French armies since 1916, had failed.

The morning of the 21st found Richthofen's airfield at Cappy shrouded in fog. Growing hope that it would soon lift saw the German pilots preparing for flight notwithstanding a heavy evening of celebration the night before following the Rittmeister's 80th victory the previous day. Despite von Richthofen having flown long and hard over the previous month, there was some good-natured horseplay on Cappy airfield, Manfred one among the many who laughed away the early morning while the mist slowly lifted.

There had been talk of him finally retiring from the battle front, a score of 80 being a nice round number at which to do so, but nothing had been decided, and there can be little doubt that the man himself would think the magic '100' a better score at which to retire.

Visibility improved. At about 1030 came the call the pilots had been waiting for. British aircraft were over the Front. No sooner had this news come than the Fokker Triplanes were started up and the snub-nosed fighters climbed into the sky.

Over the Front the usual assortment of British Corps aircraft were starting to operate, taking photographs or directing artillery fire. On this particular section RE8s of No.3 AFC (Australian Flying Corps) were operating, and of course RAF fighters

Right: O C LeBoutillier.

were beginning to patrol.

The Squadron that would be in the forefront of the coming air battle, No.209 (formally No.9 RNAS which had become 209 once the RFC and the RNAS merged on 1 April 1918), took off from its base at Bertangles, just north of Amiens. Cappy was 32 kilometres from Amiens in a straight line over the meandering Somme River which flowed almost due west at this point. They started taking off at 0935, so as German time was one hour ahead of the British they were becoming airborne just about the time JG1 were preparing to fly.

No. 209 Squadron were flying a High Offensive Patrol (HOP) in three sections of five as follows:

A Flight

- Capt A R Brown DSC B7270
- Lt W J Mackenzie B7245
- Lt W R May D3326
- Lt Lomas D3340
- Lt F J W Mellersh D3329

B Flight

- Capt O C LeBoutillier D3338
- Lt R M Foster B3858
- Lt M A Harker B7272
- Lt M S Taylor B7200
- Lt C G Brock D3328

C Flight

- Capt O W Redgate
- Lt A W Aird
- Lt E B Drake
- Lt C G Edwards
- Lt J H Siddall

Below: Lt W J Mackenzie.

Half an hour into their patrol, Mellersh dropped out with engine trouble and returned to Bertangles, changed Camels (to B6257) and at 1010 was back in the air meeting up with the others over the Front. Oliver LeBoutillier (an American from New Jersey) and his Flight, found and engaged two Albatros two-seaters over Le Quesnel, about ten kilometres south of the straight Amiens to St Quentin road. With Foster and Taylor, he engaged one of them and they set it on fire. It crashed at Beaucourt-en-Senterre, just to the north-west of Le Quesnel, at 1025.

This action occurred at the southern most section of their patrol line, so the Camels turned and headed north, but not before conducting a quick search in the clouds for the second two-seater. As the main formation headed north, von Richthofen and his pilots were heading west from Cappy both to cover any German two-seaters working near the lines, and to engage the British Corps aircraft doing similar work.

They were in company with Jasta 5 aircraft, von Richthofen leading one Kette (Flight) flying with his cousin Wolfram von Richthofen, Oberleutnant Walther Karjos, Vizefeldwebel Edgar Scholz and Leutnant Hans-Joachim Wolff. Leutnant Hans Weiss led the second Kette, which included Leutnant Richard Wenzl. As the clouds parted, the Germans saw the RE8 machines of 3 AFC and they moved to engage but at that moment, the Camels of A and B Flights of 209 Squadron arrived on the scene (C Flight had become separated). Wolff later described how they saw one small group of Camels below them, near Hamel just south of the Somme, while the Jasta 5 machines were some way off, over Sailly-le-Sec, about four kilometres to the north-east, just the other side of the river. Shortly afterwards, Wenzl saw some more Camels – Oliver LeBoutillier's B Flight.

The Fokkers of Jasta 11 and the Albatros DVs of Jasta 5 began to duel with the Camels. For once the wind (usually the

Below: Lt W R May, who so nearly became victory No.81.

prevailing wind was west to east, a distinct disadvantage for Allied flyers who would be blown east towards the German rear areas, and then have to battle against the same wind to fly back over the lines) was blowing east to west, reversing the problem.

In the ensuing fight, Lieutenant Mackenzie was wounded in the back from fire from what he described as a brown-fuselaged Triplane with blue spots on the wings (fuselage was possibly dark red but it was not von Richthofen) and although he fought this Fokker down, he had to break off due to the pain of his injury. Francis Mellersh, who had rejoined Roy Brown, dived on to the Triplane and Albatros fighters and shot at a blue-tailed Fokker which he saw go down and crash near Cerisy, right by the river. (The pilot was thought to be Scholz, although he did not crash!) He was then attacked by two more Triplanes but managed to get away by spinning down to about 50 feet. Returning then towards Bertangles, he saw a bright red Triplane crash quite close to him and looking up saw Roy Brown's Camel.

Meantime, LeBoutillier engaged Triplanes over Cerisy and fired without result at one and then fired on a red one which was then shot down by Brown, LeBoutillier reporting it crashed by Brown on the Allied side of the lines. Taylor and Foster, breaking away as the fight ended, then chased three two-seaters they found near Albert but they dived east and were not pursued due to shortage of ammunition.

As has often been related before, Wilfred 'Wop' May, from Edmonton, Alberta, hovered on the edge of the fight where, being a novice, he had been advised to stay if a scrap started; suddenly he had the opportunity to have a crack at a Fokker (thought to be that of Wolfram von Richthofen) that came tantalizingly near. However, he was then attacked from behind by another and broke away, heading for the British lines. He would have had no idea who the German pilot was and, indeed, there has never been any suggestion that 209 Squadron's pilots knew they were engaging either von Richthofen or elements of JG1 until much later.

Von Richthofen must have become disorientated, either by the wind direction – or at least, by having drifted further west than he might ordinarily have done – or by diving down on the Camel and seeing the Somme River below, and he may have

Below: Capt A R Brown DSC, credited with bringing the Red Baron down.

thought the Camel pilot was heading east rather than west. Whatever the reason, and it could have been as simple as just being too intent on getting No.81, he now made one of his rare mistakes. He pursued the Camel, at low level, along the Somme and across the British line, held by Australian troops. Uncharacteristically he chased the British machine for far too long and became separated from his men.

Many of the ground troops fired up at the red Triplane as it flew by, both because it was a German and to help the Camel pilot. Machine gun and rifle fire was aimed at Richthofen's Fokker as he pursued the young Canadian down the river valley, but by now both had been spotted by Captain Roy Brown. There has never been any dispute about the fact that Brown now disengaged from the main fight and dived after the Triplane whose pilot seemed so intent on disposing of his fellow Canadian; not just a fellow Canadian, but also a new member of his Flight and an old school pal from Alberta College South, albeit more than two years his junior.

Brown closed and fired upon the Triplane, and, as his combat report indicated '... (it) went down vertical and was observed to crash by Lieutenant Mellersh and Lieutenant May.' Later, Oliver LeBoutillier also recorded that he'd seen the red Triplane go down and crash after Brown's attack, and at this stage there was no reason to believe that Brown had not got it. LeBoutillier would later say he saw tracer from Brown hit the Fokker and that it lurched as it was hit. One question that rarely seems to be faced, when the alternative theory is voiced that Richthofen was brought down by ground fire and that Brown was nowhere near when this happened, was why Brown would even consider breaking away after taking the trouble to chase after the Triplane in order to save May unless he was satisfied that (a) he had hit him, and (b) May was out of danger.

Whatever actually happened, von Richthofen was hit by a single bullet, and although some experts have stated he would have died instantly, we can never know that for certain. That he seems to have switched off his engine and tried for a landing would indicate that while he was certainly dying, he was not yet dead. That the engine was off is shown by the fact that if the engine was on and the pilot dead, the rotary-engined Fokker Triplane must surely have whipped over with the torque of the engine and immediately spun into the ground, rather than making a flat approach. That the wheels were torn off in the crash-landing could indicate that Richthofen became unconscious or died an instant before contact with the ground.

No sooner had the Triplane come to a standstill than nearby troops infested the area, and as soon as it was realised who the dead pilot was, souvenir hunters quickly stripped the Triplane of most of its fabric. The loss of this fabric also precludes anyone knowing if, while Richthofen himself was hit by just one bullet, others may have passed through the Fokker's canvas. The angle of the fatal bullet itself is no proof of it coming from the air or the ground, unless one could be absolutely sure of the angle of the Triplane the moment it was hit; and again, there can be no certainty of that. Von Richthofen's last moments were spent chasing May, weaving and turning along the Somme valley, climbing over trees and high ground then dropping once more to a lower level.

The Triplane came down in a mangel – or fertiliser beet – field alongside the Corbie to Bray road, in the British 5th Brigade area. The lifeless body was taken to the aerodrome at Poulainville, the base of No.3 AFC Squadron, just north of Amiens and about 15 kilometres from the crash site. At about 1600 the following afternoon, Australian officers of the Squadron formed a guard of honour as the body was taken to Bertangles cemetery just up the Amiens-Doullens road. Here Rittmeister Baron Manfred von Richthofen was buried with full military honours. The career and life of the Red Baron were over.

BUCKINGHAM PALACE

1918.

The Queen joins me in welcoming you on your release from the miseries & hardships, which you have endured with so much patience & courage.

During these many months of trial, the early rescue of our gallant Officers & Men from the cruelties of their captivity has been uppermost in our thoughts.

We are thankful that this longed for day has arrived, & that back in the old Country you will be able once more to enjoy the happiness of a home & to see good days among those who anxiously look for your return.

George R.I.

Left: A letter from King George V and Queen Mary sent to all returned Prisoners of War at the cessation of hostilities.

WHERE THE VICTIMS FELL

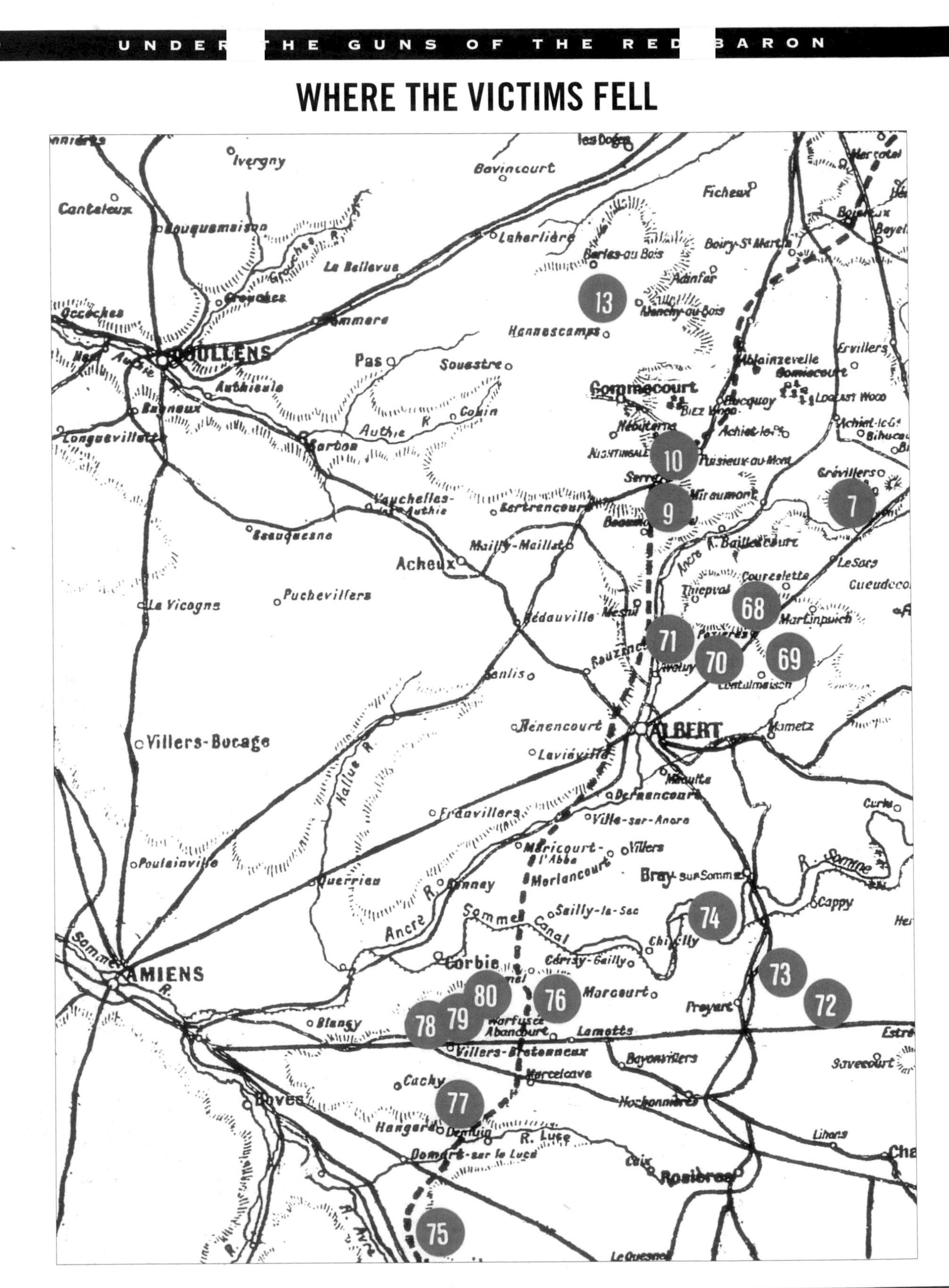

WHERE THE VICTIMS FELL

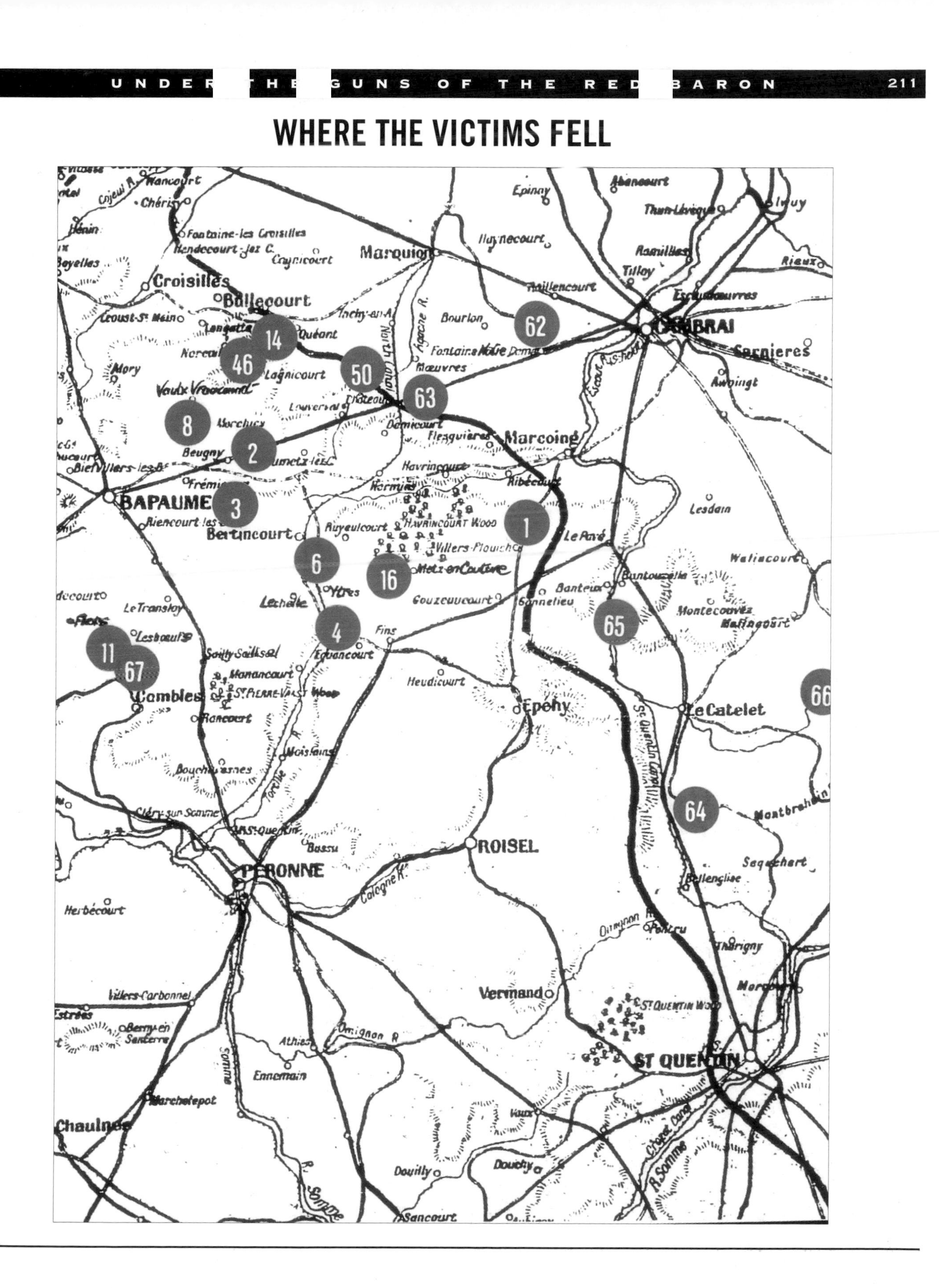

WHERE THE VICTIMS FELL

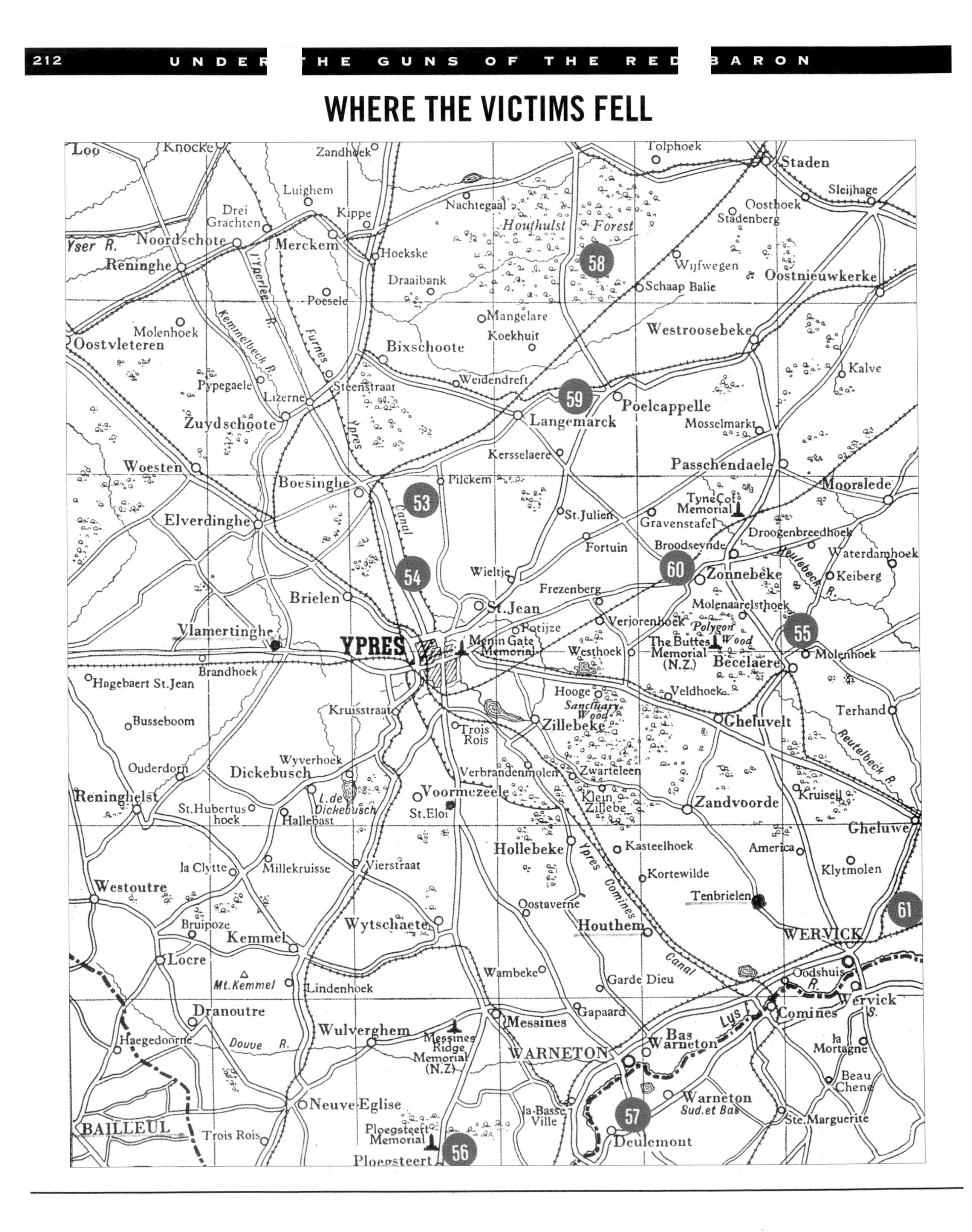

WHERE THE VICTIMS FELL

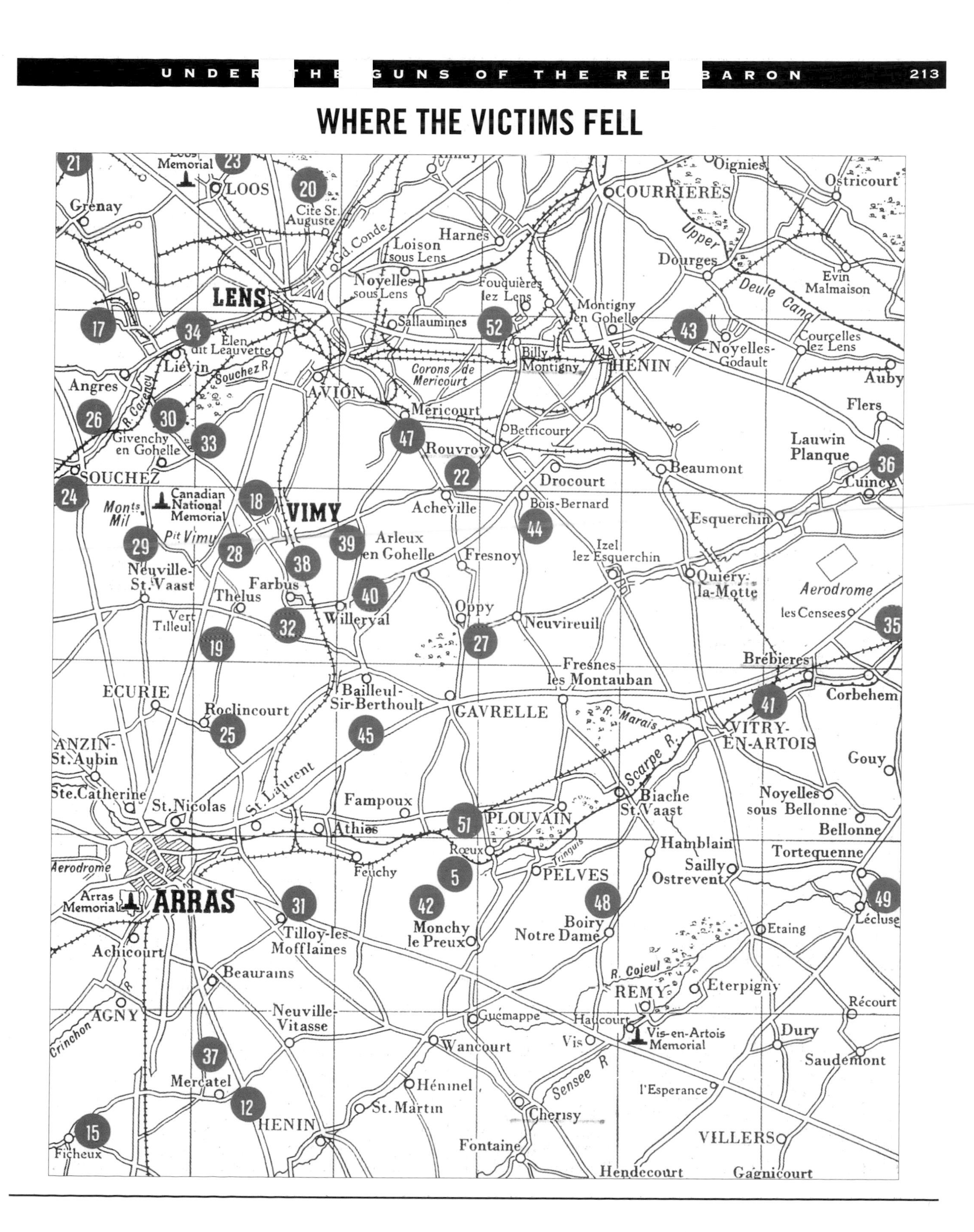

APPENDIX I

THE KILLING FIELDS

On the Western Front (a misnomer in itself – it was, after all, the Eastern Front for the Allies) the war in the air followed the war on the ground. Chronologically listed below are the main land battles and their broadly generic component actions in the British Sector during the period covered in this book.

THE SOMME, 1916

Albert	1 to 13 July
Bazentin Ridge	14 to 17 July
Delville Wood	15 July to 3 September
Pozières Ridge	23 July to 3 September
Guillemont	3 to 9 September
Ginchy	9 September
Flers Courcelette	15 to 22 September
Morval	25 to 28 September
Thiepval Ridge	26 to 28 September
Transloy Ridge	1 to 18 October
Ancre Heights	1 October to 11 November
Ancre	13 to 18 November

BAPAUME, 1917

Capture of Bapaume	17 March
Vimy Ridge	9 to 14 April
1st Scarpe	9 to 14 April

ARRAS, 1917

2nd Scarpe	23 to 24 April
Arleux	28 to 29 April
3rd Scarpe	3 to 4 May

OPPY, 1917

Capture of Oppy Wood	28 June

BULLECOURT, 1917

Bullecourt	3 to 17 May

HILL 70, 1917

Hill 70	15 to 25 August

MESSINES

Messines	7 to 14 June

YPRES, 1917 ('PASSCHENDAELE')

Pilckem Ridge	31 July to 2 August
Langemarck	16 to 18 August
Menin Road Ridge	20 to 25 September
Polygon Wood	26 September to 3 October
Broodseinde	4 October
1st Passchendaele	12 October
2nd Passchendaele	26 October to 10 November

CAMBRAI, 1917

Cambrai	20 November to 3 December

THE GERMAN SPRING OFFENSIVE COMMENCES ON 21 MARCH, 1918

SOMME, 1918

Pozières	26 to 27 March
1st Arras	28 March
Avre	4 April
Ancre	5 April

LYS, 1918

Estaires	9 to 11 April
Messines	10 to 11 April
Hazebrouck	12 to 15 April
Bailleul	13 to 15 April
1st Kemmel Ridge	17 to 19 April
Bethune	18 April
2nd Kemmel Ridge	25 to 26 April
Scherpenberg	29 April

VILLERS BRETONNEUX, 1918

Villers Bretonneux	24 to 25 April

APPENDIX II

VON RICHTHOFENS VICTORIES

	NAME	SQD	TYPE
1	Morris; Rees	11	FE2b
2	Bellerby	27	Martinsyde G.100
3	Lansdale Clarkson	11	FE2b
4	Fenwick	21	BE12
5	Thompson	19	BE12
6	Fisher	21	BE12
7	Baldwin Bentham	18	FE2b
8	Cameron (JG)	12	BE2c
9	Clarke; Lees	15	BE2c
10	Hall; Doughty	22	FE2b
11	Hawker	24	DH2
12	Hunt	32	DH2
13	Knight	29	DH2
14	D'Arcy Whiteside	18	FE2b
15	McCudden	29	DH2
16	Todd	N8	Sopwith Pup
17	Hay	40	FE8
18	Grieg MacLennan	25	FE2b
19	Murray; McRae	16	BE2d
20	Bennett; Croft	2	BE2d
21	Bailey Hampton	2	BE2c
22	Crosbee; Prance	2	BE2d
23	Green; Reid	43	Sopwith 1½ Strutter
24	Gosset-Bibby Brichta	16	BE2e
25	Pearson	29	DH2
26	Smyth; Byrne	2	BE2d
27	Boultbee; King	25	FE2b
28	Watt; Howlett	16	BE2g
29	Quicke; Lidsey	16	BE2f
30	Baker	19	Spad VII
31	Gilbert	29	Nieuport XVII
32	Powell; Bonner	13	BE2d
33	Warren; Dunn	43	Sopwith 1½ Strutter
34	McDonald O'Beirne	25	FE2d
35	Lechler; George	48	BF2a
36	Adams (AT) Stewart	48	BF2a
37	Smart (GO)	60	Nieuport XVII
38	Heagerty; Cantle	43	Sopwith 1½ Strutter
39	McKenzie Everingham	16	BE2g
40	Derwin; Pierson	13	BE2c
41	Stuart; Wood	59	RE8
42	Cunniffe; Batten	11	FE2b
43	Bates; Barnes	25	FE2b
44	Russell	60	Nieuport XVII
45	Pascoe (A) Andrews	13	BE2e
46	Franklin Fletcher	11	FE2b
47	Welch Tollervey	16	BE2f
48	Follit; Kirkham	13	BE2e
49	Applin	19	Spad VII
50	Stead; Beebee	18	FE2d
51	Davies Rathbone	12	BE2e
52	Cuzner	N8	Sopwith Triplane
53	Ellis; Barlow	9	Re8
54	Farquhar	23	Spad VII
55	McNaughton Mearns	57	DH4
56	Bowman Power-Clutterbuck	53	RE8
57	Whatley; Pascoe (FGB)	53	RE8
58	Williams (WHT)	29	Nieuport XXIII
59	Williams (CP)	19	Spad VII
60	Madge; Kember	6	RE8
61	Bird	46	Sopwith Pup
62	Boddy	64	DH5
63	McGregor	41	SE5a
64	Clutterbuck (LCF); Sparks	62	Bristol F2b
65	Heath	73	Sopwith Camel
66	Ivamy	54	Sopwith Camel
67	McCone	41	SE5a
68	Cameron (D)	3	Sopwith Camel
69	Denovan	1	SE5a
70	Reading; Legget	15	RE8
71	Sharpe	73	Sopwith Camel
72	Smart (ET) Barford	2	AWFK8
73	Harding	79	Sopwith Dolphin
74	Taylor Betley	82	AWFK8
75	Jones; Newton	52	RE8
76	Smith	46	Sopwith Camel
77	Gallie	73	Sopwith Camel
78	Adams (RGH)	73	Sopwith Camel
79	Raymond-Barker	3	Sopwith Camel
80	Lewis	3	Sopwith Camel

APPENDIX III

CALENDAR OF COMBAT 1SEPTEMBER 1916-21 APRIL 1918

	1916 Sept	Oct	Nov	Dec	1917 Jan	Feb	Mar	Bloody April	May	Jun
Mon					1					
Tue					2				1 L	
Wed			1		3				2 L	
Thu			2		4 **16**	1 **19**	1		3 L	
Fri	1 JASTA 2		3 **7**	1	5	2	2		4 L	1 L
Sat	2		4	2	6	3	3		5 L	2 L
Sun	3	1	5	3	7	4 L	4 **22,23**	1	6 L	3 L
Mon	4	2	6	4	8	5 L	5	2 **32,33**	7 L	4 L
Tue	5	3	7	5	9	6 L	6 **24**	3 **34**	8 L	5 L
Wed	6	4	8	6	10	7 L	7	4	9 L	6 L
Thur	7	5	9 **8**	7	11	8 L	8	5 **35,36**	10 L	7 L
Fri	8	6	10	8	12	9 L	9 **25**	6	11 L	8 L
Sat	9	7 **4**	11	9	13	10 L	10	7 **37**	12 L	9 L
Sun	10	8	12	10	14	11 L	11 **26**	8 **38,39**	13 L	10 L
Mon	11	9	13	11 **12**	15 JASTA 11	12 L	12	9	14 L	11 L
Tue	12	10	14 L	12	16	13 L	13	10	15 L	12 L
Wed	13	11	15 L	13	17	14 **20,21**	14	11 **40**	16 L	13 L
Thu	14	12	16 L	14	18	15	15	12	17 L	14 L
Fri	15	13	17	15	19	16	16	13 **41,42,43**	18 L	15 L
Sat	16	14	18	16	20	17	17 **27,28**	14 **44**	19 L	16 L
Sun	17 **1**	15	19	17	21	18	18	15	20 L	17 L
Mon	18	16 **5**	20 **9,10**	18	22	19	19	16 **45**	21 L	18 **53**
Tue	19	17	21	19	23 **17**	20	20	17	22 L	19
Wed	20	18	22	20 **13,14**	24 **18**	21	21 **29**	18	23 L	20
Thu	21	19	23 **11**	21	25	22	22	19	24 L	21
Fri	22	20	24	22	26	23	23	20	25 L	22
Sat	23 **2**	21	25	23	27	24	24 **30**	21	26 L	23 **54**
Sun	24	22	26	24	28	25	25 **31**	22 **46**	27 L	24 **55**
Mon	25	23	27	25	29	26	26	23 **47**	28 L	25 **56**
Tue	26	24	28	26	30	27	27	24	29 L	26
Wed	27	25 **6**	29	27 **15**	31	28	28	25	30 L	27
Thu	28	26	30	28			29	26	31 L	28
Fri	29	27		29			30	27		29
Sat	30 **3**	28		30			31	28 **48**		30
Sun		29		31				29 **49,50, 51,52**		
Mon		30						30		
Tue		31								

L = Leave W = Wounded R = Russia

APPENDIX III

CALENDAR OF COMBAT
1SEPTEMBER 1916 -21 APRIL 1918

													1918							
	July		Aug		Sept		Oct		Nov		Dec		Jan		Feb		Mar		Apr	
Mon							1	L											1	
Tue							2	L					1	R					2	75
Wed			1				3	L					2	R					3	
Thu			2				4	L	1				3	R					4	
Fri			3				5	L	2				4	R	1	R	1		5	
Sat			4		1		6	L	3		1		5	R	2		2		6	76
Sun	1		5		2	60	7	L	4		2		6	R	3		3		7	77,78
Mon	2	57	6		3	61	8	L	5		3		7	R	4		4		8	
Tue	3		7		4		9	L	6		4		8	R	5		5		9	
Wed	4		8		5		10	L	7		5		9	R	6		6		10	
Thur	5		9		6	L	11	L	8		6		10	R	7		7		11	
Fri	6	W	10		7	L	12	L	9		7		11	R	8		8		12	
Sat	7	W	11		8	L	13	L	10		8		12	R	9		9		13	
Sun	8	W	12		9	L	14	L	11		9		13	R	10		10		14	
Mon	9	W	13		10	L	15	L	12		10		14	R	11		11		15	
Tue	10	W	14		11	L	16	L	13		11		15	R	12		12	64	16	
Wed	11	W	15		12	L	17	L	14		12	L	16	R	13		13	65	17	
Thu	12	W	16	58	13	L	18	L	15		13	L	17	R	14		14		18	
Fri	13	W	17		14	L	19	L	16		14	L	18	R	15		15		19	
Sat	14	W	18		15	L	20	L	17		15	L	19	R	16		16		20	79,80
Sun	15	W	19		16	L	21	L	18		16	L	20	R	17		17		21	
Mon	16	W	20		17	L	22	L	19		17	L	21	R	18		18	66	22	
Tue	17	W	21		18	L	23	L	20		18	L	22	R	19		19		23	
Wed	18	W	22		19	L	24		21		19	L	23	R	20		20		24	
Thu	19	W	23		20	L	25		22		20	L	24	R	21		21		25	
Fri	20	W	24		21	L	26		23	62	21	L	25	R	22		22		26	
Sat	21	W	25		22	L	27		24		22	L	26	R	23		23		27	
Sun	22	W	26	59	23	L	28		25		23		27	R	24		24	67	28	
Mon	23	W	27		24	L	29		26		24		28	R	25		25	68	29	
Tue	24	W	28		25	L	30		27		25		29	R	26		26	69,70	30	
Wed	25	W	29		26	L	31		28		26		30	R	27		27	71,72,73		
Thu	26		30		27	L			29		27		31	R	28		28	74		
Fri	27		31		28	L			30	63	28	R					29			
Sat	28				29	L					29	R					30			
Sun	29				30	L					30	R					31			
Mon	30										31	R								
Tue	31																			

L = Leave W = Wounded R = Russia

THE PAINTINGS EXPLAINED

VICTORY NO. 1
11 Squadron FE2b 7018 flown by Lionel Morris and his observer Tom Rees, 17 September 1916. Morris, mortally wounded, brought his machine down by an airfield near Villers Plouich.

VICTORY NO. 6
21 Squadron BE12 6629, shot down near Bapaume, 25 October 1916, piloted by Arthur Fisher, who was killed.

VICTORY NO. 15
The DH2 flown by Sergeant James McCudden of 29 Squadron goes spinning down inverted above Fisheux, 27 December 1916 following an attack by von Richthofen. McCudden survives unharmed.

VICTORY NO. 33
No. 43 Squadron's 1½ Strutter A2401 attacked by von Richthofen over Givenchy, 2 April 1917. Despite his assertions otherwise, Sergeant Dunn, the observer, died in the air, Peter Warren being forced down into captivity.

VICTORY NO. 44
Already crippled in an attack on a two-seater, William Russell's Nieuport (A6796) is finished off by von Richthofen, 14 April 1917, and he becomes a prisoner. 60 Squadron lost four pilots in this action.

VICTORY NO. 52
In a fight with Nieuports, Spads and Triplanes, on 29 April 1917, von Richthofen brings down Canadian Albert Cuzner's Sopwith of 8 Naval Squadron, ending his Bloody April spree of 22 victories.

VICTORY NO. 62
Above the Battle of Cambrai, 23 November 1917, von Richthofen attacks DH5s ground strafing and is credited with bringing down 64 Squadron's James Boddy. Boddy loses a leg but is rescued by a brother officer.

VICTORY NO. 70
Von Richthofen's priority are the Corps' aircraft working along the Front. On 26 March 1918 an RE8 crew from 15 Squadron fall in flames east of Albert while carrying out their duties.

VICTORY NO. 73
An American, George Harding, falls under the guns of von Richthofen during Germany's 1918 March Offensive. Although claimed as a Bristol Fighter it is in fact a Sopwith Dolphin.

VICTORY NO. 76
Von Richthofen catches out Captain Philip Smith of 46 Squadron, whose Camels are attacking ground targets around Villers-Bretonneux on 6 April 1918. D6491 falls in flames.

ARTIST'S NOTES

The ten colour paintings included in this volume were created with as much regard for authenticity as possible. However, reference material for this period and subject is patchy at the best, and in many cases controversial.

The combat scenarios have been taken from translations of von Richthofen's reports or his biographical works. Some of the reports contain references to the markings of his aircraft but it has been difficult to illustrate his aircraft with certainty, particularly the earlier machines.

His first Albatros, DII 491/16 seems to have escaped the attentions of photographers so its appearance has been based on photographs of an aircraft in the same batch – 497/16 *(illustrations 1 and 2)*. This was the first of his aircraft to be painted red, but to what extent is not known. I have opted to show it with a red fuselage and tail, with the national markings still just visible through the red paint *(illustration 3)*.

Albatros DIII 2253/17 *(illustrations 4,5, & 6)*, is now generally agreed to have been painted red on the fuselage and tail surfaces with the wings left in their camouflage colours (green/mauve upper and light blue lower surfaces). There is some doubt as to the exact appearance of the national markings which may have been thinly over-painted or completely covered and inefficiently re-marked.

The Albatros D V, 4693/17 *(illustration 7)* is known to have had a red nose and tail and may well be the aircraft which appears in the oft-published photograph of von Richthofen visiting *Marine Feldfl Abt 2*. The extent of the red nose paintwork is based on this photograph; at least one earlier DV had the red limited to the spinner and the metal cowling immediately aft.

The Fokker DrI triplanes flown by von Richthofen are better documented but there is still argument over their exact appearance. Neither of the two "all red" aircraft (152/17 and 425/17, in which he died) feature in the illustrations; 477/17 *(illustration 8 & 9)* and 127/17 *(illustration 10)* both carried standard olive/turquoise finishes with red upper surfaces to the top wings and red tails, rear fuselages, cowlings and wheels. Photographs of these latter two aircraft have not been positively identified and so some doubt exists as to the extent of the red on their fuselages and rudders. National markings were in the process of change during March/April 1918 and, although there is no hard evidence to show the precise date of change, I have shown 127/17 with its upper wing crosses in *Balkankreuse* form rather than the earlier *Cross Patee* style.

Other than the rudder of Sopwith 1½ Strutter A2401, photographs of those of Richthofen's victims which appear in the illustrations have not been traced. Their markings therefore, have been based on similar machines in service with the appropriate units as near as possible at the same time. Unit markings have been included where thought to be fitting but if individual letters or numerals were probably carried, they have been omitted rather than included as guesses. In this category are the DH5 *(illustration 7)* which most likely carried a large white letter below the cockpit,the RE8 *(illustration 8)* whose unit normally marked white one or two digit numerals forward of the fuselage roundel, and the Dolphin *(illustration 9)* which may have had a white letter alongside the unit's white square. Camel D6491 *(illustration 10)* is believed to have carried the letters "RG" but their exact form and positioning is not known – they have been shown positioned as similar markings on 46 Squadron aircraft.

Artistic license has been (sparingly) employed in one or two cases. The FE2b *(illustration 1)* is shown with white markings on the nacelle in a form exhibited on a similar machine belonging to the same unit which was captured by the Germans in September 1916, although it is not known if this was an individual or unit marking. The Nieuport 17's of 60 Squadron were seen in both PC10 camouflage and aluminium paint schemes; I have chosen the latter as being more associated with the type.

The foregoing is, of course, a powerful invocation of Murphy's Law. I cheerfully await the arrival of the first photograph showing one of these aircraft taken immediately before take-off on its last mission...

CHRIS THOMAS

BIBLIOGRAPHY

TITLE	AUTHOR/PUBLISHER
A Contemptible Little Flying Corps	*I McInnes & J Webb, London Stamp Exchange*
Above the Lines	*Franks/Bailey/Guest; Grub Street, 1993*
Above the Trenches	*Shores/Franks/Guest; Grub Street, 1990*
Activities of the British Community in Argentina During the Great War	
Alumni Felstedienses, 1890-1950	
Before Endeavours Fade	*Rose Coombs, MBE; After the Battle, 1993*
Bloody April	*Alan Morris; Jarrolds, 1967*
Book of Remembrance and War Record of Mill Hill School, 1914-1919	
Burke's Landed Gentry	
Charterhouse College Register	
Cheltenham College Register	
City of Coventry, Roll of the Fallen	
Clifton College Register	
County Borough of West Hartlepool, Roll of Honour, 1914-1919	
Cross of Sacrifice, Volumes I and II	*SD & DB Jarvis; Roberts Medals Ltd*
Deeds That Thrill, The Empire Volumes 1 to 5	
Dulwich College War Record, 1914-1919	
Durham University, 1914-1919	
Edinburgh Academy Register, 1824-1914 (and War Supplement)	
Fettes College Register	
Flying Fury	*JTB McCudden; Aviation Book Club*
Historical Records of the Cameron Highlanders, Volume VII	
History of the Dorsetshire Regiment, 1914-1919	
In Memoriam, Royal Grammar School , Newcastle on Tyne	
Kelly's Handbook to the Titles, Landed and Official Classes	
King's Royal Rifle Corps Chronicle, 1917	
Lancashire Fusiliers - Salford Brigade - Roll of Honour	
List of British Officers Taken Prisoner in the Various Theatres of War, 1914-1918	*London Stamp Exchange (Reprint) 1919*
Liverpool's Scroll of Fame	
Loretto Register	

TITLE	AUTHOR/PUBLISHER
Loretto Roll of Honour, 1914-1920	
Malvern College Register	
Manchester University Roll of Service	
Manfred Von Richthofen, The Man and the Aircraft He Flew	*David Baker; Outline Press, 1990*
Marlborough College Register	
Moncton Combe School Register	
Naval Eight	*EG Johnstone; Arms and Armour Press, 1972*
Officers Died in the Great War	*JB Hayward (Reprint), 1990*
Officers of the Durham Light Infantry	*Malcolm McGregor*
Oundle Memorials of the Great War, 1914-1919	
Over the Balkans and South Russia	*HA Jones, MC; Vintage Aviation Library (Reprint)* 1987
Radley College Register	
Record of Service of Solicitors and Articled Clerks, 1914-1918	
Richthofen - Beyond the Legend of the Red Baron	*Peter Kilduff; Arms and Armour Press, 1993*
Richthofen, The Red Knight of Germany	*Vigilant (Claude Sykes); Hamilton*
Roll of Honour and War List, 1914-18, of University College School, Hampstead	
Roll of Men from Southend on Sea & District who Fell for their Country, 1915-19	
Royal Air Force, 1918	*Edited by C Cole; Kimber & Co, 1968*
Royal Flying Corps, 1915-16	*Edited by C Cole; Kimber & Co, 1969*
Royal Flying Corps, Honours, Decorations, Medals, etc	
Shrewsbury School Register	
Shrewsbury School Roll of Service, 1914-1919	
Squadron Histories, RFC; RNAS and RAF, Since 1912	*Peter Lewis; Putnam & Co, 1968*
St Andrew's University Roll of Honour, 1914-1919	
St Lawrence College Register	
Summerfields Register	
The Air Defence of Britain, 1914-1918	*C Cole/EF Cheesman; Bodley Head, 1984*
The Ceylon Roll of Honour and Record of Service in the Great War	
The Connaught Rangers, Volume III	
The Court Journal, 1917	
The Distinguished Service Order, 1886-1923	*JB Hayward & Sons (Reprint), 1978*
The Graphic	
The High School of Glasgow; The Book of Sacrifice and Remembrance	

TITLE	AUTHOR/PUBLISHER
The History of 60 Squadron, RAF	*Group Captain AJL Scott: Wm Heinemann, 1920*
The Honourable Artillery Company in the Great War, 1914-1919	
The Illustrated London News	
The Inns of Court OTC During the Great War	
The Magdalen College Register	
The Manchester Grammar School Book of Remembrance	
The Manchester University Roll of Honour	
The Oxfordshire & Buckinghamshire Light Infantry Chronicle, Volume XXVI	
The Records of Old Westminsters, Volume I and II	
The Red Airfighter	*Manfred Von Richthofen; Greenhill (Reprint) 1990*
The Red Knight of Germany	*Floyd Gibbons; Cassell & Co*
The Roll of Honour, Volumes I to V	*The Marquis de Ruvigny; The Standardart Book Co*
The Scottish Pictorial	
The Sphere	
The Times	
The Victorian Cross, 1856-1900	*JB Hayward & Sons (Reprint) 1985*
The War in the Air; Official History of the War, Volumes I to VI	*HA Jones; Clarenden Press, 1937*
The Watsonian War Record, 1914-1918	
Tonbridge School and the Great War of 1914-1919	
Univ College London, Univ College Hospital & Medical Record, A Record 1914-19	
University of Edinburgh Record of Honour, 1914-1919	
University of Liverpool Roll of Service, 1914-1918	
University of London OTC Roll of War Service, 1914-1919	
Unpublished Letters - Cyril Douglas Bennett	
Unpublished Private Papers and Documents - Captain Sidney Philip Smith	
Von Richthofen and the Flying Circus	*Harleyford Ltd, 1958*

AT-A-GLANCE NAME INDEX